Custom Cabinets

S. Blackwell Duncan

TAB Books

Division of McGraw-Hill, Inc.
Blue Ridge Summit, PA 17294-0850

FIRST EDITION
FIRST PRINTING

© 1994 by **TAB Books**.
TAB Books is a division of McGraw-Hill, Inc.

Library of Congress Cataloging-in-Publication Data

ISBN 0-8306-4172-6
ISBN 0-8306-4171-8(pbk)

Acquisitions editor: Stacy V. Pomeroy
Editorial team: Robert Burdette, Editor
              Susan Wahlman, Managing Editor
              Joanne Slike, Executive Editor
              Joann Woy, Indexer
Production team: Katherine G. Brown, Director
              Rose McFarland, Layout
              Tara Ernst, Proofreading
Design team: Jaclyn J. Boone, Designer
              Brian Allison, Associate Designer
Cover design: Denny Bond, East Petersburg, Pa.   HT1
Cover illustration: Brent Blair   4240

CONTENTS

7 Woodworking joints   158

THE PURPOSE of this book is not to guide you through a series of cabinetmaking projects but to show you by example the fundamentals of cabinetmaking and teach you how to assemble those fundamentals into a cohesive whole of your own choosing. An old saying goes that if you give a hungry man a fish, his hunger will be assuaged for a brief time, but if you teach a man how to fish, he need never go hungry again. Once you learn the basics of building cabinets, you can build whatever you want.

Two underlying premises are involved here. The first, not provable but reasonable enough, is that most folks with an interest and some aptitude can learn basic cabinetmaking and expect to turn out creditable work.

The second premise is that the skills, materials, tools, and essential principles of cabinetmaking are the same for all cabinetry and can be extended to general woodworking. Details differ from project to project, but the broad outline remains. When you understand what cabinetmaking is all about, you can build a simple cabinet. When you have learned how to do that, you can progress to more complex designs requiring more advanced skills. With the basics mastered, if you can build one cabinet, you can build any cabinet—not with equal ease, of course, and not without some experience behind you, but that's the essence of it. And I'm not talking of just cabinets but also of certain kinds of fine furniture that are part of the cabinetmaking craft.

This book is arranged in several sections, though not so designated. The first chapter, an introductory pep talk of sorts, suggests that cabinetry of various kinds can help you achieve a more comfortable, convenient, and trouble-free home environment. It points out that the reader can define and develop cabinet projects, design the units, and build them with no previous experience.

The next six chapters deal, sometimes literally, with the nuts and bolts of cabinetmaking: tools and equipment, basic materials, and the accessory and decorative materials you can include if you wish. Included is information on essential hardware, fasteners, and adhesives. The last of these chapters deals with the crux of cabinetmaking—joinery.

The next part of the book covers the various ways several vital components of cabinets are made. You will learn how to make cabinet doors and drawers and discover the ramifications of shelving. One chapter is devoted to cabinet tops and countertops.

Chapter 11 pulls together all the previously explained bits and pieces and adds a discussion of how to construct cabinet carcasses of several types, all in project form. Here is a mix of ideas, techniques, procedures, and methods. Neither they nor the projects are meant to be followed or imitated exactly, though you can do so if you wish. Rather, this chapter is intended to present you with a series of varied steps that illustrate how you can construct different kinds of cabinetry, ranging from simple utility to furniture quality, designed to fit your needs and suit your concepts of decorative niceties.

Finally, a fairly lengthy but by no means exhaustive discussion of finishing and finishes closes the book. Usually it is this final operation, the finishing, that makes or breaks a cabinet project. This material is meant to be closely examined, then varied as required.

The best way to use this book is first to go through the entire text, stopping to browse at points of particular interest. This method gives you a broad, quick overview of cabinetmaking. Then you can go back and concentrate on those parts that are of special importance. The information is not necessarily categorized and lumped together; rather, myriad details are scattered throughout the text wherever they seem most appropriate.

This book is certainly not the last word in cabinetmaking, nor for that matter is any other. This huge subject has a vast body of information available, especially in books and periodicals as well as sets of cabinet-furniture plans that have been tried and tested. You might have questions or problems or interests that are not covered here—I would be surprised if you did not. In that case, further research at your local library can get you started on a regular research course that you will find virtually endless and will point out numerous new avenues you can travel.

That, of course, is part of the fascination and the challenge of cabinetmaking. No matter how skilled you become, how many projects you build, and how much knowledge and lore you absorb, there is always more.

Enjoy.

The case for custom-built cabinets

ANY MENTION of cabinets immediately brings to mind an array of those most familiar to us—kitchen cabinets. That's reasonable enough because every modern house and apartment, no matter how small, has at least a small complement of base cabinets fitted with a countertop plus a few feet of wall cabinets mounted above them.

Sometimes, especially in older houses, these cabinet sets are built-in. That is, they were built from scratch on-site, attached to the building as they were fabricated piece by piece. More often, the cabinets are actually modules, sections of like appearance that were produced in a cabinet shop or a factory to a standard design, then transported to the site and installed with shims and matching filler panels and trimwork to become a permanent part of the kitchen.

In many homes, maybe most of them, the use of cabinets, whether prefabricated or site-built, is confined to the kitchen. Decent cabinets may be found nowhere else, except perhaps for the bathrooms, where minimal storage capability may be provided by a medicine cabinet and maybe a vanity. And for the most part, custom-built cabinetry is found today only in recently built, upscale, expensive houses or in houses that were built several decades ago when on-site custom cabinetmaking was more commonplace.

Most cabinets and so-called built-ins (distinguishing between the two is sometimes difficult) are no longer built at the job site. Instead, they are mass-produced at a factory, ordered from a catalog or a showroom, shipped to the jobsite, and assembled, anchored in place, and trimmed out. In a short time they become a permanent part of the structure, set up by two or three installers in a matter of hours. The main reason for following this course is simple enough—cost. Expert finish

1

carpenters are expensive and hard to find. Custom fabrication on-site often extends the overall job time by a certain amount. Added materials, paperwork, and headaches are always involved. And the added costs can be substantial. So the contractor finds it much easier to install (or have someone else install) a batch of factory-built units that serve the purpose well enough, at least from his standpoint, with a minimum of fuss and bother.

But this system often has drawbacks for the homeowner. Top-quality general-merchandise lines of kitchen cabinets are expensive, and the cheap ones are just that. The buyer is restricted to a few designs and appearances and a particular set of units from which a complete complement of cabinets can be assembled, none of which may appeal. Most of the commercial kitchen cabinetry is not especially adaptable for use in other parts of the house. The same is true of cabinets designed for bathroom use and furniture-type cabinetry for other purposes. And many varieties of cabinets that can be custom-made you will never see for sale in any store.

As far as built-in cabinets are concerned, of course, none can be bought from factories or salesrooms. Built-ins are exactly what the name implies. They must be constructed on the jobsite, attached to the structure as they are assembled piece by piece, to answer a particular requirement and conform to a certain set of dimensions. Shop-built custom cabinets may be built in a home shop by an amateur cabinetmaker—you—or professional cabinetmakers in a local custom cabinet shop. Either way, they are built to fulfill particular needs and for specific locations and to particular dimensions and designs that may never be duplicated. It seems apparent that the only reasonable way to attain a satisfactory complement of cabinetry, whether built-in or freestanding, is to design the units yourself and have them built by someone else or do the job yourself.

If home for you is just a place to hang your hat, designing and building a bunch of cabinets is probably not of much interest. But if your home is your castle and if you are like most other folks, an array of strategically located and well-designed cabinets throughout the house can contribute importantly to making your life a bit easier and more pleasant.

If you are a do-it-yourselfer with a woodworking bent, the challenge of building your own cabinetry is hard to pass by. All kinds of cabinets can be designed into a new house during the planning stages with little added effort and built as the job progresses or added when the house structure is complete. Similarly, all manner of cabinetry, frequently unique, can be designed for and built into older houses without any undue difficulty, often resulting in a remarkable transformation from a house that is hard to live in to one that is a delight.

Consider: There is not a room in the house that cannot use some cabinet space for storage or display. Even an existing kitchen, which presumably already has cabinets, deserves a hard look. The cabinets may be there, but are they effective, efficient, big enough, attractive enough? Are they doing the job you want done, and are there enough of them in the right locations?

Stock kitchen cabinets can be improved upon in many ways, and the kitchen cabinetry commonly found in many houses leaves a lot to be desired. This is especially true of smaller houses built more than a decade or so ago, in which skimpiness seems prevalent. And in a kitchen remodel or a kitchen in a new house, all the cabinetry can be designed ahead of time to fulfill all sorts of special needs, ideas, or even whims.

Instead of having four blank walls, a library or den can be fitted out with various kinds of shelving, display cabinets, cupboards, drawer space, built-in worktops or desks, or what have you. The same can be done in a living room or a great room; lots of shelves and cupboards are imperative in a well-designed rec room. Bar cabinetry; audio and video cabinetry; and special storage for tapes, records, and other such items may be important here. A dining room or area needs storage space for linens, tableware, crockery, glassware, table accessories, and a host of odds and ends.

Freestanding units can take care of many of these needs, but there is no substitute for a big built-in sideboard or server with a working countertop and a set of wall cabinets above. A pantry consists of an entire room full of cupboards and cabinets, with working countertop space as well. All bathrooms should have plenty of built-in storage space in addition to a vanity cabinet or built-in, good countertop space, and enclosed shelving for medicines and such. The master bath, or some other convenient location, needs space for toweling, linens, sick-room equipment, and general supplies.

Bedrooms, sadly enough, are seldom fitted out with anything beyond a closet, and that may be small. Here are opportunities for cabinetry in the form of armoires, highboys, bureaus; underbed rollouts, headboard storage units, and numerous other furnishings. Closets can be fitted with stacks or drawers; separate compartments for shirts, sweaters, and other apparel; racks for shoes, hats, ties, and belts; and other special stowaway spots.

Children's rooms are more livable and convenient if they include storage areas, either built-in or freestanding, for toys and sports equipment, desks, and shelves for books and all the paraphernalia that children like to have. Workshops cry out for cabinets and storage units for all manner of purposes, and so do garages. Entry halls, mudrooms, laundries, studios, and similar special-use areas have their own needs for supply cabinets, bootracks, worktops, and numerous other items.

People with a penchant for collecting things like old bottles, antique inkwells, china, or other collectibles have a couple of problems in particular—display space and storage space. Not much enjoyment can be gained from a fine collection of art glass wrapped in newspapers and stuffed in a cardbox box under the bed. All such items need the protected display space that good cabinetry affords. Those interested in hunting, fishing, gardening, and myriad other outdoor activities need ways to store their gear, and hobbyists who indulge in model railroading, radio-controlled airplanes, gunsmithing, or whatever have similar requirements. Indeed, the list of uses for custom cabinetry is just about endless.

The cost of custom-made cabinets and built-ins constructed on-site by professional finish carpenters or cabinetmakers is high. The cost of very fine furniture-type cabinetry, such as a mahogany captain's bed, an oak rolltop desk, or a walnut secretary, is stratospheric. Top-quality materials like exotic hardwoods and solid brass hardware are expensive today, but the labor that goes into creating fine cabinetry is even more so. Most home cabinet projects, even a substantial piece of furniture like an armoire, do not require an enormous outlay for materials. But the cutting, assembly, and finishing of such a piece requires many hours of labor.

It follows, then, that if *you* provide those hours instead of a professional, several thousand dollars' worth of cabinetry, maybe many thousands, can be put together for a cost of only several hundred. Furthermore, the results will be exactly as you want them to be, not as someone else thinks they should be. And if you are willing to take the time and patience necessary, you will find that those results are every bit as good as those that are likely to be produced by the average professional cabinetmaker. (It must be said, however, that museum-grade pieces made by some master cabinetmakers and furniture makers are in a different realm altogether and probably should not be considered part of the workaday world.)

What does it take to achieve your proposed cabinetry goals? Not much, really, when you analyze the situation and put it into perspective. First, you need motivation. You need some incentive to undertake the work, especially at the outset if you have never done anything of this sort. And if that is the case, you also need some underlying confidence in your woodworking abilities, real or potential, or at least your level of manual dexterity. You might undertake the work as a hobby, an enjoyable pastime, or a response to a creative urge to develop something of your own design and build it with your own two hands. Or you might tackle some cabinetwork as a matter of necessity, a pressing need with no one available to do the job. Maybe you feel that you can do a better job than anyone in your locale who might be available.

Your financial state might be the determining factor: time and aptitude there, but not enough ready cash to attain your goals. There is also the point that you can always take quality freestanding cabinetry along with you and possibly sell at some future date for a fair sum. The quality cabinetry that you build into your present home will always in some way enhance the salability and the value of the property. So if you have the time and the inclination for cabinetmaking, chances are good that you have a win-win situation with no real downside.

Specific skills are not necessary at the outset, although they would be a plus. You do need a certain degree of mechanical aptitude and manual dexterity, but even that can be developed. Even those who complain of having five thumbs on each hand will find that with a little practice and experience they can do a respectable job, especially with all of the remarkable workshop aids that are available today. And most folks possess a lot more mechanical and manual know-how than they give themselves credit for. Motivation of some sort, along with a willingness to learn, will just about always overcome the initial fumbling and head scratching, and you will find that you can really do a lot better job than you originally thought possible. You just have to give yourself some elbow room and a good chance to prove out. In any event, there is no such thing as an instant cabinetmaker, and understanding that fact at the outset will prepare you to allow for some occasional discouragement. Learning, knowledge, experimenting, and experience are the principal ingredients of good craftsmanship.

Besides motivation and fundamental manual skills, you need time and patience—bundles of each, and especially the latter. Cabinetmaking is not a slap-dash, zip-bang deal like whacking together a sandbox for Junior or putting up a lean-to for your pet goat. The phrase *care and patience* cannot be repeated too many times in this endeavor. This work requires big chunks of time, although usually not very much in any given session.

But even small projects, especially if intricate or ornate like a top-opening, multidrawer, lined jewelry case of myrtle or manzanita, require hours and hours of labor. There is no way around this. No cabinetmaking project can be hurried, even by an expert. (An expert wouldn't try that anyway.) Each job will take a certain time under the given conditions, and that's that. The old adage "haste makes waste" is valid in this field.

Most cabinetmaking projects proceed in slow steps. Those steps, except for the simplest of projects, involve careful planning, accurate and detailed layout, double-checking dimensions, thoughtful selection of materials, precise cutting and trimming, careful shaping and fitting of joints, certain periods for glue or finish curing, seemingly endless sandpapering and rubbing, and unhurried, intensive scrutiny throughout the entire job.

Sound difficult? It's not, really—just time-consuming. The end result of high quality, even if not perfection, makes it all worthwhile. Before you attempt any cabinet project of consequence, undertake a little attitude adjustment and tell yourself that you will not push the job and will do it correctly. That is the way to achieve excellent results, and that is what every true artisan aims for. The eventual actuality may well turn out to be something less than the original hope—if you are a perfectionist, it nearly always will—but after all, that is normal, and the next project will probably turn out better.

Aside from the woodworking and cabinetmaking skills involved, most of which are gained through experience, perhaps your greatest asset will be the knowledge you seek and absorb. Learn as much as you can about woodworking particulars, especially the facets that interest you most but also those that may be secondary. You cannot learn too much. You must find out what sorts of materials are available to you, what their characteristics are, how well you can work with them, and which are best for your particular purposes. You must have a good grasp of the uses and potentialities of the hardware and fasteners that will best help you in your projects and what sources you can tap for them. You must know something about surface preparation, applied finishes, and finishing procedures.

You need a working knowledge of the various joints used in cabinetry and furniture building, how to make them with the equipment you have available, which work best for various applications, and the other aspects of joinery. You must become acquainted with the hand and power tools, some specialized and some not, used in cabinetmaking. You need to understand, where appropriate, how to set them up for different procedures, how to use these tools most effectively, and how to care for them.

You must learn how various kinds of cabinets are assembled and the procedures and techniques employed to assemble them, not only so that you can do the assembly work but also so that you can use the knowledge to design your own cabinetry projects. The more information you have at your fingertips, the easier your tasks will be and the more successful the finished results.

Finally, even for rudimentary projects you must have a certain amount of equipment. A large and extensively equipped workshop is not an essential for making cabinets; many exquisite pieces of cabinetry and furniture have been turned out with only a few hand tools. Although a big shop would be nice, you do not really need a small one so long as you have some corner where you can set up a small workbench or even a couple of sawhorses topped with planks or plywood. For built-in projects, this might be the site itself.

You can start with simple projects using just hand tools and perhaps a couple of small portable power tools. If you discover that you enjoy cabinetmaking and become more involved in it, your projects will become larger and more complex. As that occurs, you will probably want and need additional equipment. Often, purchasing tools and equipment is fully justified when balanced against time and effort saved, accuracy and quality gained, and cost savings if the job would otherwise have to be farmed out. So you might just as well assume at the beginning that eventually you will be laying out cash for more tools and accessories and perhaps even developing a formal workshop before your cabinetmaking days are over.

How do you get started in cabinetmaking? Not by rushing out and collecting a chestful of tools and a truckload of lumber. It would be foolish to say that cabinetmaking is simple, something you can dive right into and accomplish grand things. It is not simple. Assuming you want good results, it is detailed and precise, even in the beginning stages, and an enormous amount of information must be absorbed and skills acquired before one can expect to become a superior cabinetmaker, much less a master.

On the other hand, there is nothing arcane about cabinetmaking. Even complex projects are best approached as a series of straightforward steps. Complicated procedures can be reduced to individual operations carried out in logical sequence. Anyone with sufficient interest can learn the basics of the craft in a relatively short time, at least to the point where a creditable job can be done, and then accumulate further expertise with continued experience. The level of cabinetmaking skills, craftsmanship, and artistry depends entirely upon the individual.

To begin with, you need to identify the requirements or desires (maybe both) for cabinetry in your home. Then you need to acquire an entry-level understanding of the cabinetmaking craft, not only by studying the remainder of this book but by absorbing additional material. Excellent sources are books on cabinetmaking, furniture making, and general woodworking from your local library or bookstore and periodicals on woodworking from the supermarket magazine racks. Also, send for two or three catalogs from mail-order tool and woodworking supply houses; they can be very instructive. Do some on-the-spot investigating at local hardware stores and lumberyards to discover what is available to you in tools, hardware, and materials. Once you have all this information in hand, you can begin to design the cabinetry projects that will fulfill your needs.

But you can learn only so much through reading and research, especially at the outset when everything seems to come at once and there is little or no basis for a practical understanding of what you are taking in intellectually. A lot of what you absorb will shortly disappear unless you use that knowledge in practical applications. There comes a time, usually sooner rather than later, when you learn and retain best by doing, so you must commit yourself to starting a project.

One intermediate step that is most useful, if you can make the necessary arrangements, is to observe a professional cabinetmaker or finish carpenter at work. If you can get some personal instruction at the same time, so much the better. Hiring on as an apprentice or helper for a while would be an ideal arrangement. Even a brief lesson or two learned from a topflight professional is valuable, especially if you are starting out as a rank beginner in woodworking. Another possibility along these same lines is a hands-on course in woodworking or cabinetmaking. Such courses are frequently available as part of adult education programs, crafts workshops, and similar situations. They are sometimes advertised in woodworking magazines.

Whether or not any of these arrangements is possible, you must eventually repair to your workshop area all by your lonely self, pick up your tools, and start to work. In the early stages you would be wise to proceed slowly and carefully, referring to instructional materials whenever you feel the need. If you are not quite sure about how to do something, don't just barge ahead. Stop and research the problem or find someone to question.

The folks who staff your local hardware and lumber supply outlets are usually most helpful with ideas and suggestions, instructions, and general information. Many have had long experience in the field and may be accomplished artisans.

As you build your projects, you will gradually gain confidence, skill, and solid knowledge of procedures and operations, techniques, and materials, and not much time will pass before you become reasonably self-reliant. Most if not all of what you have learned will not desert you, and in time you will become far more expert than you thought possible at the outset.

There will be problems, setbacks, frustrations, and probably some results that are far less desirable than what you had hoped for. That is inevitable. Expect it. But remember that thousands of people have traveled this route successfully before you, including many a master cabinetmaker and woodworker, so don't get discouraged.

Time-saving tools

CABINETRY of all kinds can be constructed and finished entirely by hand, using no power equipment, just as it was a century and more ago. Indeed, some expert woodworkers do just that today, preferring time-honored tools and methods simply for the challenge and the satisfaction of exercising their skills and craftsmanship. But for most of us, the time, patience, and skills essential to that process are not only lacking; the whole idea is out of the question. Any aids we can use in completing a cabinetmaking project with the best results in the least time, commensurate with the complexity of the job and the desired quality of the result, are much appreciated. And if a little money can be saved, so much the better.

To achieve this desirable situation, a would-be cabinetmaker has to be prepared to equip the workshop with a full complement of good tools, both hand and powered. Purchasing top-quality brand-name tools and machinery is extremely important if excellent finished cabinetry is the goal. Assuming that proper care and maintenance is provided, doing so means that cutting edges will retain their keenness for a reasonable period; bearings will hold up; cuts will be true, smooth, and clean; measurements will be accurate; operation will be easy and safe; and all other aspects of the equipment will be of high order.

As a starting point, every cabinetmaker's tool racks and chests should contain the usual assortment of ordinary hand and power tools you might expect to find in any active do-it-yourselfer's shop. This means a normal collection of screwdrivers, hammers, nailsets, wood chisels, pliers, clamps, an electric drill and twist bits, files, measuring devices, a plane or two, squares, and various handsaws. Such a shop is also likely to feature a table saw or a radial arm saw. A pad or similar sander is another likelihood. All of these general-purpose tools will see service in cabinetmaking; together they form a functional equipment base.

But for cabinetmaking (as well as fine-finish woodworking and furniture making), some of the general-purpose items should have certain characteristics, and numerous special-purpose tools can make the work go faster and easier. The availability of such equipment will afford better results. However, no shop needs all such tools and accessories, pleasant as that situation might be. Purchase them only as needed and only if they will be of genuine assistance in your projects. Otherwise you'll end up becoming a tool collector instead of a cabinetmaker. Some of the equipment mentioned in this chapter is stocked only by the larger hardware and woodworking supply stores or is available by mail order.

Marking & measuring tools

Precise layout and dimensioning are crucial to producing good cabinetwork, and that requires a number of marking and measuring devices (FIG. 2-1). Exactly what items might work best for you depends on what you are building and what materials you are using. Although some of the devices mentioned here are used only for measuring, most are also employed in layout work.

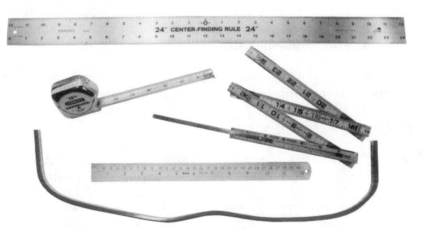

2-1
Linear measuring devices: center-finding rule, steel tape measure, carpenter's folding rule, steel bench rule, and flexible rule.

For linear measuring, the common carpenter's steel tape measure, although handy at times, just does not get the whole job done. A top-quality 12-inch steel ruler, called a *bench rule*, is very useful, as is a steel or anodized aluminum yardstick or 1-meter rule. *Centering rules*, available in 12-, 18-, and 24-inch lengths, eliminate both guesswork and dividers; they start with a zero in the middle and read to left and right. You need a carpenter's *folding* or *zigzag rule* for taking inside measurements. A *flexible curve* is sometimes handy for measuring along a curved line. A carpenter's or *framing square*, if it is of top quality, is also useful.

Exact thickness of materials is often crucial, and this can be determined easily with an *outside-reading* or *dial slide caliper* or a *direct-reading planer gauge*. These are also available now in electronic digital-readout models, which are highly accurate. Standard inside and outside calipers, available in several sizes, are widely used for this purpose, especially in wood turning. Depth or height, as of a groove, is most precisely measured with a caliper that can be used as a height gauge, a depth gauge, or *Incra gauge*, or in many instances with a *combination square*. Measurements can be checked or stepped off with dividers. Figure 2-2 shows some of these tools.

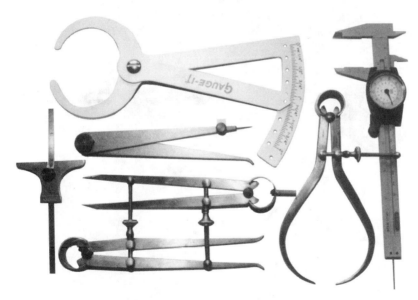

2-2
Measuring devices: middle row, top to bottom—thickness or planer gauge, hermaphrodite caliper, dividers, inside caliper; left— depth gauge; right—outside caliper and dial slide caliper.

Working with angles requires a different set of tools and instruments. The square is used to measure, check, or lay out right angles, and there are several choices (FIG. 2-3): *try square, speed square, carpenter's* or *framing square, engineer's square, T square, double square,* or combination square, as well as a very handy device called a *Squangle*. For determining, laying out, or

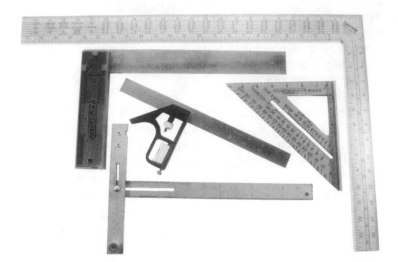

2-3
Squares: rafter, framing, or carpenter's; try; speed; combination; Squangle.

transferring other angles, you can use a *standard* or *long-arm protractor*, a *sliding bevel square*, a combination square with a *protractor head*, the Squangle, or the speed square, a *universal angle finder*, or a *Mite-R-Gauge* (FIG. 2-4). Some of these devices allow greater accuracy than others.

2-4 *Other angle-measuring devices: left to right—Squangle opened to an angle, protractor, universal angle finder, Mite-R-Gage; above—sliding bevel square; below—combination square with protractor head.*

Layout work obviously requires marking instruments (FIG. 2-5). Although a number-2 pencil is useful and a good supply of them should be on hand along with a sharpener, there are better ways. A traditional *marking gauge* does a fine job, and newer, larger models are made of steel and are easier to adjust. One key to accuracy is scribing a very fine line to cut or measure against, and you can do that with a *marking knife*. One side of the blade is flat, to be held against a straightedge, and the other is beveled to a fine edge to make the mark. A *scratch awl* can be similarly used but is less accurate; the awl can also be used for marking a point. A *striking knife* combines the two functions, with a double marking blade at one end and a scribe at the other. For laying out from a pattern, a set of *pounce wheels* makes either marking or tracing easy. For laying out small circles or other geometric figures, a *drafting* or *direct-reading compass* or a pair of *dividers* will do the job. These instruments are also used for stepping off equal distances. For larger circles as well as some kinds of straight layouts, move up to a *yardstick compass* or a set of *trammel heads* mounted on a beam.

A few more miscellaneous devices are often handy (FIG. 2-6). A *variable-form curve*, a curved aluminum ruler, allows you to draw smooth curved lines easily. A set of *french-curve templates*

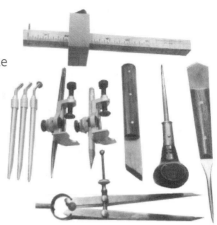

2-5
Marking devices: left to right—pounce wheels, trammel heads, marking knife, scratch awl, striking knife; above—marking gauge; below—dividers.

2-6
Miscellaneous layout devices: left to right—french curve templates, zero-zero center finder, profile gauge; above—rolling ruler; below—pantograph.

is equally useful. A *zero-zero center finder* marks the exact center of any circle up to an 8-inch diameter. *Profile gauges* copy the contours of moldings or other complex shapes so they can be duplicated on a pattern or a workpiece. Use a *pantograph* for enlarging or reducing a pattern, drawing, or plan. And finally, for a wide variety of measuring and layout chores, you might like to try a *rolling ruler*. This curious instrument performs many functions well.

Jigs, guides, & gauges

A wide variety of jigs and guides are available, all intended to position and hold a tool or a workpiece to allow a clean, accurate cut or other operation every time. Their importance should never be underestimated, especially since they are such a great help to relatively unskilled or inexperienced woodworkers. Besides affording a better-quality finished product, they save time, mistakes, and waste. All but a few are designed to be used in conjunction with power tools.

Honing and *sharpening guides* abound. These items allow you to keep your bits and blades sharp-sharp-sharp with little time or effort. Sharpness is extremely important for safety and accurate, smooth boring, cutting, shaving, and trimming. A similar *grinding jig* allows easy grinding and shaping of plane and chisel blades.

Several useful gadgets can help you bore accurately positioned holes. *Precision drill guides* make it possible to drill properly aligned holes not only on flat surfaces but also into narrow edges, curved surfaces, and spheres. *Pocket-hole drill guides* allow drilling accurate pocket holes, often required in cabinetry and furniture. If you plan to build extensive adjustable-shelf units, a *shelf-drilling jig* will save you a lot of time and effort (but the unit is fairly expensive). There are numerous designs of *doweling jigs*, a virtual necessity for edge-doweling mating pieces. You might use a *dowel center set* instead if you need to drill only a few holes, but the results are not apt to be as good. Another device worth considering is a precision drill guide— there are two or three models—that allows accurate boring at variable angles with an electric hand drill.

Setting a blade, knife, or cutter to cut to a certain depth is a frequent chore. The trial-and-error method is a waste of time when guides and gauges are made for the purpose (FIG. 2-7). A *universal tool-setting gauge* allows quick and accurate height-depth adjustment of table or radial-arm saw blades as well as router and shaper blades. Another device sets jointer knives; yet another, planer knives. A *router depth gauge* is a quick and easy device to use, and a *step gauge* is excellent for setting up a table, band, or radial-arm saw.

2-7
Left—radial-arm or table-saw blade setting gauge; right—router-bit setting gauge.

There are numerous devices designed to position the workpiece relative to a cutting edge. For example, the *Paragauge* is an extremely accurate accessory that spaces and aligns the rip fence of a table saw vis-à-vis the blade. A *Poly-Gauge* sets up miter cuts for several power tools. *Incra Jigs* are renowned for their versatility and accuracy in workpiece positioning for sawing, drilling, and routing. *Stop rods* are available in a variety of configurations to allow repetitive identical cuts.

Using special jigs for some operations makes the work easier and the results uniform and accurate. For example, there are several varieties of jigs or templates for making half-blind and through dovetails. For cutting tapers on a table saw, use a *taper jig*. A *right-angle miter gauge* for your table saw results in perfect miter cuts; a *precision miter gauge* gives you better cuts no matter the angles set, and a *90-degree universal clamping fixture* allows cuts you could not otherwise safely make. A device with the unlikely name of *Rig-A-Mortis* allows making repetitive, uniform mortise cuts, as for joints, every time. With another special jig you can turn out mortise-and-tenon joints with ease. *Finger-joint templates* transform that otherwise difficult and tedious chore into a much simpler one.

Clamps

You can't make cabinets without a collection of clamps on hand. Ordinary *C-clamps* in their various sizes are often useful in cabinetmaking—they must be set with protective pads or blocks—but there are several other types to consider. One is the *deep-throat C-clamp*, which has a greater versatility than the standard models. A close cousin, the *three-way* or *edging clamp*, allows you to apply pressure upward, downward, and across simultaneously, often necessary when applying certain kinds of edgings to flat surfaces.

A collection of *pipe clamps* is sometimes indispensable when assembling casework and a must for gluing wide flat workpieces from several smaller ones. Purchase the clamp fixtures for either ½-inch or ¾-inch pipe. Have sections of black iron or galvanized water pipe cut to whatever lengths you desire; make sure that one end of each piece is threaded. Assemble the clamps, and you're in business. If you buy at least one set of reversible fixtures, you won't regret it. Assembled backward, this tool lets you push workpieces apart or temporarily spread them for further work.

Bar clamps are similar to pipe clamps but are more costly because the steel I-bar that replaces the pipe is furnished with each clamp. They come in several sizes, as well as a deep-reach type, and are very handy. A variation is a *pistol-grip* type that works very well, especially for smaller clamping jobs. Special pads are available for use with both bar and pipe clamps to prevent marring of the workpiece.

The traditional clamping device of cabinetmakers is the *adjustable handscrew*. It is very versatile and effective, once you get the hang of adjusting it. Several sizes are available, and you can also purchase hardware kits for making your own handscrews; you furnish and shape the wood parts. *Cam clamps* have similar wood jaws but a spring-steel adjusting bar instead of spindles, and they lock with a strong cam-action arrangement. These come in several sizes.

At times, the only effective way to provide uniform and readily adjustable clamping pressure is with a *web* or *band clamp*. These devices consist of a long (15–20 feet) nylon or canvas strap and a self-locking cam-action or screw-action tightening mechanism. The band is looped all the way around the pieces to be clamped together, hitting all the pressure points along the way, and snugged down to whatever degree is needed.

Three other special clamps are worthy of consideration. The *Bessey angle clamp* allows you to clamp two workpieces of different sizes together at an angle while they are being secured. The *Kant Twist clamp* applies great pressure to a pair of workpieces so that they cannot twist out of alignment. It can also be used to bring uncooperative pieces into proper alignment. And if you plan to apply veneer in substantial expanses, you can use *veneer pipe clamps* to good advantage. These clamps are designed to slide onto your pipe clamps. The pipe clamps span the workpiece, clamped at the edges, and the veneer clamps press down on the veneer surface.

Drilling equipment

Most cabinetmakers today do their hole drilling with an *electric drill*. A ⅜-inch reversible model with speed control is about the handiest; a ¼-inch right-angle or 45-degree-angle drill is also a time-saver occasionally. Sometimes it is easiest to pick up a *hand-powered breast* or *"eggbeater" drill* or even a *Yankee screwdriver* with a bit fitted on. Cordless drills are useful for the odd small hole or two, but they drill slowly.

The drill bits (FIG. 2-8) are most important here. Standard *high-speed twist bits* are widely used, but for many purposes there are better choices. For example, a type of twist bit known variously as *pilot point*, *brad point*, or *spur point* is much superior. The bit starts without wandering and cuts fast and cleanly, leaving crisp entrance and exit edges. The best are high-speed steel with long flutes and center points. Usually sold in sets, they are

2-8
Drill bits: left to right— gimlet, two types of countersinks, spring-loaded centering bit, Fortsner bit, brad point bit, screw or countersinking bit; above— ordinary twist-drill bit.

available in standard-length fractional sizes, 10-inch and 12-inch lengths for deep boring, and metric sizes for use with the increasingly popular European cabinet hardware. In addition, certain sizes can be obtained in carbide-tipped form, the best bet for heavy use or a lot of drilling in particleboard and similarly abrasive substances that quickly dull ordinary bits. And to go along with all of these bits, you can purchase *stop collars* for setting hole depths.

Screw drills, also called *countersinking drills*, are handy when many holes must be drilled for wood screws. They drill the pilot hole and shank-clearance hole, countersink, and will counterbore for recessed screw heads, all in one pass. And they are adjustable for hole depth. In straight twist-bit style, they are sold in sets of 4 or 5 to match screw sizes 4, 6, 8, 10, and sometimes 12. The *tapered twist-bit* variety comes in sets of 7, and the *flat-spade* type is available in sets of 21 bits for varying depths.

One of the most useful types of larger bit is the *Forstner pattern*. These carbon-steel spur-cutting bits, equipped with a center point for accurate centering, are designed primarily for low-speed cutting (unless specifically designated as made for higher speeds). They cut sharp-edged, clean-sided holes with flat bottoms and cut pocket, angled, or overlapping holes with ease. They are available in ¼-inch to 3-inch diameter, individually or in sets of various sizes, sometimes cased.

Other specialty items sometimes needed are *countersinks*, which are available in several standard screw sizes, and *plug cutters* for making wood plugs to cover recessed screw heads. *Tenon cutters* are similar, and some models combine the two functions. There are *spring-loaded self-centering bits* for drilling holes for hinge screws and others for cutting mortises. If you need only to make small starter holes for screws in soft wood and don't want to bother getting out the drill, a *gimlet* (available in sets of several sizes) will do the job. And if you have occasion to drill very deep holes, you need twist bits, sometimes called *bellhanger bits*, about 18 inches or more long.

Most sawing chores in cabinetmaking, and woodworking in general, are done with a *table saw* (probably the most versatile machine) or *radial arm saw*; many shops have both and perhaps a *band saw*. Occasionally a *power jigsaw* or *saber saw* sees use, especially if the saw has to be brought to the workpiece instead of the other way around. But there are times when none of these will work adequately and traditional hand-powered types are needed (FIG. 2-9).

2-9
Saws: miter box with long back saw, offset dovetail saw, veneer saw, coping saw, carpenter's crosscut handsaw.

Sometimes a *standard carpenter's handsaw* is the answer. The kind generally preferred by cabinetmakers is the *short* (about 22 inches) *crosscut* with a taper-ground blade and moderate set to the teeth, 10 or 12 teeth per inch (TPI).

For closer quarters or finer cuts, a *backsaw* is the choice. These saws feature a rigid blade with a heavy steel or brass backing and run about 8–14 inches in length and 13–21 TPI. Depth of cut is limited because of the backing, but the cuts are fine and smooth with a very narrow kerf (width of cut).

Dovetail saws are similar but smaller yet, typically about 10 inches long with 15 TPI. They are also available in right or left offset or reversible styles, sometimes a great advantage. These saws make fine joinery cuts.

The *veneer saw* is smaller yet, with the handle compound offset and a double-curved blade with teeth on each side. There is no set to the teeth, so the kerf is narrow and flush or vertical cutting is easy.

Occasionally a situation arises in cabinetmaking where a coping or other intricate cut must be made. In this case an ordinary *coping saw* will likely serve, and so will the slightly more sophisticated *fret saw*. The replaceable (and easily broken) blades for these saws are usually 5 inches long and vary from 16 to 32 TPI.

Much miter-cutting of moldings and face-frame parts is done today with a *power-miter* or *"chop" saw*, some of which are less expensive than a top-grade hand-operated miter box. A table or radial arm saw will also do the job, but the miter box still has its place in the shop, and using it is often easier than setting up a power tool.

Planing

Purchasing your wood stock already nicely planed is the easiest course, but that is not always the final answer, and smoothing is only part of the picture. Trimming, chamfering, leveling, and shaping also have to be considered, and they require planes (FIG. 2-10).

2-10
Planes: multiplane with sets of interchangeable blades, jack plane, radius plane, block plane, and blind nailer.

A *block plane* is almost essential for a lot of small tasks. All run about 6 inches in length, and the low-angle type with the iron (blade) set to about 12 degrees seems most versatile. For edge trimming, chamfering, leveling joints, smoothing end grain, and similar chores, they can hardly be beat.

There are several other types of flat-bladed hand planes, along with the block plane, collectively called *bench planes*—smoothing, jack, fore, and jointer in increasing width and length—but unless you plan on doing a great deal of handwork using the old traditional methods, you probably will not have much use for them. An exception might be using a *jointer plane* to true and freshen edges of stock for edge-joining.

Some specialty planes are worth considering, however. A *radius plane* or *cornering tool* is one, a most useful item that allows you quickly and cleanly to ease or "soften" sharp edges to a rounded form with one pass. Four sizes are generally available: 1/16-, 1/8-, 3/16-, and 1/4-inch radius. An almost identical plane is available to cut uniform edge chamfers.

If you do not have a power jointer for trueing and trimming stock edges and don't trust your accuracy with a jointer plane, an *edge-trimming plane* is the answer. The shoe of this plane is formed in a right angle, and the skewed blade is set to 12 degrees, so that accurate and clean edge-trimming is possible on all but the worst of grains, and tear-out is seldom a problem.

You might also consider a *hand router plane*. It is a handy tool if you cut only a few grooves from time to time and don't want to bother setting up a power saw or other machine. You can hand-cut smooth, precise dadoes, stop-dadoes, slider grooves, or rabbets with ease; several models are available. For rabbeting only, consider one or more of the many *rabbet planes* now available.

One of the problems in working up a nailed-and-glued face-frame assembly is hiding the holes left when the nailheads are set. One answer is to use a tiny planelike device called a *blind nailer*. The specially ground blade, when pushed upon, raises but does not remove a tiny chip in the wood face. The nail (or screw) is driven and set in the slot, then the wood chip glued back down. Properly done, the fastening becomes invisible.

Cutting and finishing inside or outside curves can be a tedious chore, but a *compass plane* can make the job easier. This plane has a flexible steel sole that can be adjusted to follow and cut convex or concave surfaces.

At times, though, the easiest tool to use is a small *spokeshave*. This traditional woodworkers' smoothing tool is available in numerous sizes, but a 10-inch length seems the most versatile. Blade configurations are flat, round or concave, half-round, radius, or combination.

Finally, there is the *multiple-cutter plane*. This complex little device, which takes a bit of practice to use, can be fitted with any of about two dozen standard cutters, and other shapes can be custom-ground. This tool allows you to make up by hand moldings ranging from simple to intricate for application to your cabinetry and to incise custom patterns directly into your casework, face frames, tops, or whatever. Many woodworkers prefer this method to a power router or shaper; many use all three, depending on the circumstances.

Shaping & smoothing

Some of the tools already mentioned, such as the multiplane, are used for shaping the workpiece, but there are others that cabinetmakers often employ. For example, one of the handiest devices for final shaping of finials or other decorative items is a *detailing file*. This tool has a double-ended taper with a half-circle profile, bastard-cut on one end and fine-second-cut on the other for easy flip-flopping.

Standard *cabinet rasps*, curved on one side and flat on the other, remove stock rapidly and accurately. They are available in several sizes and cuts. Although you can buy them individually, a woodworker's full set of five or eight files is often most advantageous.

For fine work in finishing cabinet embellishments, *riffler files* are the best bet. They come in a variety of shapes and either rasp or file cuts in varying degrees of coarseness. The double-ended variety is perhaps most common, but you can also obtain single-ended styles with wood handles. Rifflers can be bought singly, but sets offer greater versatility.

Neither hand planes nor power planers leave a surface smooth enough to take a final finish. Unless the final result is intended to be rough or have some sort of texture, further smoothing must be done. The usual procedure is sanding. This can be done with a power sander, but many cabinetmakers prefer to hand-sand, at least in the final stages. And power sanding is not always possible where intricate detailing is involved.

For flat sanding, you can use a block of scrapwood, provided its working surface is perfectly plane. For better results, though, use a *molded-rubber sanding block*. For tricky surfaces like small inside or outside curves, inside angles, and V-grooves, a *teardrop* or flexible *sanding block* is most useful. And for complex moldings, your best bet is to get a set of *contour sanding grips*. All of these forms are fitted with whatever sandpaper you wish to use, cut to appropriate size.

Another possibility is *sanding sticks*. These handy gadgets come in sets containing a variety of sizes with special sanding belts, grit sizes 120–600. Use them for all sorts of smoothing in awkward and hard-to-reach spots.

Sanding is not the only way to smooth a workpiece. Many cabinetmakers prefer to use *scrapers,* which are available in several varieties. Probably the best known are simple cabinet scrapers that consist of a flat plate of rigid top-quality steel, typically about 80 millimeters thick. Several configurations are available, and they are often sold in sets.

Some scrapers are stiff, sharp blades attached to a shanked hardwood handle. Some are *shavehooks*, each blade configuration with its own handle. Others, called *scraper systems*, have several blades that can be attached to a single handle. They are particularly useful for smoothing odd shapes and moldings and can be employed for removing old finishes. The *Maute scraper*, for the same purposes, has a single blade whose position on the handle can be changed to suit different shapes.

A *scraping plane*, which looks a bit like a smoothing plane but has a nearly upright (adjustable) blade, is another option for fine smoothing. A *two-handled cabinet scraper*, which looks like a spokeshave but has an upright blade, is another possibility. Perhaps the finest (and certainly the most expensive) of this type of scraper is the cabinetmaker's *finishing scraper*. It is a sizable wood-bodied, planelike tool that holds a special scraper blade at a 5-degree angle and is designed for one-handed use.

For scrapers to work effectively, they must be sharpened so that the blade edge, besides being absolutely true, has a tiny lip of metal on one side, called the *curl* or *hook*, that does the scraping work. It is developed by dressing the blade edge with a fine stone if necessary, then a *burnisher*. A wheel burnisher is best for a straight blade because of its unerring accuracy. For shaped blades, and straight ones, use either a triangular or a round hand burnisher, whichever works best.

Fastening

A few special fastening tools are useful in cabinetwork. For example, a hammer is not just a hammer, and the ordinary 16-ounce carpenter's *claw* or *ripping hammer* won't serve you well in cabinetmaking. But a 12- or 13-ounce claw model will work quite well. At times an upholsterer's tackhammer is very handy for driving brads in small moldings.

A good alternative is to obtain a set of the traditional *cabinetmaker's* or *Warrington hammers*, usually available in 10-ounce, 6-ounce, and 3.5-ounce sizes. These hammers have a broad face for nailing and a wedge-shaped peen for starting small finish nails or brads. They are excellent for all kinds of cabinetmaking chores and not expensive.

The screws used traditionally in cabinetmaking have been slotted brass or steel wood screws, and traditional *cabinetmaker's screwdrivers* are best if you enjoy the time-honored methodology. These screwdrivers are made of tool steel and have hollow-ground blades and flat waists where a crescent wrench can be applied for more driving torque. The best models have tips ground to fit specific screw sizes and are fitted with ferruled hardwood handles.

Today, however, several new screw patterns are becoming increasingly popular. Changes in thread designs make driving easier and increase holding power, and changes in head designs require different kinds of drivers. The traditional straight-slotted head is still in use, as is the Phillips head, which requires a Phillips screwdriver in sizes 1, 2, or 3, depending upon the screw size. The *Robertson Drive* head is usually referred to as *square drive*; the sizes are 0, 1, 2, and 3. *Recex screws* are designed to be driven with either a square or a Phillips driver. *Clutch-head screws*, however, require special drivers. You will sometimes encounter *Posidrive* and *Allen* types of fasteners; the latter requires special Allen wrenches, which come in numerous sizes and are usually sold in sets.

Miscellaneous hand tools

Numerous miscellaneous hand tools come in handy. Much depends on your personal preferences and the tasks involved. For example, many cabinetmakers work with veneers, which means acquiring a set of specialized tools such as a *veneer hammer*, *rollers*, *trimmers*, *punches*, and an *inlay cutter*.

Other tools have more general woodworking purposes, such as *corner chisels*, which are designed to square off the rounded corners of mortises. *Dogleg chisels* are useful for a variety of tasks, and *nooker knives* (three sizes are commonly available) are great for cleaning out corners and crevices.

Glue applicators, injectors, brushes, and rollers suited to your tasks are good time-savers. A wide array of *woodworking mallets* is available in woods of several species, several hardnesses of plastic, and rawhide that comes in handy for different striking or assembly operations that must be mar-free. A small, soft-faced *dead-blow hammer* in 8-ounce size works well for driving tight joints together.

Installing cabinets, or building them in place, requires a *plumb bob* for dropping plumb lines to achieve true vertical position and levels to ensure the horizontal lines. An ordinary bob and a 2- or 4-foot *spirit level* can do the job, but a more accurate and easier method (albeit more expensive) is to employ one of the new "smart" *electronic levels*. Instead of eyeballing a bubble in a vial, you can see a highly accurate digital readout of the level's position.

Specialized power tools

2-11 *Plate joiner.*

Over the past few years several specialized power tools have become available at prices affordable for the amateur woodworker. One of the best of these is the *Lamello machine*, now better known as a *plate joiner* or a *biscuit joiner* (FIG. 2-11). The purpose of this machine is to cut matching slots in two mating workpieces into which special splines called biscuits or plates are inserted. The system is fast and precise, simplifies even simple joints and makes complex ones easy, and best of all is practically foolproof. You can get along fine without a biscuit joiner, but once you have used one, you will wonder why you didn't get one sooner.

In the sawing department, *floor table saws* have long been standard shop machines and probably always will be. Nowadays, though, you can purchase even a small *benchtop model* and be assured of good quality and accuracy. Some of the new "cutting systems" and saws with sliding tables now available at affordable prices bear investigating if you are in the market for a new saw. Also, the current prices of quality *benchtop* or *portable bandsaws* and *radial arm saws* (FIG. 2-12) make them viable options for even small home shops. Some of the radial arm saws can double as sanders, planers, and routers when fitted with the proper accessories.

2-12
Radial arm saw.

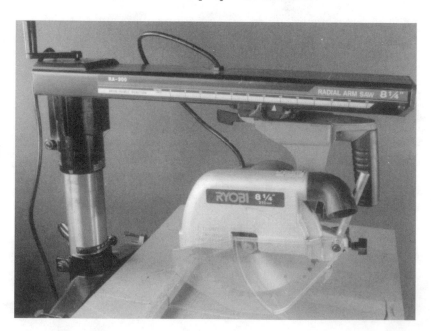

Perhaps one of the handiest power saws to come along in years is the *power-miter* or *"chop" saw* (FIG. 2-13). Several sizes are available, and while most make only single-angle cuts, some models can make compound cuts. A chop saw is most useful, especially if set up on a special miter-saw bench, not only for cabinetmaking but for general woodworking and rough and finish carpentry in house building.

Power sanders (FIG. 2-14) are almost essential in a modern home shop. Most woodworkers are familiar with *belt sanders* and *pad sanders*—the latter has always been especially popular for cabinetmaking. But there are innovations in the sanding field too. The new *random-orbit disk sanders* outperform all the old styles. They remove stock rapidly when necessary but also produce a very fine, smooth surface. Several models are on the market, all good quality, both *in line* and *right-angle* types with several features. For extensive cabinetmaking, this type of machine is an enormous help.

2-13 *Power miter or "chop" saw.*

2-14
Power sanders: half-sheet pad sander, random orbit sander with dust collector, small belt sander, triangular-head finishing sander.

Time-saving tools 29

Another interesting innovation is the *finishing sander* with a triangular pad mounted well forward. Working in the close quarters and tight inside corners so common to cabinetmaking has always been a difficult chore, but this machine answers the problems.

There is also a new (and relatively inexpensive) generation of *combination belt and disk sanders*. The benchtop models—there are about a dozen—are the most suitable for the home shop, but a stationary floor model is worth considering. Sanders come in two general types: *narrow-belt*, with a 1-inch-wide belt and a disk typically of 5-, 6-, or 8-inch diameter; *wide-belt*, which typically has a 4-inch belt and a 6-inch disk. Floor models are usually fitted with 6-inch-wide belts and 9-inch-diameter disks, or 12-inch disks in the heavy-duty type. The wide-belt type is particularly useful in a cabinet shop.

For edge and narrow surface sanding there is a similar tool called an *oscillating edge sander*. This machine carries a 4-by-24-inch belt mounted sideways to an angle-adjustable table. The belt rotates like any belt sander but also oscillates rapidly up and down, producing a fine finish. The benchtop machine could see a lot of use in a cabinet shop; large floor models are also available.

Depending upon suppliers to provide you with smoothly planed; zero-defect; warp-, twist-, and cup-free stock of exactly the right matching thicknesses is a chancy proposition at best. The solution to the problem is having your own *thickness planer*. Heretofore, these machines have been beyond the means of most home-shop owners. Today they proliferate because the price has come down and the usability factor has gone up.

A planer like the *Ryobi* 10-inch portable model or one of its similar cousins now can be part of even a small shop. It is an invaluable adjunct, especially if you recycle used stock, buy rough-sawn material, or want to work up some of your own plank stock from logs. Several models are available at reasonable cost in sizes from 10–20-inch plank-width capacity. Some can be fitted with special cutters to produce moldings in various profiles. If woodworking is an ongoing interest, a planer is one machine that can soon pay for itself.

While carpenters' hand planes are fine for many chores, a *power plane* (FIG. 2-15) is more practical and a good deal faster. The cuts are apt to be smoother and more accurate in the hands of an amateur (some practice is necessary to get used to the tool, though). A small *power block plane* is excellent for light work and can make very delicate, precise cuts; one-hand operation is easy. The larger models are designed for two-hand operation and can tackle almost any kind of planing job.

2-15
Power plane with 3¼-inch-wide blades.

Another valuable tool for the cabinetmaker is a *router* (FIG. 2-16). There are three kinds: *standard base*, *plunge*, and *trimmer*. The standard base or conventional type has been the most common until recently. This workhorse sits on a flat, round base with the cutter projecting below the base to whatever depth is desired. The entire machine is lowered onto

2-16 *Router.*

the workpiece to make the cuts. The plunge router, however, sits above a spring-loaded base with the cutter well clear of the workpiece. To make the cuts, the machine is positioned and the head pushed slowly down, driving the cutter into the workpiece. This machine is readily controllable and especially good for making mortises. The trimmer router is used primarily for trimming the edges of laminates applied to countertops or other components, although it can be used for any similar purpose and on all ordinary materials.

Conventional and plunge routers are available in both ¼- and ½-inch collet sizes for cutter bits of those shank diameters. Horsepower ratings range from ¾ to 3. The smaller machines are adequate for occasional light use; a ¾–1¼-horsepower router with a ¼-inch collet is good for general purposes. To drive ½-inch shank bits, you need more horsepower; 1½–2 horse is a good size for cabinetmaking, running long moldings, and such moderately heavy-duty tasks.

A router can be used at the bench or brought to the workpiece. There is a vast array of cutter bits for all sorts of purposes, including raised panel sets for door making and numerous individual configurations for veining, chamfering, dovetails, V-grooving, rounding, and slotting. And there are many jigs and guides that allow great flexibility of cuts in making joints of various sorts.

By mounting your router in a special table, you can turn it into a fixed benchtop machine that operates like a small jointer or shaper. Several such models are now available in varying degrees of sophistication. In addition, there are a couple of small, discrete *benchtop router-shapers* being produced that include an integral, nonremovable router motor serving the same purposes with a bit less flexibility.

The small *laminate trimmer* is cost-effective only if you will be applying substantial quantities of plastic laminates such as Formica to your cabinetry. For only a few feet of edge trimming (a single countertop, for instance) a hand trimmer or even a file can do the job at little cost. Beyond that, a power trimmer is most helpful, and a standard router can do the job.

A *jointer* (FIG. 2-17) is a fine machine to include in any cabinet shop. Its primary purpose is to create clean, fresh edges. This is necessary when two edges are to be glued, for example. It is also always wise to cut an edge on the jointer before making a rip cut on the table saw to ensure that the edge against the fence is true. The jointer also surfaces any stock narrow enough to run through the machine (but a planer does a better job). And once you learn how to make the setups, you can cut wide rabbets, raised panels, bevels and chamfers, tapers, recesses, tenons, and even relatively complex shapes. For most home shops, the 4-inch size is adequate, although a 6-inch jointer with extra cut depth is more useful.

2-17
Small jointer.

The *shaper* is perhaps one of the most misunderstood and little-used of the power tools available for home shops. What it can do for the cabinetmaker, once proficiency in use is attained (and that is not hard), is amazing. Unlike the router, which takes shanked bits fitted into a collet, the shaper has an upright shaft or spindle, solid and fixed on small machines and hollow and interchangeable on many larger ones, onto which three-lip cutters are secured.

A myriad cutter shapes are available, and special configurations can be ground to suit. Some cutters are single-purpose, such as *glue-joint* and *bead cutters*. Others are combination types that will produce differing profiles depending upon the extent or depth of the cut. Still others are matching sets, like the cabinet set used for making mating cabinet-door stiles and rails. There are numerous sizes of shapers available, but for a home cabinet shop a ¾- or 1-horsepower machine with a ½-inch-diameter spindle is suitable.

Power-tool accessories

Dozens of power-tool accessories allow you to perform many added operations with various power tools. By picking and choosing with care, you can handle the maximum number of tasks of most value to you with the fewest power tools. The usual trade-off is that a good bit of time is needed to make the setups or conversions for each operation, and added time may be needed to perform each operation.

A secondary consideration is that there may be limitations to what or how much you can do, what degree of complexity you can undertake, or how good the final results will be. Nonetheless, it pays to keep an eye out for such accessories. Just make sure they are top quality and will perform as advertised.

For example, one handy device that has been around for many years and is a proven performer is the *Safe-T-Planer*. This inexpensive device will plane, rabbet, tenon, make raised panels, and do other chores with precision and safety. One model fits any kind of drill press with a ½-inch chuck; another is for radial-arm saws with ⅝–1-inch spindles; and a third fits Sears radial-arm saws. It is designed to operate at speeds of 3,000–6,000 RPM.

Many items can be fitted to a table saw. A large sanding disk is one example. You can mount a molding head with several profiles of interchangeable cutters to any good 8–12-inch saw that operates below 5,200 RPM so it can be used as either a shaper or a jointer. For cutting dadoes, simply fit a set of combination dado blades, or a single adjustable blade, to any ⅝- or ¾-inch arbor saw that operates below 6,500 RPM.

A drill press, depending upon the size and model, can be fitted with a special mortising machine of excellent accuracy. Special bit and chisel sets are available in ¼–⅝-inch sizes, and allow mortise depths of up to 3½ inches.

Another attachment that can be fitted to a floor or benchtop drill press centers and holds an air-filled *contour* or *drum sander*. The sander is a cylinder usually about 2 to 3 inches in diameter and 4 or 8 inches long (depending upon drill-press size). It is inflatable and covered with a removable sandpaper sleeve. Once inflated to a suitable pressure with a compressor or even a bicycle tire pump, the surface will conform to whatever shape is pushed against it to be sanded. These are also made for wood-turning lathes.

Vacuum systems

One of the biggest problems in cabinetmaking, and woodworking in general, is that great quantities of sawdust accumulate in a very short time. This can be a serious fire hazard, especially where clouds of airborne wood flour develop during extensive sanding operations. The stuff is pervasive, getting into everything, and is also explosive under some conditions. Sawdust is a health hazard, causing all manner of respiratory problems; some exotic woods are particularly toxic; and sawdust or any other kind of dust raises hob with fine finishing processes.

The obvious solution is to corral as much of the dust as you can. Some equipment available at reasonable cost helps greatly in that respect. There are three general approaches: collecting sawdust, shavings, and chips as they are generated at each machine; collecting debris after it falls from various hand or portable power-tool sanding or cutting operations; and filtering the air in the workshop on a continuous basis.

Much cabinetwork is done in place, when cabinets are fitted and installed or perhaps built in place. And much work is done on cabinet assemblies with hand and small power tools. Either way, sawdust and other debris accumulates on the workpiece and the surrounding area.

The best way to keep ahead of an excessive pileup is to vacuum everything frequently with a powerful canister-type shop vacuum that is always kept at hand. A hose with a crevice nozzle gets into the cracks and crannies, and a round furniture or upholstery brush will do a good job on flat surfaces. The key is to use a machine of 1½–2 horsepower or more that has plenty of suction.

To clean flat surfaces in preparation for finishing, a shop vacuum with a wide brush on the hose will do a good job. Just pop the brush off and use the hose alone to get into the corners. Another possibility for all-around cleanup is the Royal Dirt Devil hand-held minivacuum, available at many housewares stores. This machine is unique in that it features a power brush, weighs only 3½ pounds, and has an extension hose and crevice nozzle.

Keeping the shop clean and the air relatively clear during power-tool operations requires a different approach. First, as many hand-held power tools as possible should be equipped with dust-collector bags, preferably with dust collection hoses or outlets that can be attached to a shop vacuum. With the latter arrangement, the dust is immediately sucked safely away, and the workpiece is kept relatively clean at the same time.

Stationary or benchtop tools, such as the table saw, planer, jointer, belt-disk sander, or radial arm saw, should be tied into a central dust-collection system. The heart of the system is a base-mounted impeller driven by a motor ranging typically from 1 to 3 horsepower, generating a tremendous suction. The smallest models have but one bag, but most have an upper and a lower bag. One is a separator to take out large particles, and the other is a filter to catch dust.

For a small shop, a 1-horsepower two-bag collector (FIG. 2-18) that handles one machine at a time should be adequate, although a midsized two-machine collector with greater bag and air-handling capacity might be better. All of the higher-quality collectors, unlike a shop vacuum, have a relatively low sound level.

Rigging up a dust-collection system takes a bit of ingenuity, although there is nothing difficult about it. The standard inlet size of the collector is 4-inch diameter, so connections can be made with standard 4-inch flexible collector hose, or you can substitute ordinary clothes-dryer hose for light-duty service. In some cases a machine may work better, or be already equipped with a smaller outlet or hose; 2-inch and 3-inch collector hose is available for those situations, as are reducer fittings.

2-18 *Dust collector.*

Dust hoods are used at the machine to channel the waste material into the hoses, and these can be rigged in any number of ways, depending upon the particular machine. Also, you can fabricate your own machine-dust collectors from plastic, sheet metal, plywood, or whatever else works. Several types of fittings are available, and they can be joined with band clamps; or to make airtight connections (which results in greater suction), you can use tape.

Devices called *blast gates* can be inserted into the collection lines as needed to control or redirect airflow. Thus, you can simply hook up each machine to a single hose as you use it or engineer a permanent system with each machine connected to the collection hoses and ready to be on line at the push of a gate.

Keeping the air in the workshop clear of dust is partly accomplished by employing the two methods just described to the fullest extent possible. To achieve a greater degree of purification requires further measures. The simplest is to introduce a strong forced draft by means of a fan or blower that pulls fresh air into the shop area from outdoors or another part of the building, sweep it through the area, and exhaust it to the outdoors. This method can be effective in some circumstances but is not a good constant-duty solution, especially in locales where mechanical heating or cooling is in operation much of the time.

Another method is to recirculate the air in the workshop, which should be relatively tightly closed, through *filter panels*. The volume of air should be high to drive as much as possible through the filters in as short a time as practical. Ordinary furnace filters can be used, and vacuumed or washed out often.

Another possibility is to set up both arrangements and use them separately or together as conditions indicate. And in some instances an air-filtration system can be tied in with the central heating or air-conditioning system. Regardless of the specifics, your local heating, ventilating, and air-conditioning (HVAC) contractor can probably furnish you with both ideas and equipment.

Safety considerations

You may be tired of hearing assorted safety and health warnings. We seem to be inundated with cautions and caveats about everything these days. As has often been said, living can be hazardous to your health. Unfortunately, this rash of dire admonitions is so thick around us, and so many of them seem so ridiculous (don't run your electric drill while taking a bath), that most are routinely ignored.

In spite of that, there are some safety rules appropriate for cabinetmaking and woodworking that bear repeating:

- Keep all cutting edges, regardless of which tools or machines they are in, as sharp as you can. Dull blades not only produce poor quality work, but are dangerous to the user.

- Run all power machinery at appropriate speeds for the tasks at hand.

- Always have safety guards and shields in place on power machines unless they must be removed to perform some operation (often the case).

- Fit your power machines with accessory safety devices such as antikickback rollers and hold-downs on the table saw and pushpads for the jointer.

- Whenever you work with any tools or equipment that might produce flying debris or use finishing liquids that might spatter, wear safety spectacles, wide-vision goggles, or a full flip-up face shield. If you already wear glasses, consider shatterproof lenses.

Hearing protection is now recognized as considerably more important than previously thought. A chain saw operates at about 120 decibels, a table saw at only slightly less, and either can cause hearing loss. Even a router, at 100 decibels, is considered very loud, as is the piercing whine of a shop vac. A safe level of continuous sound is usually considered about 85 decibels. This means that for workshop use, you need hearing protection with a noise reduction rating (NRR) of at least 25 decibels. Earplugs are best, some of them providing a NRR of over 30 decibels. Wraparound earmuff types typically run about 20 NRR.

For many of us, especially those with respiratory ailments or allergies, a respirator is a must. So many dusts and vapors, especially from exotic woods or various applied finishes, can cause problems that there is no sense in taking a chance with any of them. There are two considerations here: dust and particulates, and fumes or vapors. Some respirators, or masks, are proof against one or the other, some against both. There are many different kinds on the market, so check the specs carefully, look for MSHA and NIOSH approval, and select a model suitable for your purposes for which you can get replacement filters or cartridges. For many purposes, the small, lightweight throwaway particle masks are adequate. For total protection, a sealed positive-pressure respirator that completely covers the face and has a belt-mounted blower is best.

Certain kinds of woods, waxes, finishes, or even steel-wool pads can give some people skin rashes, and some finish components can be absorbed into the skin to create worse problems. The answer is simple: Wear rubber gloves or disposable (and very inexpensive) vinyl gloves. The rubber ones are more durable; the vinyl allow a better sense of feel and touch; but both work well.

Finally, forget about working in the shop if you are tired or stressed out, and certainly don't do so if you have had a couple of drinks. Watch the tube instead.

CHAPTER 3

Basic materials

ALL THE ANTIQUE cabinetwork you see is made entirely of solid wood, except for the hardware. Several decades ago, plywood products began to appear, and kitchen cabinetry made of enameled sheet steel became popular. Then came various reconstituted wood products and plastics. Today, only a small percentage of the materials used in cabinetry, especially the commercial variety, is solid wood. Its most common application is in visible parts like face frames, drawer fronts, and doors.

Softwood plywood is now widely used in hidden parts of cabinets, and plywood veneered with various woods is popular for visible portions. Wood products like oriented strand board (OSB), particleboard, chip- or waferboard, hardboard, medium-density fiberboard, glass, ceramic tile, laminated plastics, simulated and real stone, acrylics, and even sheet vinyl are employed in various combinations to serve just the right purpose with exactly the desired appearance. There are numerous choices in most of these materials, along with a huge array of hardware. The more you know about them, the greater will be your success in designing and constructing cabinetry to fulfill your needs.

Solid wood

The chances are good that you will want to use at least some solid wood in your cabinetmaking projects, especially if you enjoy working and finishing wood to bring out its natural beauty. It is perhaps the most versatile of all building materials and a pleasure to work with once you understand its properties and characteristics.

Composition

Although wood appears to be a simple material, it is complex. The details of its structure determine not only the appearance of any particular species but its other characteristics as well, such as how it can be worked, machined, and finished.

The basic structure of a tree, including roots, trunk, and branches, is an enormous collection of tiny cells, all bonded together and formed with a substance called *lignin*. At any given time, most of the tree is dead, supported by these cell walls. Only the root tips, buds and flowers, leaves, seeds, and a very thin layer of cells beneath the bark (the *cambium*) are alive. Once the tree is fashioned into lumber, it is the cellular structure we work with.

A cross section of a log reveals a series of concentric circles, layers of materials with different appearances (FIG. 3-1). The outermost is the outer bark, a protective layer. Beneath that is the inner bark (*phloem*, or *bast*), which carries liquid nutrients upward as sap. Next is the growth portion, the cambium, which produces new wood and bark. All of these layers are disposed of during the manufacture of lumber to become waste, garden mulch, or some other by-product.

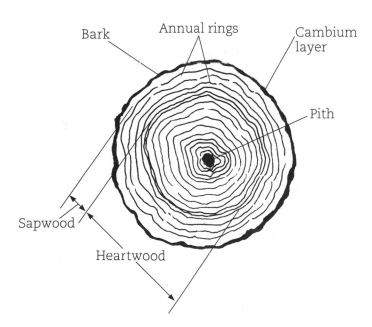

3-1
Cross section of a log.

The cambium produces little bark but develops a very visible, measurable layer of new wood called *sapwood*. The cells of this wood carry water upward to the leaves. The center portion of the trunk, varying in diameter depending upon the species, is usually a different color (also characteristic of the species) and is called the *heartwood*. This is mature dead wood and is difficult to differentiate from the sapwood in some species.

Spring is the time of fastest growth, tapering off during the summer and ceasing in early fall. The quick growth is composed of large light-colored cells and is called *springwood* or *earlywood*. The slower growth, made up of smaller cells of darker color, is called *summerwood* or *latewood*. In many species, this results in highly contrasting rings called *growth* or *annular rings*; counting them will give you the age of the tree because unless growing conditions are extremely unusual, there is one set each year.

Characteristics

The cellular structure and composition of each species of wood is responsible for a number of discernible and measurable characteristics and properties. Of most interest to cabinetmakers are those that govern two main features—workability and appearance. Cost and availability are two principal factors, but those are market-oriented and highly variable.

Density

An important but often ignored property of wood is its density. Although the cell walls of most woods are about the same composition, the space within the cells varies widely; even among trees of the same species. Density is determined by measuring specific gravity. A certain volume of wood, typically 1 cubic foot, is compared with a like volume of water at a temperature of 4 degrees centigrade. The result is expressed as a ratio of the weight of the wood to the weight of the water.

Various test methods and parameters can be used. The exact density depends upon the moisture content of the wood, obviously a variable characteristic. For example, red maple at 12 percent moisture content has a specific gravity of 0.54, a bit more than half the weight of water.

The value of this figure lies in its comparison with those of other woods. First, it is an indicator of the relative strength of the wood; second, an indicator of relative hardness; and third, an indicator of how well the wood will resist withdrawal of a fastener. In all cases, the higher the specific gravity, the harder and stronger the wood and the more resistant to fastener withdrawal.

Also, the greater the density, the greater the likelihood that the wood may split when a fastener is driven into it. Thus, white oak, at 0.68, is harder and stronger than the maple cited, while eastern white pine, at 0.40, is considerably softer and weaker. These factors can be important when considering how well a certain wood will perform in certain applications and how it might be handled and finished. Some relative densities of common woods are shown in TABLE 3-1.

Table 3-1 Approximate weight, ounces, per cubic foot of some common woods at 12 percent moisture content.

Ash, white	42	Hickory, shagbark	52	Pine, sugar	25
Ash, black	34	Lignum vitae	80	Pine, western white	27
Aspen, quaking	27	Locust, black	48	Poplar, yellow	30
Beech	45	Lauan	31	Redwood	28
Birch, paper	38	Mahogany, Honduran	35	Rosewood, Bolivian	50
Birch, yellow	43	Maple, red	38	Satinwood	67
Butternut	27	Maple, sugar	44	Spruce, red	29
Cedar, white	31	Oak, red group	45	Spruce, white	28
Cherry, black	35	Oak, white group	48	Sycamore, American	34
Chestnut	30	Pecan	47	Teak	44
Douglas fir	35	Pine, eastern white	24	Walnut, black	38
Elm, American	35	Pine, lodgepole	28	Walnut, claro	30
Fir, balsam	25	Pine, Ponderosa	28	Walnut, European	34
Fir, white	27	Pine, slash	41	Willow, black	27
				Zebrawood	48

Hard versus soft

Loose use of the terms *hard* and *soft*, mixing them with *hardwood* and *softwood* can cause confusion. As we've just seen, hardness is relative to specific gravity or density. The relative hardness or softness of a wood indicates its strength, toughness, resistance to scratching or denting, proclivity for splitting, and other factors not of consequence in this context, such as insulating value.

A wood with a specific gravity of 0.13, like balsa of model-making fame, is a real featherweight and extremely soft. On the other hand, lignum vitae, the choice for carvers' mallets, with a specific gravity of about 1.09, is terrifically hard and will not float in water.

Hardwoods and softwoods, however, are different classes of trees. Hardwoods are often referred to as *deciduous* or *broadleaf* species, trees that lose their leaves more or less all at once each year: maples, oaks, beeches, birches. The softwoods are commonly called *conifers* or *evergreens*: pines, firs, spruces. Neither definition is exact. Specifically, hardwoods are all angiosperms, and the softwoods are gymnosperms (following the exact botanical definitions given to those classifications).

In fact, some hardwoods are soft, and some softwoods are hard. The broadleaf hardwood quaking aspen might weigh in at 0.38 specific gravity, and the black cottonwood is even lighter. Certain subspecies of the conifer Douglas fir can run 0.50 and longleaf and slash pines about 0.60.

Grain Another loosely term, *grain*, can mean several things. Although in some senses grain has a bearing on some of the mechanical properties of wood, to a cabinetmaker, it is mostly the factors that affect the final appearance that count. Thus, *grain* can be used in the sense of texture, either coarse or fine across the annual rings, or surface appearance in general.

It can also relate to the presence or absence, or the size or quantity, of open pores exposed on the surface of the wood. A wood with many large pores (oak) is called *open-grained*; a smooth, unpored wood (white pine) is called *fine-grained* or *tight-grained*.

Grain is also used to denote the natural directional lie of wood fibers. When undisturbed, regular growth takes place; the cell structure is predominantly parallel with the tree trunk. In this case, or in any piece of wood where the wood fibers lie parallel with the long axis of the piece, the wood is called *straight-grained*.

Various growth problems can cause other fiber patterns. In *wavy-grained* wood, the fiber pattern undulates; in *curly grain*, the fibers appear as clusters of curls or whorls, sometimes called *birdseye*. *Fiddle-back* grain is a wavy pattern found in some maple, for example, and *spiral-grain* barber-poles along the length of the tree trunk or branches, twisting to right or left. Engelmann spruce does this sometimes.

In *interlocked grain*, the fibers grow first in one direction, then another, then back again, and are difficult to work. In *cross-grained* wood, the fibers lie at angles to the long axis of the log instead of parallel, and the angles may be variable. All of these grains are important to the cabinetmaker because of the way they affect the workability and finished appearance of the cabinetry.

Grain is also a term used in conjunction with the way the wood is cut, and this will be considered later.

Texture

Each species has its characteristic texture, and this characteristic is closely allied with the common conceptions of grain. A number of factors may be involved, but the chief determinant is cell size. The smaller the cell, the finer and smoother the texture; the larger the cell, the coarser and rougher the texture. The open- or fine-grain terms discussed earlier, with respect to visible pores or open cell cavities on the surface of the wood, also play a part in texture. And any other conditions that affect the planeness and smoothness of the wood surface, whether natural or introduced, can vary the perceived texture of the wood.

Figure

Figure is a characteristic that is often especially important to the cabinetmaker who seeks a pronounced visual effect in a clear- or natural-finished workpiece. This is a highly variable and indeterminant patterning of the wood that is unimpressive or even unnoticeable in some woods but extremely emphatic in others, sometimes even in woods of the same species.

There can be several causes for this, alone or in combination. Staining caused by the presence of extractives, fungi, or other elements can play a part, as can other natural coloration such as variances between heartwood and sapwood. Pronounced growth rings or ring irregularities are possible. In some species, cell structures called *rays*, which radiate outward laterally from the center of the tree, are distinctive; when pronounced, this is called *ray fleck*. Knots and assorted growth defects may add character. Odd and disoriented growth patterns are common contributors to figure, resulting in such distinctive patterns as *quilting, blister, birdseye, burl, roe, dimple,* and various kinds of *crotch* figure. Note that these may also be referred to as *grain*.

In addition, figure may be revealed or enhanced by the way the boards are cut from the log. Depending upon the angle of the cut to the fibers, the grain and figure will take on different appearances. The figure may be unnoticeable if the slice is made in one direction, very pronounced if made in another.

Color   In many cabinetmaking projects, the color of the wood is a consideration. If the finish will be natural, the wood may have to blend in with other furnishings or surroundings. If a stain finish is contemplated, selection of the stain color will depend upon the color of the wood. Sometimes two contrasting or perhaps compatible colors of woods are desired.

Color varies not only among species but also between trees of a given species, and even between parts of the same log. Most of the species commonly used in cabinetmaking exhibit characteristic colorations that are quite uniform. The colors in many of those less readily available woods that might be used, however, as well as some that are common, can be quite dissimilar. This means that careful selection, piece by piece, is sometimes an important consideration.

Wood color is caused by pigments embedded in the wood. Because these pigments are likely to be more plentiful in the heartwood, that part of the tree is often darker, sometimes to a great degree, than the sapwood. This is not always the case, though; in some species only a tiny bit of darker heartwood is visible.

Another point to keep in mind is that nearly all woods will darken when exposed to air and light because the pigments will slowly oxidize. A clear finish does not eliminate the process, which is much more noticeable in some species than others. Eastern white pine, for example, is notorious for this. Almost white when freshly cut, it will eventually turn a golden brown.

Anyone who works with solid woods soon discovers that there are several other properties that have an impact on the projects and are best learned through experience. For example, some woods are excellent for some purposes, not for others. Western larch is fine for many construction projects but not suitable for cabinets; eastern white pine can be used for either purpose. Beech is particularly good for fashioning food containers because it transfers no tastes or odors to the contents, but it has a terrible shrinkage problem.

The heartwood of redwood and cedar both have high natural resistance to rot and insects, and both can be used in cabinetry if the surfaces are not subject to hard usage, like a countertop. Many species, like walnut, cherry, oak, mahogany, butternut, zebrawood, and maple, have long been favorites for making furniture and cabinets because of their natural beauty and distinctive appearance.

Also important to the cabinetmaker is the way the wood will react to different machining operations because this dictates to some extent how difficult a project will be to complete and how it will look when finished. For instance, white pine is fine-grained; soft, and easy to work with either hand or power tools. Sugar maple will turn easily on a lathe despite its hardness, and planes, mortises, and otherwise machines well. Yellow poplar machines only adequately, holds stains well, and will seldom split when nailed. Lauan ripsaws nicely, but cottonwood leaves fuzz and fibers no matter how it is sawed or machined. Birch sands well and finishes nicely.

Miscellaneous properties

Woods have other pecularities and idiosynchrosies that may or may not be important to the task at hand. For example, steel fasteners in oak will eventually leave an ugly black stain from a chemical reaction. White pine, as well as some other conifers, may have hidden pitch pockets that will suddenly ooze a gummy mess. Hemlock knots can be so hard that they will take chunks out of chisel or plane blades.

You can find occasional "reaction wood," either the compression or the tension variety in almost any species. You may encounter defects of many kinds in almost any species. The fundamental constant of woods is the seemingly limitless range of variables.

Cuts

The angle at which a board is cut from the log, together with its relative position within the log, makes a considerable difference in the surface appearance of the wood. These differences are much more noticeable in some species than in others.

Several cutting methods are possible, depending on the size and kind of log, general procedures of the mill doing the cutting, and the intended use of the lumber. For the visible parts of cabinetry intended to have a natural finish, the cuts that exhibit the most pronounced grain or figure are often the most desirable. The terminology is a little confusing, but important nonetheless.

The simplest method of sawing a log into lumber is to square up the log by sawing off the barked slabs from the outside. Then the log is run back and forth on the carriage, with a board being cut away on each pass (FIG. 3-2). Or a few passes may be made on one side, a few on the other, and the remainder of the log rotated 90 degrees and sliced up.

3-2 *Slash sawing pattern.*

This is called *slashsawing* and produces tangential surfaces. The boards are usually termed *slash-grained* or *slash-sawn*, *flat-grained* or *flatsawn*, or *side-grained* if the wood is a softwood (FIG. 3-3). If a hardwood, it is often called *plainsawn*. The sawing is done parallel to the *pith* (the small, soft core approximately at the center of the tree) and tangent to the growth rings at angles of 45 degrees or less. This results in free-flowing patterns across the faces of the boards.

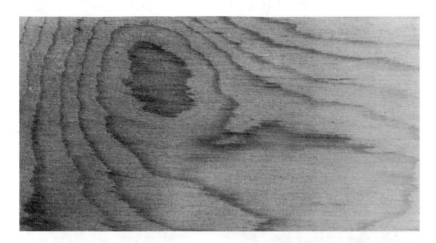

3-3
Slash sawing results in this appearance in softwoods, called flat-grained.

Another method is to quarter the log, then saw boards from each quarter so that the annual rings all lie at angles between 45 and 90 degrees to the faces of the boards (FIG. 3-4). This is called a *radial surface*, and the wood is termed *edge-grained* or *vertical-grained* if a softwood, *quartersawn* if a hardwood. The growth-ring lines run parallel with the grain and the long axis of the board, creating a distinctive pattern (FIG. 3-5). When present, rays appear as small flakes along the board edges.

A third and much less common method of cutting involves shifting each cut in a log quarter so that it is made between angles of about 35 to 45 degrees (FIG. 3-6). This cut also has a distinctive appearance in some species, and the boards are called *riftsawn*. Because this method is wasteful—a wedge-shaped gap is left between each board—it is expensive and usually confined to special orders and small quantities. The appearance of such stock, however, can be impressive.

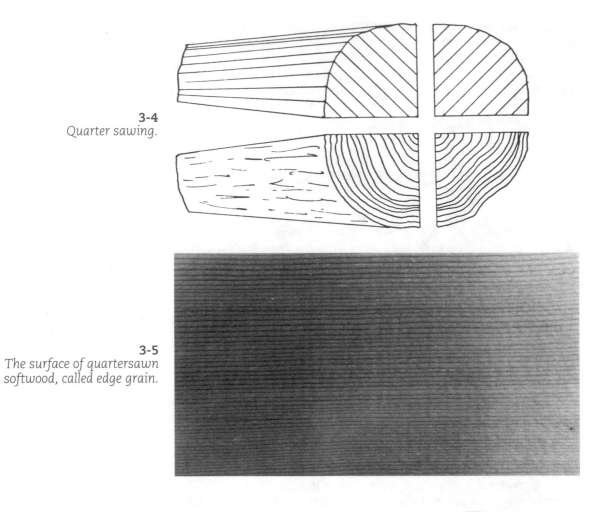

3-4
Quarter sawing.

3-5
The surface of quartersawn softwood, called edge grain.

3-6
Rift sawing, the most expensive and wasteful method.

Green wood, especially when cut in the spring, contains an enormous amount of water. When the logs are sawed and the planks allowed to air-dry, the free moisture within the cell cavities evaporates. When the liquid content of the wood gets down to about 28 percent (the fiber saturation point) and the cells are empty, moisture begins to leave the cell walls, and the wood starts to shrink. The shrinkage takes place in all directions, but not uniformly and not equally in different species or even in lumber of the same species.

To reduce the possibility of a host of problems, such as stain, rot, checking, and various kinds of warping (cup, bow, twist, crook, kink, diamond, crown, etc.), freshly cut stock must be carefully seasoned using certain procedures. Most commercial seasoning is done by either air-drying or kiln-drying, so that when the wood reaches the consumer, it has largely stabilized. That, at least, is the theory. In practice, wood movement is a constant problem that confronts every cabinetmaker.

Because there is no way to avoid the problem, you must learn to live with it. Different woods act differently, so becoming thoroughly familiar with the woods you work with is important. Study the details of wood movement and how it can be handled, a complex subject when seen in its entirety. But if you wish to harvest some of your own woods, perhaps noncommercial species that are otherwise unavailable, the ins and outs of seasoning will be of considerable concern.

Exercise the best craftsmanship, and assemble components of your cabinetry with tight, well-fastened joints; with appropriate fasteners and adhesives (especially the latter); with matching, mating, or opposing shrinkage or movement patterns (called *balanced construction*).

In some cases you can make allowances for expansion and contraction, which is a continual process in solid woods. This can often be done by design, as in frame-and-panel cabinet doors where the center panel "floats" in grooves cut into the inner frame edges (FIG. 3-7). The degree of dimensional change of many species can be calculated at various percentages of moisture content, and tables of coefficients are available for the purpose.

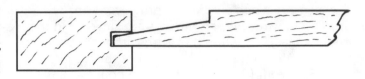

3-7
*Center panel mounted in a
cabinet frame-and-panel
doorframe like this "floats"
and is not bothered
by expansion.*

On an easier level, there are a few things to keep in mind.
When you purchase commercial stock for cabinetmaking,
make sure that it has been kiln-dried. The percentage of
moisture content of such wood may be as high as 19 or 20, and
a 14–15 percent rating is common. However, in nearly all parts
of the United States, the moisture content for cabinet woods
should be 8 percent, 6 percent in the arid Southwest; along the
lower Atlantic and Gulf Coast regions it can be as high as 10–11
percent (FIG. 3-8).

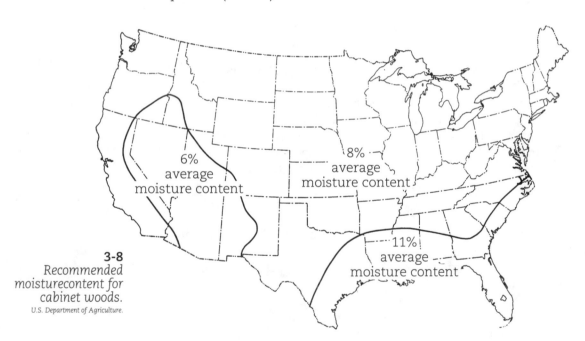

3-8
*Recommended
moisturecontent for
cabinet woods.*
U.S. Department of Agriculture.

But although these are the recommended levels, the wood you
buy may not be at that point, even if so rated, because wood
shrinks and swells with changes in atmospheric moisture
conditions, picking up and releasing moisture in cycles that lag
local humidity readings. To help stabilize the wood you buy,
you can "season" it yourself.

The material you purchase from a local lumberyard, or perhaps a faraway mail-order source, will probably have been stored in conditions different from those where the finished cabinetry will be installed. Therefore, buy your stock well ahead of time and store it well stacked and separated so that air can reach all surfaces, preferably under conditions identical to those at the eventual installation location. Leave it for at least a month to adjust to local conditions.

If the stock is unusual or cannot be readily matched with more, be sure to buy extra—10 percent at least—to substitute for pieces that shrink or warp and become unusable for your project. Under no circumstances should you store the material in your garage or crawlspace where conditions are probably adverse.

Also, you can deliberately select species that are less susceptible to expansion and contraction or warping. Lauan, for example, is substantially more stable than eastern white pine. Note too that plainsawn or flat-grained boards tend to shrink in width but not much in thickness. Quartersawn or edge-grained boards tend to shrink considerably less in width, not much in length, and have less tendency to warp. And you can use finishes that either seal the wood or allow it to breathe, whichever is more beneficial. No finish, however, is permanently impervious to moisture transfer into or out of the underlying wood.

Most commercial lumber stock is classified and graded by various agencies or associations under various sets of guidelines or specifications, and the details are extensive, complex, and sometimes confusing. Also, changes are made every so often. Even so, some reasonably uniform general standards are in effect at any time. Going into great detail is unreasonable here, but a brief look at some of the points of importance to a cabinetmaker is worthwhile.

Lumber is separated into several main classes of manufacture. *Rough* lumber is sawed, trimmed, and edged, but not planed smooth. *Surfaced* or *dressed* lumber has been smoothed by a surfacing machine on one or more surfaces and is designated

Classification & grades

accordingly, S1S means "surfaced one side"; S1E means "surfaced one edge"; S2S means "surfaced two sides"; and so on. *Worked* lumber has been dressed and shaped, as in molding stock. These last two categories are the ones of interest to cabinetmakers. Other classes may include *blanked, ripped, resawn, patterned,* and others.

Lumber is further classified by use. Softwoods are typically classed as *yard* lumber, *structural* lumber, and *factory* and *shop* lumber. Hardwood classes are *factory lumber, dimension parts,* and *finished market products.* Lumber is also classified by size groups (softwoods) or cutting sizes (hardwoods). But the grading into quality levels is most important to the cabinetmaker. Here again, there are differences between hardwoods and softwoods.

Softwoods are subdivided into two major categories: *construction* and *remanufacture.* This has given rise to many more grade names and definitions. You will probably have need for some materials from the *nonstress* and the *appearance* subdivisions of the construction category; the two often overlap. One of the principal uses of appearance grades is cabinetry, and there are several grading systems. From the top grade downward, the designations in the category (frequently called *select*) are *Select-B&BTR* (B and better) or *1&2 Clear; C Select; D Select.* Or you may encounter *B&BTR, C&BTR, D.* Or *Superior Finish VG* (vertical grain), *FG* (flat grain), or *MG* (mixed grain); *Prime Finish VG, FG, MG; E Finish.* In the lower-grade category, usually called *common,* the grades rank downward from *No. 1 Common* to *No. 5 Common.* The higher the number, the lower the quality and the worse the appearance.

The hardwood quality grades are also complex, but they reduce to a relatively simple system that largely prevails throughout the industry. The grades are based mainly on appearance and refer to the poorest face. They rank downward typically as *Firsts, Seconds, Select, No. 1 Common, No. 2 Common, No. 3A Common,* and *No. 3B Common.*

In practice, Firsts and Seconds are almost always combined as FAS, and the wood is about 80 percent clear (no knots or appreciable defects, according to a complex set of parameters) in each board. There are numerous other gradings for different species of hardwoods and hardwood products, so specific details are important; check them out.

As you select stock for your cabinetry projects, keep in mind that the price of the material is related to the grade. The lower the grade, the lower the price. Therefore, the lower the grade that will fulfill your needs regardless of the species, the lower your project cost. Also, the higher the grade, the more difficult it is to obtain the material, especially in quantity.

Note too that the grade of a particular piece may bear little relation to the purpose you intend for it. If you order some hardwood for cabinet doorframes without specifying grade, you might well receive FAS—prime stock for a prime price. But you might be able to get along just as well for a lot less money with some sticks of No. 2 Common, which in most cases is a good grade for general cabinetwork.

Remember that the grade given to each piece of hardwood is based upon the poorer face. Thus, a piece of No. 3 Common could be No. 2 Common on one face. If one face of that piece will be hidden in its final location and the grade—or more to the point, the appearance—is satisfactory, there's no need to pay the added price for a higher grade.

On the other hand, softwoods are most often graded on the basis of both sides. This can result in neither face being suitable for a particular purpose, necessitating a higher grade.

The final point to remember about grading is that each piece of stock is graded according to the characteristics of the whole length and width. Because of some serious defects in part of the piece, the whole may be graded low, but a large part of the piece may be fine. Perhaps you can buy the piece cheaply and use the good part where appearance matters and the rest where it doesn't.

When purchasing cabinetry stock (or any other, for that matter), it makes good sense to handpick each piece if you can, inspecting it carefully. Many dealers do not allow customers to pick through the stock, but you can always refuse to take any pieces you consider unsatisfactory.

If you are ordering by mail, you have to rely on the judgment of others, but often you can talk with a company representative or salesperson and explain in detail your particular needs. Then at least an informed selection can be made by the supplier.

Size   When dealing with lumber, you will see that there are often two sets of dimensions (TABLE 3-2). The nominal dimensions consist of *trade sizes* that are industry reference standards. Thus, a 2 × 4 in theory measures 2 inches thick and 4 inches wide, a 1 × 6 measures 1 by 6 inches.

Table 3-2 Dimensions of lumber.

Softwood

Nominal (trade)		Actual	
Thickness	Width	Thickness (in.)	Width (in.)
1	2	¾	1½
1	4	¾	3½
1	6	¾	5½
1	8	¾	7¼
1	10	¾	9¼
1	12	¾	11¼
2	4	1½	3½
2	6	1½	5½
2	8	1½	7¼
2	10	1½	9¼
2	12	1½	11¼

Hardwood

Nominal (trade) sizes are given in either fractions or whole inches and sometimes quarter-inches for thickness. Widths are given in inch fractions and wholes. Actual dimensions vary depending upon species and grading rules.

Note: Actual thicknesses and widths often vary slightly from the listed actual dimensions because of shrinkage.

In fact, those are the real dimensions only when the wood has just been cut, and sometimes not then. The real measurements are called the *actual dimensions* and are something less than the nominal dimensions. How much less depends upon how much the wood has dried and whether it is rough-cut, dressed, worked, or resawn and what grading standards are in effect for that lumber.

Note, however, that measurements of piece length are considered actual, although they may not be fully accurate. For example, a 10-foot board can be expected to be 10 feet long. It almost never will be less, but may be fractionally more.

Occasionally wood is sold by the piece (such as blanks for wood turning) and sometimes by the square foot; for rare woods or specialty pieces, even by the linear inch. The usual measure of quantity for woodworking lumber, however, is the *board foot*: 1 nominal board foot measures 1 inch thick, 12 inches wide, and 12 inches long. Thus, a 10-foot 1-x-6 equals 5 board feet; a 10-foot 2-x-6 equals 10 board feet. Actual board footage does not signify. Prices are typically quoted and calculated on the basis of 1,000 board feet, designated as M. Thus, material at $900/M costs $900 per thousand, or 90 cents a board foot.

Softwood lumber is made in even-foot lengths in increments of 2 feet, with 8 feet usually being the shortest and 16 the longest readily available, although lengths sometimes go to 20 or even 24 feet, depending upon the product. The widths and thicknesses are largely standardized; although presently given in inches, standards may be changed to metric in the near future.

Hardwood lumber lengths are largely random, from as short as 18 inches or so to 16 feet or more. Many more standard thicknesses are available. For some kinds of stock, the thickness may be designated in terms of ¼-inch increments, written out as 2/4, called *two-quarter* (½ inch thick); 5/4, called *five-quarter* (1¼ inches thick); or 8/4, called *eight-quarter* (2 inches thick). Widths are typically random unless the product is a specific manufactured one, such as a flooring strip, and might run anywhere from 1½ to 12 inches or more. Larger pieces are harder to get and more costly, and this varies with the species.

The length and width of the stock you purchase is easy to control. Just order lengths and widths that will cover your needs. Overwide stock can be ripped to size; overlong trimmed down. Narrow pieces can be glued to make wide pieces, a common shop process.

But thickness variations can cause problems, and the actual thickness of both hardwood and softwood stock can vary considerably for the same nominal thickness, even if all the stock is from the same batch from one mill. This is caused by a number of factors like shrinkage, species variables, and processing-machine setup differences. A difference of just a few thousandths of an inch in two mating pieces in a cabinet face frame can be most unsightly. If you fail to spot the difference before assembling the parts, trying to erase the problem can be very difficult, sometimes impossible.

If you do not have a way to reduce thickness, such as a thickness planer, be watchful of the thickness variations in the stock you purchase. This holds true for both plain and worked materials.

Check mating pieces before assembling them. When there are variations, you may be able to match the visible faces, any offset hidden from view where it doesn't matter. Mating pieces can be cut from the same board. Mismatches can be carefully hand-planed or sanded away if not too great, and joint adjustments can be made.

If you have the opportunity to handpick your stock, take an accurate thickness gauge along and check each piece. If there are variances, select as many like-thickness pieces as possible and fill out with thicker ones that can be taken down. Any well-equipped commercial woodworking shop can do this for you for a small fee.

As you can readily see, however, having your own power thickness planer would allow you to match all your stock for thickness, saving a lot of time and trouble. And in addition you would be able to tailor stock thicknesses to your projects.

With very few exceptions—those being extremely hard, mineralized, or fractious woods like ironwood, lignum vitae, or anything with squirrely grain and fiber—both hardwoods and softwoods can be worked with the entire range of ordinary hand and power tools. However, as you can see from TABLE 3-3, the workability of different species varies considerably.

Veneer

The term *veneer* in general means an overlay or facing applied to, or capable of being applied to, another surface. In woodworking, it invariably refers to very thin wood sheeting. This is solid wood in the sense that its makeup is only wood in its natural state, but unlike the solid wood just discussed, it is extremely thin and cannot be used alone.

Veneer woods are cut from dozens of different species, most of them hardwoods and many of them exotics (imported from other countries; species from this country are called *domestics*). Because small pieces of veneer can be butted together and glued upon a large substrate with handsome effect, even species that are rare, not commercially viable, or grow too small to be otherwise usable can be employed in cabinetry and furniture making.

As with solid woods, the way the veneer is cut from the tree, and the part of the tree from which it is cut, result in grains and figures of different patterns and emphasis. In square footage, most veneers are softwoods of ordinary appearance, such as fir. They are used in numerous kinds of plywood destined mostly for the building trades, accounting for perhaps 80 percent of production.

Of prime interest to the cabinetmaker is the small percentage of fancy veneered plywoods (more about that subject later) and the veneers themselves. Many species are available, and by using them, the amateur cabinetmaker who is willing to take the time and effort to become proficient at veneering can

Table 3-3 Machinability of selected hardwoods.

Kind of wood[1]	Planing— perfect pieces pct.	Shaping— good to excellent pieces pct.	Turning— fair to excellent pieces pct.	Boring— good to excellent pieces pct.	Mortising— fair to excellent pieces pct.	Sanding— good to excellent pieces pct.	Steam bending— unbroken pieces pct.	Nail splitting— pieces free from complete splits pct.	Screw splitting— pieces free from complete splits pct.
Alder, red	61	20	88	64	52	—	—	—	—
Ash	75	55	79	94	58	75	67	65	71
Aspen	26	7	65	78	60	—	—	—	—
Basswood	64	10	68	76	51	17	2	79	68
Beech	83	24	90	99	92	49	75	42	58
Birch	63	57	80	97	97	34	72	32	48
Birch, paper	47	22	—	—	—	—	—	—	—
Cherry, black	80	80	88	100	100	—	—	—	—
Chestnut	74	28	87	91	70	64	56	66	60
Cottonwood	21	3	70	70	52	19	44	82	78
Elm, soft	33	13	65	94	75	66	74	80	74
Hackberry	74	10	77	99	72	—	94	63	63
Hickory	76	20	84	100	98	80	76	35	63
Magnolia	65	27	79	71	32	37	85	73	76
Maple, bigleaf	52	56	80	100	80	—	—	—	—
Maple, hard	54	72	82	99	95	38	57	27	52
Maple, soft	41	25	76	80	34	37	59	58	61
Oak, red	91	28	84	99	95	81	86	66	78
Oak, white	87	35	85	95	99	83	91	69	74
Pecan	88	40	89	100	98	—	78	47	69
Sweetgum	51	28	86	92	58	23	67	69	69
Sycamore	22	12	85	98	96	21	29	79	74
Tanoak	80	39	81	100	100	—	—	—	—
Tupelo, water	55	52	79	62	33	34	46	64	63
Tupelo, black	48	32	75	82	24	21	42	65	63
Walnut, black	62	34	91	100	98	—	78	50	59
Willow	52	5	58	71	24	24	73	89	62
Yellow poplar	70	13	81	87	63	19	58	77	67

[1]Commercial lumber nomenclature.

create cabinetry of unique and handsome appearance. This is a method of including the natural beauty of woods that are not obtainable in any other way.

Some of the readily available domestic species are maple, cherry, ash, pecan, elm, butternut, and oak. Popular exotics include rosewood, bubinga, purpleheart, wenge, ebony, zebrawood, and eucalyptus. There are many others (TABLE 3-4).

Table 3-4 Commonly available veneer woods

Type	Cut	Color
Ash, white	flat cut	white to cream
Anigre	figured	yellowish-white to lt. brown
Aspen, quaking	stripe	yellowish-white to lt. tan
Avodire	stripe	white to gold
Beech	straight grain	whitish-brown
Benge	straight grain	med. brown w/dk. stripe
Benin	stripe	yellowish-brown
Birch	flat cut	white
Bubinga	straight grain	pink w/lt. purple streaks
Butternut	leafy grain	warm tan
Cedar, aromatic red		lt. red w/lighter streaks
Cherry, African	close grain	pinkish-brown to blood red
Cherry	straight grain	plain sliced—lt. reddish-brown
Ebony, macassar		dk. brown to black
		yellowish-brown to gray streak
Elm	strong growth pattern	lt. grayish or pinkish-brown
Eucalyptus		colors widely variable
Gumwood, red	figured	reddish-brown w/dk. streaks
Goncalo alves	fine rays	dark w/black bands and dark streaks
Hickory		white to cream—brown lines—tan heartwood
Holly	extreme close grain	pure white
Kelobra	large figure w/wavy lines	brown w/greenish cast
Koa		golden brown w/dk. streaks
Lacewood	flaky grain	lt. pink
	large rays	
Mahogany, African	various	various
Mahogany, Honduran	flat cut	various colors
Maple	various cuts	predominantly white
Maple, bird's eye	medium to small eyes	
Narra	stripe	rose to deep red
	distinctive grain	
Oak, white	various cuts	white
Oak, red	various cuts	reddish tinge
Padauk (vermillion)	quartered stripe	bright orange-red
Pecan	flat cut	reddish-brown

Table 3-4 Continued.

Type	Cut	Color
Pine, white	flat cut	cream
Purpleheart	even texture	deep purple w/stripe
Prima vera		yellow-white to yellow-brown
Rosewood	various	various
Satinwood	stripe	pale gold
Sycamore, white	mottle	white
Tamo	varied grain	tan to lt. brown
	varied figure	
Teak	flat cut	yellowish to dk. brown
	fine wavy grain	
Tulipwood	straight grain	pink to yellowish
Walnut	various	various
Wenge		dk. brown w/fine black veining
Yew, English		white to pale lemon or pink to orange and rose
Zebrawood	straight grain	alt. lt. to dk. brown stripe

Veneers are typically available in thicknesses of ⅟₂₈ and ⅟₄₀ inch, occasionally in others such as ⅟₁₆ or ⅟₁₀ inch. Certain flexible veneers are ⅟₆₄ inch thick. Most softwood and much hardwood veneer is cut from tree trunks, but specialty pieces are taken from tree stumps, burls and other disfigurements, reaction wood, butts, and crotches—all of which exhibit unusual, emphatic, and wild figures or grains.

Veneers are cut in several ways (FIG. 3-9). *Rotary-cut* veneers result from rotating a log on its long axis against a knife, thereby "unpeeling" the log in a continuous blanket; this is a typical method for producing softwood plywood veneers. *Plain-sliced* veneers are also sliced from a log, but in straight sections that are in effect very thin boards. *Quarter-sliced* veneers are also slabbed straight from the log, but the log has first been quartered, and the knife is angled against the quarter cuts. *Semirotary-sliced* veneer is peeled from logs sliced in half. All of these cuts show different and characteristic patterns and figures. Odd pieces like burls and crotches are cut in whatever manner best suits the piece and will produce the most interesting figure, usually by plain-slicing.

Veneers are sold by the square foot, and there may be two grades available. Terms vary, but they approximate *standard* and *premium*. Actually there are numerous grades, but they are

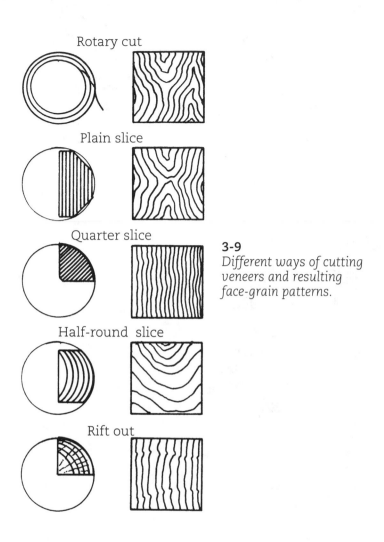

Rotary cut

Plain slice

Quarter slice

3-9
*Different ways of cutting
veneers and resulting
face-grain patterns.*

Half-round slice

Rift out

of interest primarily to industrial buyers. Most veneers are in
small pieces, in random widths of 3 to 12 inches or so and
lengths of 2 or 3 feet. Some premium pieces may be available in
lengths up to 8 feet or more. Often packages are available
containing a specified total quantity, such as 25 or 50 square
feet. Premium-grade sheets are stacked and kept in consecutive
order so that they can be perfectly matched in color, grain,
figure, and texture. Flexible veneers are made into full sheets
for easy application and typically run 18, 24, and 36 inches
wide by 4 or 8 feet long.

Tiny pieces of veneer are used for inlay work to create an infinite number of artistic designs. Smaller pieces can be used to cover small individual cabinet or furniture components. Flexible veneers can be used to cover convex or concave surfaces or large flat surfaces with ease. But the real challenge, and the fun, in employing veneers lies in the process called *matching*. This is what produces cabinetry of unique character. There are several ways to match veneer sheets (FIG. 3-10):

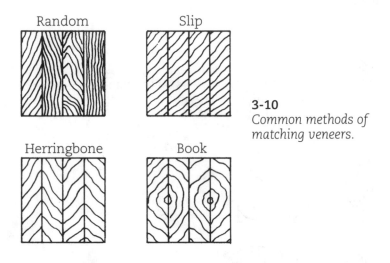

Random

Slip

Herringbone

Book

3-10
Common methods of matching veneers.

- *Random matching* involves laying out the pieces so that there is no repetitive pattern or common arrangement, just a mix. Pieces may be from the same or different logs and are not in any order.

- *Slip matching* involves placing consecutive sheets or strips of veneer side by side so that the pattern repeats and typically follows from sheet to sheet.

- *Book matching* or *book-leaf matching* involves placing alternating sheets faceup as they come from the sequentially stacked bundle (called a *flitch*). In horizontal book matching each pair lies side by side, opened out like the pages of a book. In vertical book matching they lie end to end. Where both height and width are needed, the two methods are combined.

- *Decorative* or *geometric matching* involves creating patterns with sheets or pieces of veneer, usually of like or similar visual characteristics (FIG. 3-11). Diamond matching is popular, as are reverse diamond and four-way or fourpiece. V herringbone, L, and checkerboard are other possibilities, and with the right pieces, even sunbursts are possible (but tricky).

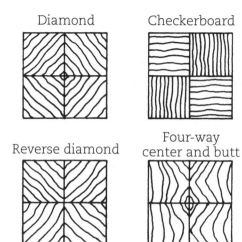

Diamond

Checkerboard

Reverse diamond

Four-way
center and butt

3-11
Methods of geometric veneer matching.

Working with veneers is a subject by itself but is not terribly complicated. Experience is the best teacher. There are several tools that are peculiar to the process, and trying to work without them is fruitless. They are not costly, however, and include such items as trimmers, rollers, special hammers and saws, punches, and clamping or pressing arrangements. With a little practice, the results can be rewarding.

Softwood plywood

The softwood plywood industry is devoted almost entirely to the production of numerous types of plywood for construction and industrial purposes. The manufacturing requirements and grading standards are voluntary under *U.S. Product Standard PS-1*, which is updated periodically. Most of the plywood produced in this country follows this standard, promulgated by the American Plywood Association (APA). A considerable amount of softwood plywood (some of which may actually include a hardwood species) can be used to good advantage in cabinetmaking, so having a working knowledge of the product is helpful.

Plywood is a sandwich made up of several thin layers of wood. *Veneer-core plywood* consists of several sheets of veneer with the grain laid at alternating right angles (*cross-lamination*). *Lumber core plywood* uses a center matrix of small sticks of wood glued together, covered with exterior veneer layers. Construction is always balanced, and because of the cross-grain pattern, plywood is very strong, stiff, and tough for its thickness and weight, and unlike most solid woods it is also quite stable. It is mostly made in sheets measuring 4 by 8 feet, but some items are 3 or 5 feet wide and lengths may go out to 12 feet in 1-foot increments. There are a few special sizes as well. Thickness depends upon the specific product, but those generally available are ¼, ⁹⁄₃₂, ¹¹⁄₃₂, ⅜, ¹⁵⁄₃₂, ½, ¹⁹⁄₃₂, ⅝, ²³⁄₃₂, and ¾ inch. There is also a 1⅛-inch thick subflooring material that makes good bench- and countertops.

There are several classifications of softwood plywood, but the one of chief interest to cabinetmakers is called *sanded plywood*. This plywood is sanded smooth (relatively speaking) on both faces during manufacture. There are three *Exposure Durability* classifications for this product: *Exterior*, in which the plies are fully bonded with waterproof glue for permanent exposure to the weather; *Exposure 1*, which will handle high moisture conditions periodically; and *Interior*, for dry interior applications only.

There are six veneer grades, which refer to the appearance of the exterior veneers (TABLE 3-5). The "best" side of the panel is called the *face*; the opposite is the *back* or *backing*. The veneer grades may be the same or different. While reference is actually to the veneer layer itself, the grade may also be used to designate the whole panel—e.g., A-C or B-B.

Each panel also has a species classification, which refers to the species used for the face and back veneers. The higher the number, the stronger and stiffer the panel. If the face is from one group and the back from another, the panel is classed in the higher group.

Table 3-5 Veneer grades of softwood plywood.

N	Smooth surface "natural finish" veneer. Select, all heartwood or all sapwood. Free of open defects. Allows not more than 6 repairs, wood only, per 4 × 8 panel, made parallel to grain and well matched for grain and color.
A	Smooth, paintable. Not more than 18 neatly made repairs, boat, sled, or router type, and parallel to grain, permitted. May be used for natural finish in less demanding applications. Synthetic repairs permitted.
B	Solid surface. Shims, circular repair plugs and tight knots to 1 inch across grain permitted. Some minor splits permitted. Synthetic repairs permitted.
C Plugged	Improved C veneer with splits limited to $1/8$-inch width and knotholes and borer holes limited to $1/4 \times 1/2$ inch. Admits some broken grain. Synthetic repairs permitted.
C	Tight knots to 1 $1/2$ inch. Knotholes to 1 inch across grain and some to 1 $1/2$ inch if total width of knots and knotholes is within specified limits. Synthetic or wood repairs. Discoloration and sanding defects that do not impair strength permitted. Limited splits allowed. Stitching permitted.
D	Knots and knotholes to 2 $1/2$-inch width across grain and $1/2$ inch larger within specified limits. Limited splits are permitted. Stitching permitted. Limited to Exposure 1, or Interior panels.

For top-grade material, select APA grade-marked panels. The stamping will tell you exactly what product you are looking at. If you need to order plywood, specify sanded, the thickness, the face and back veneer grades, group, exposure durability, panel size, and number of panels. In fact, since most lumberyards keep only a limited stock, your off-the-shelf choices may be limited. However, one can usually find a plywood that is suitable for countertop substrate, drawer boxes or bottoms, cabinet backs and floors, and various hidden components.

Hardwood plywood

The hardwood plywood industry manufactures a vast array of plywood panels in numerous sizes for a multitude of purposes. Most of the production is used in industrial, commercial, and construction applications, but it is also a prime material for furniture and cabinetry. Much of the hardwood plywood produced in this country conforms to the American National Standard for Hardwood and Decorative Plywood (ANSI/HPMA HP).

Like softwood plywood, the so-called hardwood variety is a laminated assembly. Most of the commercially available stock is in the form of panels measuring 4 by 8 feet in thicknesses of ¼, ½, and ¾ inch, with the ¼-inch perhaps being the most common form, as decorative wall paneling.

There are several panel constructions, designated by the kind of core employed (TABLE 3-6): *hardwood veneer*, *softwood veneer*, *hardwood lumber*, *softwood lumber*, *particleboard*, *hardboard*, and *special* (which means any other material). Four types are produced;. in descending degree of water resistance; *Technical* (exterior); *Type 1* (exterior); *Type II* (interior); and Type III (interior).

Table 3-6 Hardwood & decorative plywood.

Types: Technical (Exterior); Type I (Exterior); Type II (Interior); Type III (Interior)	
Cores	**Plies**
Hardwood veneer	3-ply and up
Softwood veneer	3-ply and up
Hardwood lumber	3-, 5-, 7-ply
Softwood lumber	3-, 5-, 7-ply
Particleboard	3-, 5-ply
Hardboard	3-ply
Special	3-ply and up

- Grades:Premium (A); Good (1); Sound (2); Utility (3); Backing (4); Specialty (SP).
- Sizes: Most common—48 by 84 inches, 48 by 96 inches, 48 by 120 inches; other available.
- Thicknesses; Usual range—⅛ to ¾ inch.
- Identification: By species name of face veneer, which may be either a hardwood or a softwood.

The face veneer is the key factor in most of this plywood, and there are several grades. The A *grade*, the best, may also be called *Premium*; this is the best choice for cabinetry with a natural finish. The B or *Good grade* can also be employed for this purpose, but matching is not apt to be as good. For a painted surface use *Sound grade*, or *Industrial* if you don't mind some filling and sanding. The back veneer can be almost any kind of wood. Some 50 species are commonly used for face veneers (TABLE 3-7), some of which, like the pines, are actually

**Table 3-7 Face veneers of hardwood
plywood grouped according to specific gravity (density).**

Category A species (0.56 or more) specific gravity) gravity)	Category B species (0.43 through 0.55 specific gravity)	Category C species (0.42 or less specific
Ash, Commercial White	Ash, Black	Alder, Red
Beech, American	Avodire	Aspen
Birch, Yellow Sweet	Bay	Basswood, American
Bubinga	Cedar, Eastern Red[b]	Box Elder
Elm, Rock	Cherry, Black	Cativo
Madrone, Pacific	Chestnut, American	Cedar, Western Red[b]
Maple, Black (hard)	Cypress[b]	Ceiba
Maple Sugar (hard)	Elm, American (white, red, or gray)	Cottonwood, Black
Oak, Commercial Red	Fir, Douglas[b]	Cottonwood, Eastern
Oak, Commercial White	Gum, Black	Pine, White and Ponderosa[b]
Oak, Oregon	Gum, Sweet	Poplar, Yellow
Paldao	Hackberry	Redwood[b]
Pecan, Commercial	Lauan, (Philippine Mahogany)	Willow, Black
Rosewood	Limba	
Sapele	Magnolia	
Teak	Mahogany, African	
	Mahogany, Honduras	
	Maple, Red (soft)	
	Maple, Silver (soft)	
	Prima Vera	
	Sycamore	
	Tupelo, Water	
	Walnut, American	

[a]Based on oven-dry weight and volume at 12 percent moisture content.

[b]Softwood.

softwoods. Another 100 or so species are sometimes used or can be special-ordered.

As a practical matter, the amateur cabinetmaker is in most instances confined to choosing whatever hardwood plywood— usually in the form of wall paneling—is in stock at the local supplier's warehouse or can be readily ordered from a wholesaler. Special ordering from a manufacturer is seldom feasible in small quantities, and having panels shipped from faraway sources can be cost-prohibitive. When an unusual species is desired, the best bet is to purchase the face veneer and apply it to a readily available low-cost softwood plywood or other substrate in the home shop.

Wood composition panels

Several kinds of composition panels are made from wood and wood by-products. Their greatest use is in industry and the building trades, but there are occasions when one of them serves well in cabinetry applications. The principal products are particleboard, hardboard, medium-density fiberboard, waferboard or chipboard, and oriented strand board (OSB). The latter two are chiefly construction items and not suited to cabinetwork, though they might be usable for rough or temporary storage units, for example.

Particleboard

Particleboard is made of wood chips or particles like coarse sawdust and a resin binder. There are two main kinds—*Type 1*, for interior use, and *Type 2* for exterior use, with several grades in each, depending upon the density of the board. There are numerous sizes, but the standard ones you are likely to find at supply houses are panels 4 by 8 feet and ⅜, ½, ⅝, and ¾ inch thick. There are four kinds, intended for different classes of applications. *Extruded* is the lowest density, has the lowest strength, and is the least expensive; it is often used for commercial furniture backing. *Single-layer* is the most common, widely used for various construction purposes, floor underlayment, and other noncrucial tasks; it has a homogeneous, fairly coarse makeup. *Three-layer*, on the other hand, is made of coarse particles in the center with a thin layer of fine and dense material on both faces. This works well where painted surfaces are intended or for countertops or other cabinet components to be covered with a plastic laminate. The heaviest and smoothest surfaced is the *graded-density* type, used only where those characteristics are most important; it is the most expensive.

Particleboard can be used as a substitute for plywood in many cabinet applications at somewhat less cost, although the results are not usually quite as good, and the material is a bit more difficult to work with the tools and equipment normally found in a home shop. You can construct cabinet cases or make built-in cabinetry entirely of particleboard, including the doors but excepting the face frames, and expect decent results if you work carefully and put a little extra effort into the finishing process.

Local suppliers usually do not stock a wide variety of particleboard grades; you may have only a couple to choose from. If you do have a choice, the *medium-density grades* 1-M-1 and 1-M-2 are good for cabinet cases and shelves. For doors that will be faced with a laminate, 1-L-1 works well.

One particleboard product is useful in some kinds of cabinet projects—*shelf stock*, with its rounded outer edge. This product comes in standard widths and long widths for any shelf application. However, unlike solid wood or plywood, if particleboard shelving is overloaded, it will fail, breaking in half like a cracker. Be sure to follow the loading recommendations given in chapter 10.

Particleboard does not work like wood or plywood; its properties are different. You can work with ordinary hand and power tools, however. Because the material is very abrasive, it will dull saw blades rapidly; carbide-tipped or metal-cutting blades are recommended for power saws, disposable blades for hand cutting (otherwise expensive sharpening will be required). Keep chisel and plane blades very sharp, or the material will tear and chip.

Chipping can be a problem, so use fine-toothed saw blades and tape cutlines. Surface-planing is not effective, and power edge planing can also cause problems. Again, carbide blades are necessary. You can rout particleboard with varying degrees of success, depending upon the pattern being routed and the density of the material. This should not be done on surfaces near panel edges, however, since breakage can easily occur from weakening of the material.

This material does not hold common or box nails well; ring-shanked nails are better. Screws are better yet, and you can purchase specially designed bugle-headed screws for just this purpose. Sheet-metal screws also work well. Either kind must be set in pilot holes, countersunk as necessary; otherwise, you will twist the heads off the screws.

When through-drilling, drill from the face down and place a scrap block against the back to minimize chipping-out when the drill point breaks through. If you have many holes to drill, use a carbide-tipped bit.

When sanding, use top-grade long-lived paper. To achieve a smooth finish, seal the surface first, then apply a filler that can be sanded smooth rather than attempting to smooth the raw surface.

Dense surfaces can be satisfactorily glued together, but the porous edges require a lot of glue and do not hold up well. Do not depend on glue joints alone. As for joint configuration, only the simplest kinds that make use of maximum flat surface area are effective. Complex joints are likely to break up in the making.

Hardboard

Hardboard is made from a mash of crushed and rearranged wood fibers and synthetic binders that is cooked up, rolled out, and pressed into sheets. The material is harder than most woods, and because it has no grain, it is about equally strong in all directions. It is considerably stronger and stiffer than most woods along their grain structure but less so across the grain.

Depending upon the product, it may have two smooth faces, or a smooth face and a screened or textured back. The most common panel size is 4 by 8 feet, although several other sizes are available, mostly on special order. Thicknesses range from $\frac{1}{12}$ inch to $1\frac{1}{8}$ inches, but those usually stocked by local suppliers are $\frac{1}{8}$ and $\frac{1}{4}$ inch.

There are five classes of hardboard:

- *Class 1, Tempered*: very hard-surfaced; the stiffest, strongest type and most resistant to abrasion and water.
- *Class 2, Standard*: not specially treated, as is Class 1; tempered but has relatively high water resistance and strength.
- *Class 3, Service-Tempered*: a treated material with good strength, water and abrasion resistance, hardness, and stiffness; only somewhat lower in quality than Class 2, Standard.
- *Class 4, Service*: similar to, but a considerably lower grade than Class 3, Service-Tempered.
- *Class 5, Industrialite*: a general-purpose hardboard with lower density and less strength, stiffness, and general resistance to wear and abuse than the other grades.

When selecting a hardboard grade, be guided by the intended use if you have a choice. A low grade would be satisfactory for a cabinet back, for example, but Class 1 a better choice for a drawer bottom. Again, dealers do not usually stock large quantities of hardboard, so you may be limited. You can determine the class by the number and color of the stripes painted on the panel edges: 1, one red; 2, two red; 3, one green; 4, two green; 5, one blue.

Hardboard can be worked with ordinary tools, both hand and power, but carbide blades and carbide-tipped bits are recommended because this is an abrasive material that dulls cutting edges rapidly. The material will not split, nor will it chip away or crumble like particleboard. However, it will edge-dent; corners or edges can break out or off under excessive pressure; and if bent too far, a panel will suddenly snap in two. Depending upon the kind of saw used, the upper or lower edge of the cut will feather and fuzz markedly, pushing up and out in a ridge. This can be cleaned off by beveling with a block plane.

When drilling holes, drill from the smooth face and place a block of scrap material under the back to reduce chipping and tearing when the bit comes through. High-density hardboard can be drilled and tapped and will hold coarse-threaded screws reasonably well. Sheet-metal and particleboard screws can be used; holding power for smooth nails is not especially good. Adhesives sometimes prove worthwhile, depending upon the circumstances.

Sanding will smooth cut edges, but do not sand the smooth faces; this will only roughen the surface and raise fibers, making a blemish correctable only with difficulty. Screened or textured surfaces cannot be smoothed practically. Scratches and similar damage can be filled, then scraped smooth with care. Surface sanding can be done if necessary after a couple of coats of primer or sander surfacer have been applied, using light pressure and very fine grit.

Medium-density fiberboard

Medium-density fiberboard, or MDF, is a material recently developed under the joint auspices of the National Particleboard Association and the American Hardboard Association. The purpose was to provide a hardboard of adequate strength and other suitable properties but lighter weight than other products that could be successfully employed for a wide variety of commercial purposes. Cabinetwork, shelving, doors, and paneling are among those uses.

MDF is a good material to use in cabinetry because of its reasonable weight, good strength, and good working properties. The surfaces are smooth, the edges are tight, and it takes applied finishes well and can be covered with a laminate. It is an essentially defect-free and stable material. However, it is neither well known nor widely distributed as a do-it-yourself product, so is not commonly in stock at local supply houses, especially smaller ones. This situation may improve with time.

MDF can be worked with ordinary hand and power tools. It will not hold nails; screws must be used. Sheet-metal and particleboard screws work well and can be used to hold edge-mounted hinges or other hardware, as well as some light-duty surface-mounted hardware, in thicker panels. Drilling pilot holes is necessary, as is countersinking.

Accessory materials

MUCH CABINETRY, especially individual furniturelike pieces such as bookcases, armoires, and stereo cabinets, is made entirely of the basic materials discussed in the previous chapter, save for bits of trim or hardware. But often accessory materials are incorporated as well, sometimes as a matter of practicality, sometimes for decorative or design emphasis, sometimes both. All of these materials are easy to come by and fun to work with, requiring no special expertise.

Plastics

Everywhere we turn these days plastics have invaded our lives, and cabinetry is no exception. Commercial cabinetry, especially the less expensive variety, uses plastics extensively in the form of vinyl coverings and coatings, some hardware, and occasional components. Plastics are not as common to custom or home-built cabinetwork, and many of them are suited only to industrial production methods. But four types in particular may well find a definite place in your plans.

Laminates

Plastic laminates have been around for years and are about as popular today as ever. Products like Formica and Micarta are widely used to cover the tops of kitchen counters, bath vanities, and similar cabinetry, and to surface kitchen cabinets, inside and out, including drawers, in the European style. There are also many miscellaneous uses for the material, such as drawer lining, shelf topping, cabinet-door backing, planter lining, and display-case interiors.

Plastic laminate is made of several layers of ordinary brown kraft paper, the same as your supermarket grocery bags. The bonding agent is phenolic resin, and the sheets are formed under heat and pressure. The face layer, containing the color, pattern, and texture, is of a higher-quality paper overlaid with melamine resin for toughness and wear resistance.

Laminates for these purposes are available in a great array of colors and patterns and several textures, including simulated stone, wood, leather, and fabric. The new specials are also intriguing, such as the variety that contains light-reflecting flecks of metal.

There are several grades, but the most common and most useful is *general-purpose*. Made in a ¹⁄₁₆-inch (actually 0.05-inch) thickness, it is intended to be applied to horizontal work surfaces. Another type, the *vertical* grade, is for doors, cabinet sides, and the like. The general-purpose grade can also be applied vertically, however, and frequently is.

Stock sizes vary somewhat with the manufacturer, and availability varies, but there is generally a good range of sheet sizes for you to choose from. Common widths are 24, 30, 36, 48, and 60 inches, in lengths ranging from 5 to 12 feet, usually in 1-foot increments. You may also be able to buy nonstandard sizes; commercial cabinet shops are a potential source.

When selecting a laminate, first determine what sheet sizes are available in the color, pattern, and brand you want. Then calculate the cut sizes of the pieces you will need for your project and make layout drawings to determine which sheet sizes will be the most advantageous, giving you the maximum number of pieces with the least waste. Be sure to make an allowance for waste and error, perhaps a miscut, because if you have to reorder another sheet, it may not match.

Working with plastic laminates requires some special tools. The pieces are cut, generally a bit oversized, by scoring with a special carbide-tipped knife (FIG. 4-1), then breaking it like glass. A carbide blade in a power saw will work, but it's a tricky

4-1
Plastic laminate can be scored with a special knife like this, then snapped along the line.

business because the material is so thin, limber, brittle, and susceptible to chipping and breaking. A special power laminate slitter is best.

Fine, intricate cuts can be made with appropriate kinds of small hand or power saws fitted with carbide-tipped or metal-cutting blades, sometimes with a nibbler. If holes must be drilled, use carbide-tipped bits and bore from the face side, with blocking underneath.

Edges are trimmed with a router fitted with special carbide laminate-trimming bits (FIG. 4-2), with a power laminate trimmer or with hand laminate edge-trimming planes. Certain files can also be used for small trims. Narrow edges are typically worked with special edge-banding equipment.

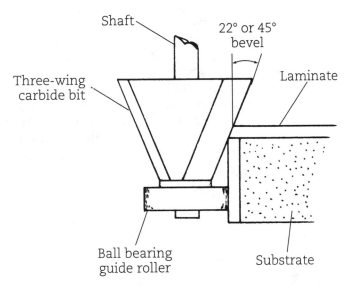

4-2
Special laminate-trimming bit in a router to trim counter edge.

Plastic laminates must be applied to a clean, dry, smooth substrate such as plywood or smooth-surfaced particleboard. The substrate should be rigid, well-supported, and plane, with defects filled and smoothed. Application is always made with contact cement; for home-shop purposes, the nonflammable, nontoxic variety is the only one to consider.

A recent variation is the solid-color plastic laminate. In this material the color permeates entirely, so that the characteristic brown edge band of a corner joint found in self-edged standard laminates does not appear. There are all kinds of design possibilities here, including inlays of various sorts. Edge joints can be built up with several contrasting solid-color laminates, both vertically and horizontally, to produce spectacular results when trimmed off. Only solid colors are available, and fewer choices of those than in the standard type. Other characteristics are about the same as for the standard material, but the cost is about triple, and the installation is trickier. Professional application is suggested, but a competent craftsperson can probably do a creditable job, especially with a bit of practice.

Acrylics

Acrylic plastics and similar types (formulations vary) can be readily obtained and can serve many purposes in home projects. These materials are available in a wide variety of sizes and shapes, in sheet, rod, tube, and block form. They are made in opaque, semiopaque, and transparent colors; tints of gray and bronze; and water-clear varieties of glazing quality. The surface may be matte, highly polished and reflective, or impressed with a decorative pattern. These are very flexible materials that can be employed to great advantage in a variety of imaginative cabinetry treatments, but they are largely overlooked.

In cabinetwork, clear polished sheet plastic makes excellent see-through doors, and the colored or patterned varieties are fine for opaque applications (FIG. 4-3). The pieces can be hinged

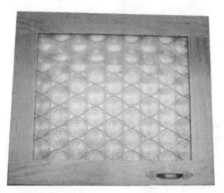

4-3
Acrylic panel, used to glaze cabinet doors.

as discrete doors, set in wood frames, or used as sliding panels. Clear, colored, or patterned sheets can be installed as sliding drawer tops to protect the contents (valuable for bulk supplies like flour or grain), as attractive drawer bottoms, or as complete protective drawer units for dry-food storage (rice, beans, etc.). Certain types of plastics can be used as counter overlays for cutting or pastry boards, or simply for protection. Semiopaques and colored transparents can be set as light diffusers in lighted cabinetry. Other kinds and forms of materials can be made into unique drawer handles and cabinet doorpulls or knobs.

These plastics can be readily worked, with varying degrees of difficulty depending upon the product, in the home shop with ordinary hand and power tools. A few important points to remember: some are very strong; some will have glass-sharp edges when cut; most tend to scratch and mar easily; and they may deform from frictional heat when being worked with a power drill, saw, or sander.

Always leave the protective paper on the material when working it. You can cut sheet plastics with a handsaw, some kinds with a power saw. Follow manufacturer's recommendations, and use fine-toothed blades. Another method for cutting sheets is to use a scoring tool, then break the material like glass.

Drilling holes is often best done with a hand drill, but you can use a power drill at low speed. Use sharp twist-drill bits and use light pressure and slow feed; back the material with scrap to prevent tear-out. You can finish rough edges by filing first, then wet- or dry-sanding, then compound buffing if necessary. Using special compounds, you can also polish plastics of this sort.

Some plastics can easily be drilled and tapped, routed, carved, or heat-formed, so you have a great deal of artistic leeway. Painting, lacquering, scribing, etching, and sand-blasting are other possibilities.

Pouring plastics

Pouring plastic, also called *casting resin,* is a two-part clear, viscous liquid poured to form a thick layer that cures water-clear. There are several kinds that might be used in cabinetwork, to cover a countertop or even to decorate door panels or drawer faces. They are tough, have excellent stain and dirt resistance, and are durable. Although they will scratch, they can be polished. This is a permanent finish that cannot be readily refinished.

One common variety is *polyester resin,* which can be poured in successive layers to whatever depth is desired. Another is *two-part epoxy,* which will form a thick, hard coat. Various brands are available at hobby and craft stores; they are used in such diverse pastimes as model railroading and decoupage.

You can pour the material over smooth-sanded raw wood, which will bring out the grain and figure, much as varnish does but with greater depth, and will protect and preserve it. Or you can treat the surface in the manner of decoupage or some variant thereof. The underlying decorative material can be anything your imagination suggests. For a kitchen counter, you might glue old menus, favorite recipes, old newspaper ads for food, stock certificates, Confederate money, or anything else to the countertop, then pour on the plastic. You can embed colored marble or glass particles, dried flowers or leaves, grains, seashells, or any of a thousand other items.

Sheet-vinyl flooring

When linoleum was in its heyday, it was frequently used to cover kitchen and pantry countertops. The top-quality material made a tough, serviceable work surface that lasted for many years and could readily be replaced when it became shabby or the kitchen decor was changed. Today you can accomplish the same purpose by installing sheet-vinyl flooring. The modern material is tough and longlasting, relatively inexpensive, and easy to handle. Note, however, that this material has a low heat tolerance—you can't park a red-hot frypan on it—and it is susceptible to knife cuts.

A great array of colors and patterns is available. Your best bet is to select a top grade with a smooth surface, or at least a minimum of crevices or pattern indentations that could easily collect soil. The vinyl surface that overlays the core and backing material should be as thick as is available for long wear and good abrasion resistance.

Sheet vinyl is typically available in widths of 6 to 12 feet and is cut from bulk rolls by the running foot and sold by the square yard. Arrange your size requirement so that when it is laid, there will be no seams on the countertop; this will probably entail some waste. To install, just cut the material to exact size, check for fit, spread whatever adhesive is recommended by the manufacturer, and lay the piece in place. Make sure there are no air bubbles underneath, and thump the entire area flat with a mallet and a short length of flat scrapboard.

Counter edges can be trimmed off with stainless steel or aluminum molding made for the purpose, or with finished wood molding. If a backing cove is installed for support at the rear wall joint, the vinyl can be wrapped up the wall to form a backsplash. It can be terminated at the top edge with a small painted wood molding or a metal molding, or it can be extended to the base of the wall cabinets above.

Glass

Glass of one sort or another frequently has a place in cabinetwork, and there are several possibilities, depending upon the application.

Clear plate or *float glass* can be obtained from local suppliers readily cut to size and often can be bought inexpensively as used or salvaged glass. It is strong and distortion-free. Although less common and more expensive, float is also available in bronze, gray, and green tints that can be useful for decorative impact. All exposed and unframed edges should be rounded over by grinding, a process that any good glass shop can do. All glass-holding hardware must be solidly anchored since it must bear a considerable weight and at the same time ensure user safety.

A thickness of $\frac{3}{16}$ inch is suitable for large unframed doors set in roller tracks, as for a gun cabinet; the ¼-inch thickness is more than enough but might be easier to get. New types of hardware also allow the ¼-inch thickness to be installed as discrete unframed hinged doors on cabinets of almost any kind. This arrangement has become popular for kitchen wall cabinets, display and curio cabinets, and stereo cabinets. Another use for ¼-inch float is as a protective covering laid directly over a horizontal wood surface such as a built-in desk or makeup counter.

A glass thickness of ⅛ inch is fine for frame-type cabinet doors. Float or plate glass has the best qualities, but you could also use ordinary *double-strength* (DS) window glass at less cost. *Single-strength* (SS) window glass is a bit thin and can shatter easily when struck but might be all right for some purposes.

Clear and tinted glass are not your only options. There are several varieties of pattern glass available, such as *ribbed, stippled, floral,* and *hammered. Stained glass,* either newly made or antique, is very popular and can be installed in cabinetry with stunning effect. *Mirror glass* also has its place, especially in display and curio cabinets where it is typically mounted on the cabinet back with adhesive and sometimes on shelves as well. *Etched glass* is another possibility. There is always a certain selection commercially available, but your best bet is to have the sizes of panes that you need custom-etched with designs of your choosing. If you feel really ambitious, learn the *sand-blast etching process* yourself and make your own etched-glass panels.

Working with glass takes some practice, and it has to be done carefully. You can successfully do your own cutting once you get a little practice and accumulate the right equipment. You can also drill glass, using bits especially made for the purpose available from tool suppliers. Edge grinding and polishing requires special equipment and is better outshopped.

Ceramic tile

Probably 99 percent of the ceramic tile used is laid as kitchen and bath countertops and backsplashes. The remainder appears as miscellaneous decorative or accent pieces on sideboard and vanity tops and similar applications.

There is an enormous range of tile products to choose from, and they can be confusing. However, your local supplier can help you select the right type. For strictly decorative purposes where the tile will be placed vertically and receives no wear and tear, any kind of tile is fine, including delicate hand-painted ones. But for service use on any kind of horizontal surface, you will need tile that will stand up to modest wear and abrasion, is stain-resistant, and has a surface that will absorb minimal moisture.

There are four categories of permeability. *Impermeable tile* will absorb less than 0.5 percent liquid by weight, and *vitreous tile* will absorb more than 0.5 but less than 3 percent of moisture and is almost entirely resistant to grime infiltration. *Semivitreous tile* can absorb 3–7 percent moisture, and *nonvitreous tile* will absorb more than 7 percent.

There are also several types of tile, six of which are suitable for cabinet-top applications. *Ceramic mosaic tile* is available in several shapes and size ranges up to 6 square inches of surface area. *Glazed wall tile*, although nonvitreous, is a popular choice. It commonly comes in the 4¼-inch size, but others are available.

Paver tile is always larger than 6 square inches and is typically much larger, up to 12-x-12 inches. It will work on countertops, but there are few matching trim pieces made, and color selection is limited. *Quarry tile*, also always larger than 6 inches square (36 square inches), is sometimes used but is really unsuitable because it stains readily and cannot be adequately sealed. Also, no trim pieces are available.

A relatively new variety, *decorative thin wall tile*, is suitable only for backsplashes since it is structurally weak. Another variety, called *monocottura*, imported from Italy, is a strong glazed tile that works especially well but has variable availability and is fairly costly. However, it is now being made in limited quantities in this country and probably will become more common.

There is a tendency to use handmade, hand-painted "designer" or "decorator" tiles for countertops. A few probably work satisfactorily; however, they should be avoided unless adequate service performance can be assured. Typically these tiles are soft, porous, weak, and fired at low temperatures, so that the glaze (and the tile) is soft. Many are also irregular and difficult to lay, almost impossible to cut and trim with good results. And they can be overly expensive.

Whatever variety of tile is laid as a countertop should be glazed, and the glaze should be very hard and abrasion-resistant. These properties are quite variable from product to product. Most tiles will show scratches if cut upon, and surfaces should not be cleaned with an abrasive cleanser, but tile is basically wear and abrasion resistant if treated with some care, and hot pots and pans will not bother it.

Note though, that if the countertop is intended for heavy-duty use, glazed wall tile probably will not hold up well; the glaze is relatively thin and soft, and the tile is somewhat weaker than the other varieties. Note too that any tile can be chipped or cracked if a cast-iron pot is dropped hard enough on it, but any breakable dropped on a ceramic-tile counter will probably do just that.

Most glazed wall tile is about 5/16 inch thick; ceramic mosaic tile is about the same, and paver tile ranges from 3/8 to 5/8 inch thick depending upon the specific type. Quarter-inch or 5/16-inch tile is more than adequate for all countertop purposes.

There is a wide range of sizes, 4¼ inches square being one of the most common. Other popular sizes are ¼-inch square mosaic, 1, 2, 6, 8, 9, and 12 inches square. Rectangular shapes are available, such as 6 by 9 inches, as well as various shapes and patterns.

Most tile lines include matching special trim shapes for finishing, such as *bullnose, cove, cap,* and *accent strip.* Small square tiles are easiest to work with in many respects, but for countertops a better arrangement is to use the largest tiles that will readily fit the countertop dimensions in order to reduce the extent of grouted joints. The sizes most often recommended for countertops in kitchen and bath are 4¼ inches and 6 inches square.

Tile joint lines are problematic because they collect dirt and grime easily, and most grout joint fillers will readily stain even when sealed. By using large tiles and placing them close together for narrow grout lines, 1/16 inch or less, and using a dark-colored grout rather than the traditional white or light gray, you can minimize the problem. Applying one of the new epoxy grouts or stain-resistant grout sealers will also help. These materials are constantly evolving, so check with your dealer for the newest and best products.

Ceramic tile is available in a huge range of colors, and as the saying goes, there is something for everyone. You can choose from solids in pastels, earth tones, primaries, and patterns. Although there are some different surface textures, the only suitable tile surface for a countertop is smooth-glazed, and the thicker the glaze, the better. You have a choice here, between *bright* (glossy), *semimatte* (semigloss), and *matte*. Bright is highly reflective; matte is not and appears almost flat or dull, and the semi is about halfway between.

Ceramic tile is not hard to lay once you get the hang of it and can be an interesting challenge. You will need some special gear, such as a *tile cutter*, a *nibbler* or *nipper*, perhaps a *glass cutter*, an *adhesive trowel*, and a *grout float*, but this represents no great outlay of cash. These and a few ordinary shop tools will see you through.

Stone

Stone has been used for centuries in cabinetwork, especially as service tops for commodes and washstands, dining-room servers and sideboards, kitchen-sink cabinets and the like. Marble was, and often still is, the classical stone of choice, but slate, limestone, and soapstone were also sometimes used.

Today you have numerous choices of materials, and the stone look has become popular and fashionable for base-cabinet and island countertops in the kitchen, vanity and bar tops, and sideboard or server countertops. You can select from slabs or tiles of *marble* in several colors and striation patterns; *granite* in grays, green, and pinks; *slate* in several colors; *limestone* in variable patterns; and *soapstone*.

Other kinds of stone might be used provided you can have it cut and polished. Or you can use *ersatz stone*, called *solid surfacing material* by the industry. Some of these materials resemble natural stone by intent, and some do not. They are made of plastic resins and mineral fillers, dense and heavy. But unlike real stone, they can be worked with tools, much like a moderately abrasive hardwood or wood composite.

Stone countertop slabs are custom-cut to suit each individual job; off-the-shelf sizes do not exist. Common thicknesses are ¾ and 1 inch, but any thickness can be ordered.

Stone is extremely durable, heat-resistant, and abrasion-proof, but depending upon its porosity and kind, can have a tendency to stain. Some stone such as granite will take a glasslike and almost impervious polish, and special sealers are also available. Stone is also extremely heavy; a granite top 1 inch thick, 30 inches wide, and 8 feet long will weigh almost 300 pounds, so your supporting cabinetry must be strong, rigid, and assembled with well-made joints. This is the most expensive countertop material by far and should be installed by a professional crew.

The situation is different with solid surfacing materials like *Avonite* and *Corian*. These products are cast in stock sizes, usually slabs 30 and 36 inches wide and 8, 10, and 12 feet long. Thicknesses are ¼, ½, and ¾ inch. It is also fairly expensive.

Where ceramic tile might run as little as $3 or $4 a square foot, $15 to $25 or more is likely for solid surfaces. These materials also are heavy, although not as heavy as natural stone. Therefore, your underlying cabinetwork must be well designed, adequately braced, and well joined.

They do have some advantages. As the name implies, the surfaces are solid—often no joint lines or seams, which makes for a hygienic and easy-to-clean installation. The material can be worked into whatever configuration is needed, much like wood. Wear resistance is excellent, and if some minor damage does occur, it can usually be sanded out or otherwise repaired. Resistance to stains, heat, water, and abrasion is very good.

In most cases, having a professional installation made would probably be a smart idea. On the other hand, a competent craftsperson should be able to do a creditable job of making a solid-surface countertop. Mistakes could be very expensive, though. Design a small cabinet project like a washstand and try fashioning a modest top before you tackle your whole kitchen.

Moldings

Often the edges of cabinets, countertops, cabinet doors, or even drawers are shaped to some form other than a straight or slightly beveled cut by means of a power router or shaper. But sometimes this is not convenient or possible, and sometimes a design may call for raised trimwork on an otherwise flat surface. In such instances, wood trim molding is needed.

Trim moldings are made in a wide variety of stock shapes and sizes, typically in "sticks" up to 16 feet long. Thicknesses and widths vary with the molding design, and often there are several proportional sizes in a molding pattern. The most common wood used is pine, often ponderosa, but you can also buy oak, mahogany, and other species; the more unusual varieties are handled by specialty suppliers.

Local woodworking or millwork shops can usually turn out custom moldings too. Local lumberyards are likely to carry only a limited supply of moldings, mostly of those patterns that are popular with area building contractors for residential and interior trimwork.

A more flexible and convenient arrangement is to equip your shop to make whatever molding patterns you like. There are more bit and cutter patterns available than there are stock moldings, and some of them are adjustable so that you can turn out custom profiles.

For small runs, the easiest and least expensive approach is to have a reasonably powerful router capable of taking bits with ½-inch-diameter shanks set up in a small router table, to which you can add plywood wings if necessary. For long runs and heavy-duty service, a *spindle shaper* is the answer if you want a wide variety of cutter patterns. These tools will allow you to cut raised door panels too. A *planer molder* is another possibility, although perhaps more limited.

Several varieties of wood moldings are of particular interest to the cabinetmaker (FIG. 4-4), and the smaller sizes are usually the most workable. *Screen mold* and *panel mold* are useful, as well as *base cap* in various forms, *base shoe*, *mullion*, and *flat astragal*. *Ply cap* framed around a thin panel simulates a raised-panel effect, and *lattice* and *corner guard* can sometimes be used. Although larger, some kinds of *casing* and *chair rail* fit in nicely. *Quarter round*, *half round*, and various forms of *glass-bead* and *stop* molding have numerous applications.

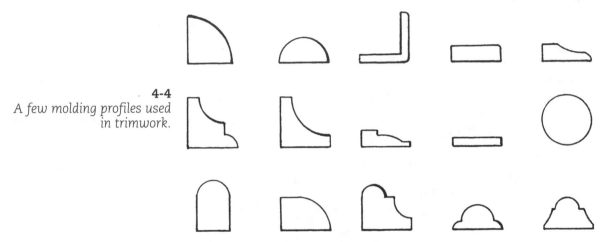

4-4
A few molding profiles used in trimwork.

Moldings can be applied in combinations (FIG. 4-5). For example, identical base-cap sections placed back-to-back make a new molding pattern. Parallel half rounds or screen molds present a different appearance. A half round centered atop lattice looks a little like flat astragal. In furniture cabinetry, *base*, *crown*, *bed*, and *dentil* moldings of various sizes sometimes figure prominently, usually in combinations.

4-5
Small moldings set back-to-back or edge-to-edge to form new shapes.

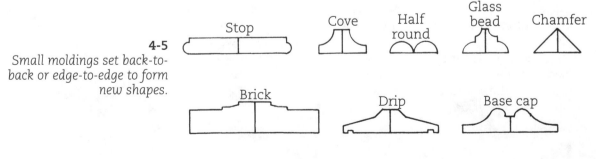

Stop   Cove   Half round   Glass bead   Chamfer

Brick   Drip   Base cap

As for specific applications, there are many. Moldings can be attached to conceal panel edges or to frame panels by insetting the panel or mounting the molding on the surface of the panel around the perimeter. They can be surface-mounted on flush door panels in all sorts of geometric or free-form designs, from simple to ornate. Moldings can be used to restrain cabinet-door glazing or fabric, cane, or screen insets in a decorative fashion.

A relatively bulky molding or combination set is sometimes installed around the base or top of a cabinet, or below an overhanging countertop edge at the joint line. Counter edges can be trimmed with molding, and so can the edges of bookcase shelves, stiles, and rails. There are other applications, and doubtless your imagination will suggest some.

Running your own molding stock takes practice and some care, primarily using the machinery safely and correctly. Working with moldings, however, is simple.

Make rough designs first, and be sure of all your dimensions. The trick is to make extremely accurate, clean cuts exactly to size at exactly the right mating angles, then keep everything in perfect alignment as you secure the parts. A power miter saw fitted with a Teflon-coated, carbide-toothed finish blade helps a lot. Fastening the molding is usually accomplished with glue and finish nails or brads.

Inlay borders

Inlay borders began to appear many decades ago on fine furniture and cabinetry, painstakingly done by hand using tiny strips and chips of exotic woods. Today, although inlay border work is still done partly by hand, the task is much easier, and the results can be fine, even when done by an amateur woodworker.

This is not a suggested addition to ordinary utility cabinets, but it is a method of dressing up your furniture-grade cabinetry, whether built-in, installed, or freestanding. And while the process looks a bit daunting at the outset, it really is not. With practice and the right supplies you can achieve some impressive results.

Modern inlay border (FIG. 4-6) comes in a variety of stock forms made in strips and ready for installation in a suitable groove in the surface of the workpiece. The strips typically are 3 feet long and about $\frac{1}{32}$ inch thick. Depending on the pattern, widths are commonly ¼, ⅜, ½, and ¾ inch; some other sizes occasionally appear.

The strips are made of woods of contrasting colors to form the pattern. You can also purchase *solid-brass border* and *pearl acetate* that is practically indistinguishable from the real thing. *Celluloid strips* come in narrow widths and can be used alone or to border other inlay strips. There are also a few varieties of plain wood strips available, like ebony and rosewood.

All of these materials are typically offered in widths of ⅟₁₆, ⅛, ³⁄₁₆, and ¼ inch. They are readily available through mail-order and large metropolitan supply houses.

Designs vary, but as the name implies, inlay borders are usually placed close to but not at the edge of a plane surface such as a cabinet top or countertop, cabinet door, or drawer face. They might also be placed in rails or stiles, anywhere your sense of design suggests might be appropriate. For best effect, though, inlay borders should be used sparingly and positioned for maximum visual impact.

Installation is not difficult. It just takes patience and care and a lot of precision. The first step is to lay out the inlay location; use strong light and a marking knife. Then cut grooves to receive the inlay strips. This can be done with a table or radial saw fitted with a dado blade or a router. You can also use a special hand router plane for strips ¼ inch wide or more; this allows precise control.

The width of the cut should be exactly the same as the width of the inlay strip, or you can make it just a hair narrower and sand the inlay to fit. The idea is to not get the groove too wide (or the strip too narrow), and all the edges should stay crisp and arrow-straight. The groove depth should be just a tiny bit shallower than the inlay thickness so that you can sand the border down flush with the workpiece surface. Clean out square corners with a small chisel, chip-carving knife, or similar sharp tool. When the strip fits properly, secure it with carpenter's yellow glue.

Field inlays

Field inlays are ready-made veneer inlay patterns of various sorts (FIG. 4-7) that can be inset anywhere in the field of a plane surface such as a cabinet top, door, or drawer front. Like border inlays, they are made up of pieces of wood of contrasting color and grain to form a design or a scene, a process called *marquetry*.

4-7
Ready-made veneer inlay assembly.

Stains or paints are sometimes employed to add color. Popular motifs include birds, butterflies, flowers, wild animals, classical scrollwork, and various geometric designs. There are even a few picturelike scenes, like a galloping horse in a field, a winter landscape, or a three-masted ship. Some of these are available in kit form so that you can put the precut pieces together yourself. There is a wide variety of sizes and shapes, too, such as ellipses, squares, wings, circles, and rectangular panels.

Like border inlays, field inlays should not be used to excess, detracting from the overall appearance of the cabinetry with too much busyness and lack of design coherence. Installation is made in the same way as border inlays. If the inlays are large and applied as complete panels, you will probably need to apply moderate uniform pressure so that the piece remains flat and intact as the glue cures.

Edge banding

The edges of composite materials that are open to view, such as plywood, particleboard, or a veneered or laminate-finished substrate, must be covered with an edging material for the sake of appearance.

Solid wood components in that position are usually formed and finished in the same way as the remainder of the piece, but there are occasions when they too are treated with an edging. This may be done for decorative contrast or to change the edge shape without milling the component itself. Edging material can take a number of forms.

A veneered substrate such as a cabinet top or door is usually furnished with a veneer edge trim, available in a number of varieties. Common species of wood like cherry, oak, and walnut can be bought in rolled-up 8-foot strips 1 or 2 inches wide in *self-adhering, glue-on,* and *iron-on* types. The self-adhering has a peel-off backing and sticks on like a label. The iron-on type is treated with a hot-melt glue backing and adheres when pressed against the workpiece edge with an ordinary household iron or a special edge-banding iron. The glue-on variety is applied the old-fashioned way by smearing the edge with yellow glue and applying, then clamping, the edging.

You can purchase 250-foot rolls of some kinds of veneer edging. Although mainly intended for use with a device called a *table edgebander*, it can be applied with an iron. Another type of edging for machine application is *preglued polyester banding*, a thin plastic material. Selection of styles is limited. For veneer surfaces of species that are not available in precut edgings, you will have to slice your own strips. This is also the method used when it is desirable to make a close match between the surface and the edges. Make the strips a bit wider than the thickness of the workpiece, then trim the banding flush with a special edge-trimmer tool.

When a laminate-covered substrate is treated with a laminate edge, the process is termed *self-edging.* Usually the edging is a strip of the same material as used in the surface cut about $\frac{1}{16}$ inch wider than the edge. However, a contrasting or complementary laminate might be applied to good effect. For countertops, which are often only ¾ inch thick, an extra piece of material is attached along the front edge to double the substrate thickness, then self-edged.

One method of edging a countertop covered with ceramic tile is to use a special "nosing" type of tile that is laid along the counter edge and rounds over to make a band. The pieces can be matching or contrasting; not all tile lines include them.

Another method is to use matching trim tiles, typically rectangular and half or less of the width of the field tile. The field tile is laid flush with the edge of the counter, and the trim tiles are mounted in a vertical band along the counter face.

Yet another arrangement, especially where the tiles are all small, is to bevel the counter edge. The bevel width equals the tile width plus grout lines. Then a row of tile is laid in a vertical band, another along the bevel face, and the remainder of the field tiles flat on the counter surface. With very small tile like ¼-inch mosaics or penny-rounds, the counter edge can be formed into a continuous downward curve.

Ceramic-tile and laminate countertops are often edged with solid wood, and the same can be done with any kind of cabinet top, whether the edge thickness is doubled or built-up or not. A fairly hard and dense wood is best, to survive inevitable bumps and bangs along the top edges without severe denting.

Another method of edge banding is less popular now than heretofore but in many instances has much to recommend it—applying a *metal edging*. There are several styles in aluminum and stainless steel; availability varies. Metal edging can be installed to trim laminate, stone, ceramic-tile, or sheet-vinyl countertops, or on wood edges for protection. These edgings, made in several widths and profiles, typically come in lengths of 8 or 10 feet or more. They are attached directly to the counter edge with screws.

Some cabinet designs may call for special forms of carved moldings or trim pieces (FIG. 4-8). These materials cannot be handily duplicated in a home shop but are readily available in a wide variety of styles from supply houses. In most cases, you

Carved moldings & trim

4-8
*Ready-to-use carved moldings
and trims.*

simply glue the pieces to the workpiece surface after the
surface has been prepped for the application of finish
materials.

One of the more popular items is the *corner curve*, also
sometimes called *French provincial* trim. These pieces come in
different widths and curve radii, forming reverse corners to be
joined by matching straight lengths. They are usually applied
to door faces, sometimes drawer fronts.

Three kinds of special cabinet moldings are also popular. One is
a relatively small freestanding type of cove, fairly ornate in
profile, designed to be installed at the very top of wall cabinetry
or tall freestanding cabinets as a cornice. It may butt against
the ceiling or not, as desired.

The second molding is called *cabinet panel molding*. Similar in
profile to plycap, it is made with a ⅜-inch rabbet in the back.
Fitting the molding around the perimeter of a ¾-inch-thick
plywood door panel or drawer front creates the appearance of
raised panel construction with little effort and no special
machining. This molding usually comes in 4-foot oak or birch
sticks. Finally, you can buy a special molding that can be
installed as a strip across cabinet doors or drawer fronts to

provide a continuous pull. The molding tenons to the rest of the panel to form a unified surface.

Carved, laser-cut, or *embossed* hardwood moldings are made mostly of beech, birch, or a similar light-colored wood that can be treated to match almost any cabinet finish, natural, stained, or painted. These moldings come in several widths, usually 4-foot sticks, and numerous patterns. Some have names, like *Greek key, rope, bamboo,* and *dentil,* but many others are nameless and only numbered patterns.

Carved trims, actually embossed wood (usually birch) ornaments with intricate shapes and fine detail, are made for surface application on cabinetry of all sorts. Numerous patterns are available from supply stores. Many are so ornate that their extensive use would create a baroque effect; a little goes a long way. Yet, properly employed on some cabinet designs, they can add much.

A relatively new item is *laser-cut filigree.* This precision-cut wood trim comes in 3-foot strips and is available in several attractive, delicate patterns. As with the other trims, it is applied to the workpiece surface with glue. The pieces, only ⅛ inch thick, are made of maple-faced plywood. Widths range from 1 to 2 inches.

CHAPTER 5

Hardware

HARDWARE IS crucial in several ways. Visible components should be selected to complement the design of the cabinet and often that of other nearby cabinetry or decor. Those items that have to be functional as well as decorative must perform both roles well.

The right kinds of hardware must be selected for various tasks because some will work better than others in a given application. And often you can develop a particular cabinet design or include a special cabinet accessory by selecting some special hardware that makes the whole idea workable. Having a good working knowledge of the whole gamut of cabinet hardware is important, even though you will use only a small fraction of what is available.

The scope of items available is astounding. There seems to be a piece of hardware to fit every situation and solve every cabinetmaking problem, yet new items appear regularly.

One problem with this is that only a small part of this collection is readily available to the home cabinetmaker. Some items are distributed only regionally; many are not well advertised or well known; and sheer numbers preclude an individual store or supplier from carrying everything or even a good representation.

Amateurs are often unaware of many hardware items that might simplify, enhance, improve, or embellish their projects, and they may be unfamiliar with specialty items that allow some unusual construction or design possibilities. This chapter will cover the general categories of cabinet hardware to give you a quick overview of the field as a starting point.

In any cabinetmaking project, your best bet is to know exactly what items are available to you locally and through catalogs and design the project or set the specifications accordingly. The wisest course is to have all the hardware in hand before starting the project because these items come and go. You are likely to need the parts for accurate placement and dimensioning.

To investigate thoroughly, first check local hardware and houseware stores. Get on the mailing lists of woodworkers' supply houses and cabinet-hardware suppliers and manufacturers; the latter are especially important if you will need period hardware such as Victorian or Early American.

A visit to the library might help, too. Look through books on furniture, cabinetry, and woodworking, and check homeowner, woodworking, and crafts magazines. For unusual or specialty needs, you can consult Sweet's Catalog, a collection of manufacturers' literature used by architects, and Thomas's Register, a compendium of U.S. manufacturers (large libraries have both sets).

Knobs

There is an enormous array of knobs (FIG. 5-1) from which you can select about any color, style, pattern, material, shape, and finish to fit any application. Sizes range from about ⅜ inch up to 4 inches or so for irregular shapes or diameter for rounds. Most extend from about ¾ to 2 inches from the mounting surface.

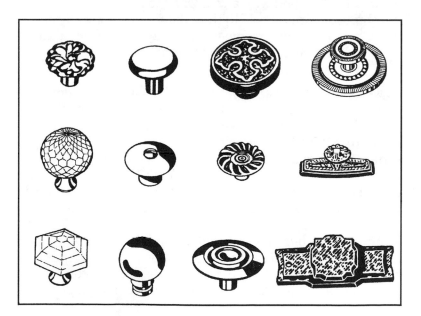

5-1
Knob patterns.

In addition to the myriad modern and conventional styles, you can find dozens of replica knobs that simulate various antique styles. These are extremely valuable when you are constructing reproduction cabinetry. Some varieties come with a matching *escutcheon*, a flat decorative plate that mounts beneath the knob body to protect the cabinet surface against soil and fingernail scratches.

If you find nothing suitable commercially, give some thought to making your own unique knobs. Here is an opportunity for the wood turner to work up knob sets of exotic woods or an amateur blacksmith to hammer out wrought-iron designs. Other possibilities are metals either cast or turned, such as copper or stainless steel, hand-thrown porcelain that may also be hand-painted, shaped wood or plastic, or cast plastic.

Knobs can be attached to the cabinetry in several ways, which may have a bearing on the design, construction, or final appearance of the piece. The knob may feature an embedded wood screw to be threaded into the workpiece from the front. Or a wood screw may extend through the knob with the head visible from the front. The knob may have an integral threaded rod to be run through a drilled hole in the workpiece and secured from behind with a nut. Or a machine screw may be run through a drilled hole to thread into the knob body from the back. Rarely, the machine screw may pass through the knob and be secured from behind with a nut.

Pulls

As with knobs, there are dozens of pulls (FIG. 5-2) that can be used on all kinds of cabinet doors and drawers. Some pulls, particularly the *ring* type, are secured with only one screw, but most are fastened at two points. Some are designed to be surface-mounted with wood screws or machine screws that pass through and are secured with nuts. Other are attached from the back with machine screws that run through drilled holes in the workpiece and into tapped portions of the pull.

Although most pulls project well beyond the mounting surface, some are designed to be recessed flush with the workpiece surface. This requires making cutouts or mortises to accommodate them. A special variety called a *finger pull*

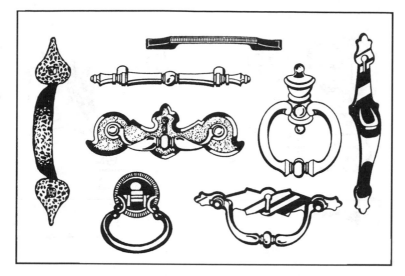

requires only a large-diameter hole; the pull is simply pressed into the hole.

Here again, there is ample opportunity for the inventive woodworker to design and fabricate pulls of unique appearance. Wood is a favorite material, of course, but heavy metal rod or wire, ceramics, plastics, pipe, and leather are workable, and even recycled items that were never intended for the purpose have been put to work.

Catches

Catches are devices installed on cabinet doors to hold them closed. They can be divided into two groups: *concealed* and *visible*. Concealed catches are utilitarian and plain, made for service; not appearance.

Visible types range from ordinary and plain to highly decorative as well as functional. *Latch-bolt catches* are visible, consisting of a handle and operating mechanism mounted on the outside of the door and a catch assembly that might be mounted on the inside or the outside.

Concealed catches come in three main types; *friction*, *roller*, and *magnetic* (FIG. 5-3). A friction catch depends upon spring-steel clips mounted on the inside of the door that clamp over a stud or prong mounted inside the cabinet, or vice versa. A roller

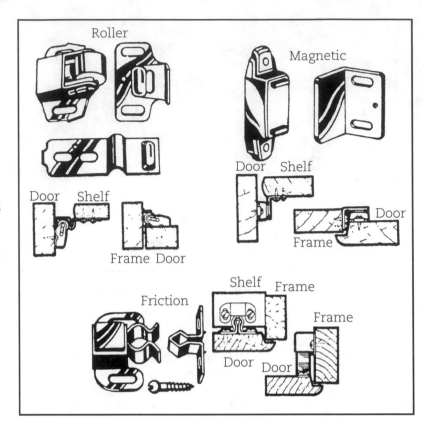

Roller

Magnetic

Door Shelf

Door Shelf

Door

Frame

Door Shelf

Frame Door

Shelf Frame

Friction

Frame

Door Door

catch has one or two spring-loaded rollers that ride onto a mating ramp or clip; which half of the mechanism is mounted on the door and which in the cabinet depends upon the design. A variant is the *bullet catch*, which has a spring-loaded ball that snaps into a mating cup opposite. A *ball catch* operates on the same principle but is a different design. The magnetic catch has a small permanent magnet in one half of the mechanism and a small steel plate as the other; the two engage as the cabinet door closes. The latter two types of catches must be augmented with doorpulls or doorknobs.

Finger or *touch catches* have become very popular. They are fully concealed but of good appearance, some magnetic and some mechanical. Once they are properly adjusted, a slight push on the door face near the catch mounting area releases the mechanism, and the door pops open slightly and remains so.

No pull or knob is needed because the edge of the door serves the purpose, so the door face is devoid of hardware.

Although some ingenuity (and occasionally an extra mounting block) is sometimes needed, almost all kinds of catches can be mounted in a vertical or a horizontal position.

Latches

The term *latch*, or *latch-set* or *lock-set*, is most often associated with full-sized passageway doors, implying the large knob and latch-bolt assembly in use almost everywhere. These latches are occasionally installed in large cabinetry, especially the built-in variety. But there are smaller cabinet-door types, some similar to standard door latch-sets, mostly with a decorative aspect. Some can be surface-mounted, but many models are designed to be mortised into the door and cabinet frame.

Unlike standard passageway sets, cabinet latches are made with a knob or handle on only one side. Many are two-part, and they are reversible so that they can be installed on either the left or right side of a door. While most catches depend upon pressure for operation, latches are operated by slide or rotary motion. The function of a latch is the same as a catch, but the cost is frequently higher, the installation more difficult, and the appearance entirely different.

Probably the most common kind of latch is the venerable *barrel bolt*, available in numerous surface-mount utility styles but also in full-mortise solid brass. The flush bolt is similar. The most common surface-mount decorative latches are the *bar latch* and the *turn catch latch*, both of usually made in solid polished brass.

Locks

There is a wide range of locks (FIG. 5-4) made for cabinetry, and some do double duty as lock and catch mechanisms. They are widely used in applications such as desk or bureau drawers, cedar chests, secretaries; gun, curio, and china cabinets; display units; and cupboard doors. Often their purpose is more for decoration or appearance, or perhaps childproofing, than security because most of the cabinetry involved can easily be broken into, locked or not.

As with other types of hardware, there is a wide range to choose from, and you can find a lock to suit just about any purpose. Among them are such items as *full-mortise drawer locks*, *disk-tumbler cam locks*, *full-mortise barrel-key locks*, *piano locks*, *half-mortise flush-mount locks*, *cedar chest locks*, and *surface-mount cupboard locks*. All of these styles have different appearances and installation requirements.

Hinges

Hinges can be puzzling because there are so many different kinds. However, having a working knowledge of what's available and different applications is important. Not only do hinges run a full range of sizes, shapes, colors or finishes, and patterns; their design must also be suited to a particular application. Apart from whatever visual impact the hinges have, you must decide how much if any of the hinge will be visible, how it will function, how it will be attached, and how well it will work.

Strap hinges consist of two elongated leaves that are nearly always surface-mounted. They are available in sizes of 2–20 inches or more (leaf length), and the leaves are usually joined at the barrel with a nonremovable pin. *T-hinges* are similar, with one elongated strap leaf and one rectangular leaf. Both types (FIG. 5-5) are available in decorative and utility styles. The most popular cabinetry use for these hinges is in the Colonial

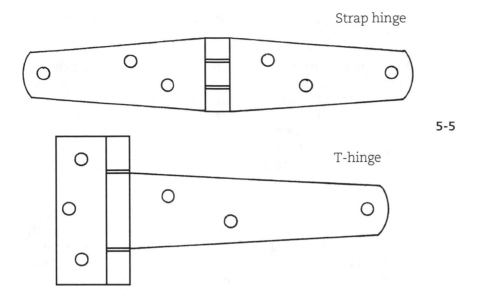

Strap hinge

5-5

T-hinge

or Early American styles of simulated wrought-iron, hammered-copper, or hammered-brass hinges.

The *butt hinge* (FIG. 5-6) is probably the most widely used of all the hinge styles, and there are many designs to fill a wide variety of applications. There are three categories, depending upon the fitting of the center pin upon which the two leaves pivot. The least common is the *loose-joint* or *two-part butt hinge*, which has the pin secured to one leaf, the second leaf pivoting freely on the pin. The two leaves can be separated by lifting the loose leaf off the pin. This kind of hinge must be made specifically for right or left hinging and cannot be used interchangeably. If left-hand hinges are installed on a right-

Butt hinge

5-6

hand door, the hinges will be upside down, and the door will simply slip off the fixed hinge pins.

A *fixed-pin (fast-pin* or *tight-pin) butt hinge* is interchangeable from right to left. The pin is secured and not removable, and the two leaves cannot be separated. These designs are rectilinear, so that there is no "right side up" and their appearance is uniform.

At first glance, a loose-pin butt hinge looks no different from a comparable fixed-pin hinge. However, the hinge leaves and barrel are constructed so that the pin can be driven all the way out, separating the two leaves. The hinge is interchangeable from left to right by merely removing the pin and shuffling the leaves so that the head of the pin is always at the top of the barrel. This also means that a door can be removed from the frame by pulling the pins from the barrels, separating the leaves without removing them from the cabinet door or the frame.

Butt hinges are also designated by the way they are mounted (FIG. 5-7), and the distinctions can be important:

- *Full-surface butt hinges* are designed to mount with one leaf flat on the surface of the cabinet door and the other on the cabinet face frame; the entire hinge is visible.

- *Full-mortised butt hinges* have both leaves inset or mortised, one into the cabinet door edge and the other into the face-frame edge; only the hinge barrel is visible.

- *Half-surface butt hinges* have one leaf surface-mounted on the cabinet door and the other mortised into the face-frame edge; the barrel and one leaf are visible.

- *Half-mortise butt hinges* have one leaf mortised into the cabinet door edge and the other surface-mounted on the face frame; again, the barrel and one leaf are visible.

There are several styles of *semiconcealed hinges,* available in both loose- and fixed-pin types but mostly the latter for simple reversing. Whereas the butt hinges just described are installed where the surface of the cabinet door is flush with the surface

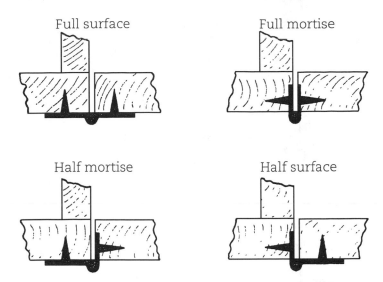

Full surface

Full mortise

Half mortise

Half surface

5-7
Four principal butt-hinge mounts.

of the face frame, there are three possibilities here: (1) flush surfaces; (2) overlay, where the cabinet doors overlap the face frame on the outside; (3) inset (also called offset), where the doors are lipped so that part of the door lies within the face frame and part overlaps it slightly. There are some variations, but most of these hinges are designed to accommodate stiles and frames that are ¾ inch thick.

There are several common semiconcealed types. The *surface-mounted* variety is available for both overlay and ⅜-inch inset (sometimes called a ⅜ *offset hinge*). Half of the hinge mounts on the back of the cabinet door, the other half on the face frame with the leaf, barrel, and mounting screws visible (FIG. 5-8). A similar type is available in both *free-swinging* and *spring-loaded snap-closing* designs, both overlay and inset, where part of one leaf and the barrel is visible but not the mounting screws. *Wraparound hinges* surface-mount, with only the barrel showing (FIG. 5-9). In the standard variety, the right-angled leaf mounts on the door edge and back, and the straight leaf is attached to the frame edge or the cabinet side. In the heavy-duty back-to-back type, both leaves are right-angled and surface-mount in the same way.

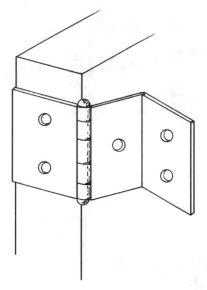

5-8
Half-visible semiconcealed wraparound hinge.

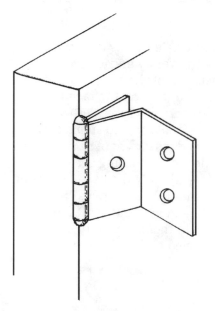

5-9
Semiconcealed wraparound hinge, barrel visible.

Another hinge that is almost entirely concealed is the *pivot* or *pin hinge* (FIG. 5-10). There are several designs. One is made for overlay doors and will mount close-fitting doors for a fully flush appearance on the cabinetry face. One is made to mount to the door back and cabinet stile, another to mount to the door back and the cabinet rail. Another type, called a *reversible knife hinge*, reveals only the pivot point, mounts to the door and

Pivot hinge

5-10

cabinet-rail edges, and opens and closes like a jackknife blade. These are available for overlay, ½-inch inset, and ¾-inch inset doors. Yet another type, for flush doors, consists of an adjustable bracket-mounted pin that attaches to the door edges. The pin extends into a small bushing pressed into a hole in the rail edge.

The *no-mortise hinge* (FIG. 5-11) is made in only limited styles, but can be handy. It is self-aligning, allows 180-degree door swing, automatically provides the proper clearance between door and stile edges, and installs easily. The type that mounts fully on the surface of a door edge is best for doors, but the kind

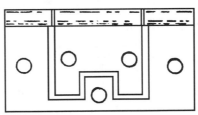

No-mortise hinge

5-11

with wraparound flanges is ideal for cabinet lids that should be hinged but tight-fitting, as for stereos.

Several kinds of cabinet hinges are completely concealed when the door is closed. Probably the best known carry the name of the manufacturer—*Soss hinges*. These multilink hinges are available in a wide variety, must be fully mortised into the door and stile edges, and are for flush applications. Barrel hinges are similar, but mount easily in two matching drilled holes. There is one size for ½-inch-thick doors, another for ¾-inch. There is a similar link type that can be surface-mounted. Another variety surface-mounts, is spring-loaded for snap closing, and can be used for both overlay and ⅜-inch inset door design. It will fit doors from ¾ inch to 1 inch thick.

The so-called European style of kitchen cabinetry (which can be used elsewhere as well) has recently become popular in the United States. The principal feature of this design is the smooth, undetailed face that the entire installation presents. No framework or hardware can be seen, and there are only hairline cracks between the doors and around the drawers. The design requires a special kind of hinge known as *European cabinet* or *EuroStyle hinges*, sometimes *Blum* or *Grass hinges* after those brand names.

There are several types of these hinges, depending upon the application. Originally made for frameless cabinetry, models that can now be face-frame-mounted. Various openings are available, such as 95, 110, or 165 degrees for different door locations. Most of these hinges mount on the surface in the cabinet, but the door portion fits into a special cup hole 35 millimeters in diameter. New product lines surface-mount entirely.

Finally, there is the *continuous hinge* (FIG. 5-12), more commonly known as the *piano hinge* because of its long use on the keyboard cover of that instrument. As the name implies, the leaves and barrel of this hinge are continuous, and they typically come in lengths of 2, 3, 4, and 6 feet. They can be cut to required length. Common widths, measured from side to side with the leaves opened out flat, are 1¹⁄₁₆, 1¼, 1½, and 2 inches. A smaller version, usually called a *jewelry-box hinge*, is only ¾ inch wide when open and is available in 6-, 12-, 18-, and 24-inch lengths. Normal finishes are bright brass, brushed brass, antique brass, and nickel plate. Matching screws are available.

Piano (continuous) hinge

5-12

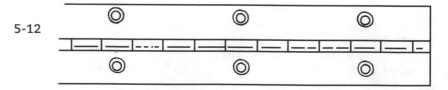

There are many occasions when the joint between two workpieces is not strong enough to meet the loading requirements of part of a cabinet or extra strength, stiffness, or rigidity is needed. Sometimes that need can be met by simply adding glued blocks, braces, or extra thickness, but often the most practical approach is to install plates or braces. They afford considerable strength with little bulk, install quickly and easily, and are low in cost.

Plates are just flat pieces of steel or brass with predrilled and countersunk screw holes. The most common shapes are *straight strap*, T, and *flat right-angle corner* or L.

Braces are usually made of steel, occasionally brass, and may be *flat strap* (angle braces) or *stamped* (corner braces). For relatively light-duty applications, plastic corner braces are available. *Miter-corner braces* have a center web and are used to reinforce mitered corners as on a cabinet door frame. *Screen-corner braces* have a turned-down lip on the inside of the angle so that they can be attached to both surfaces and edges.

In most cases, plates and braces are mounted on the surfaces of mating workpieces in hidden locations. Some specialized pieces may require some inletting, and this can be done with flat pieces if desired. There are a few decorative items, typically brass for a type of cabinetry sometimes called campaign furniture, designed to be mortised into the visible surfaces at particular locations.

Most of the cabinetry in a house, especially the kitchen, is built-in or shop-built and permanently installed. But some kinds of cabinets are fitted with casters, such as a portable bar or enclosed tea caddy, or may have glides (sometimes called feet) for floor protection, leveling, or both, as in a cased stereo system.

If the cabinet is of the utility variety, there is a wide range of casters that might be used. Most are *open-wheeled* and may be plate- or stem-mounted. Some have side brakes to lock the wheel. Light-duty models often have plastic wheels such as white styrene; some have nylon; and the heavier-duty types

Plates & braces

Casters & glides

have rubberlike tires. The better casters are equipped with ball bearings for easy swiveling.

Much the same can be said of casters suitable for modern cabinet styles, except that the caster design is also modernistic in appearance; the hooded caster is an example. For reproductions of antique cabinetry, a variety of appropriate casters are available. Most are of the stem design. Some have die-cast metal or stamped steel bodies, but the best are made of solid brass or cast iron. The wheels may be fashioned of solid brass, white porcelain, or a hardwood like maple.

Glides are usually thought of as appropriate for the tips of chair legs, but they are widely installed on the bases of various kinds of freestanding cabinetry, often to protect the floor surface or to elevate the bottom of the piece slightly so that no splintering or similar damage will occur if the piece is moved. In other cases, an uneven floor causes leveling or wobbling problems that can be solved with adjustable glides.

Some fixed glides attach to the bottom edges of the cabinet with a single short nail. They may be made of nickel-plated steel, a rubberlike material, plastic, or white nylon. Other varieties have self-adhesive backings and are usually made of felt or rubber; protection is their main purpose.

Adjustable glides come in two general types. One has a threaded center bolt about 1 inch long, typically a ¼-inch (20) or ⁵⁄₁₆-inch (18) size. They are designed to turn into matching threaded pieces installed in the bottom edges of the cabinet. The other type has a threaded center stem as long as 3 inches that threads into a companion U-bracket. The bracket is mounted to the cabinet. Most of the glides are about 1¼ inch in diameter and may be made of heavy steel or a slippery plastic like phenolic.

Brackets & standards

Brackets can serve as braces, strengtheners, or supports for shelving. They are available in numerous sizes and in decorative and utility styles. Some are made to hold wood or particleboard shelving and may be sized to accept standard shelf widths; most are predrilled for mounting screws. Other types are fitted with spring clips that will hold glass shelves, and some are made to swing to one side when not in use or fold down out of the way.

Another style, sometimes called a *pin bracket* but more properly a shelf support (FIG. 5-13), is used in pairs at each end of a shelf for easy removal or height adjustment. There are several varieties; nearly all mount by simply pushing them into predrilled ¼-inch holes in the cabinet sides. Shapes vary, but they are all small and unobtrusive. They may be made of clear or brown plastic; steel that is nickel-, brass-, or zinc-plated; or solid brass. A drilling jig is available to aid in boring straight rows of uniformly spaced holes, valuable for extensive adjustable shelving installations using these supports.

Pin brackets

5-13

A *standard*, or *shelf standard*, is a special kind of steel strip used to hold mating shelf supports in place (FIG. 5-14). Probably the most common variety is made with a continuous series of rectangular horizontal slots. The strip can be mounted on a flat surface; most models can be recessed into a groove for a flush installation. The strips are secured with nails (supplied) driven through predrilled mounting holes. Finishes are bright zinc, bright brass, and dark brown, and the lengths are 2, 2½, 3, 4, 5, and 6 feet. The matching clips lock into the slots. The standards are installed two at each end of the shelf section, and if the shelves are long, another standard can be installed at the midway point for support.

Shelf standard

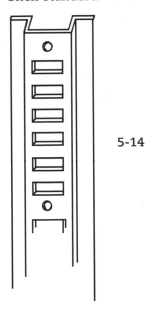

5-14

Another type of shelf standard consists of a box-shaped strip with vertical slots into which special shelf brackets lock. Various finishes are available, and the brackets are made for stock shelf widths. These standards are to be mounted at the rear of the shelves, usually on the surface, but they can be recessed, about 6 inches or so inboard from the shelf ends and at other suitable intermediate points if required.

Slides

One of the more important items in cabinet construction is the *drawer slide*. There are numerous ways to install a drawer so that it will slide in and out freely. The traditional method is to make the slide components of wood, integral with the cabinet construction. This method is still widely employed today, especially in antique reproduction work or by cabinetmakers who enjoy working with the old methods.

Most amateur cabinetmakers select one of the slide systems commercially available, especially when building kitchen and similar cabinetry that will see heavy-duty use. Although there is a cost involved, this usually results in a better-operating drawer and fewer installation or construction problems. Slides may also allow a manner of operation for a drawer or other slide-out unit that would not otherwise be feasible. One example is a full-extension drawer capable of holding 50 to 75 pounds of flour or dog food.

If cost is not a consideration, *ball-bearing drawer slides* are the most effective means for providing smooth, trouble-free operation. There are several types of such slides; one of the less expensive ones is shown in FIG. 5-15.

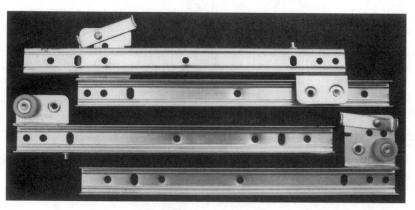

5-15
Ball-bearing roller drawer slides: mated pair (above); separated set (below).

There are four parts. A *guide track* is fixed to each side of the cabinet frame, and a mating slide is mounted on each side of the drawer. A *stop block* is provided so that the drawer cannot be pulled out completely by accident. When the drawer is fully closed, the *rollers* drop into a slight depression in the tracks so that the drawer cannot slide open, even if the guides are tilted slightly. Slides of this sort come in sets, are made in lengths of 12 to 24 inches in 2-inch increments, can be cut shorter, and require ½-inch clearance on each side between the drawer and the frame. Drawer extension is about two-thirds of the overall length of the slides.

The slides just discussed are visible when the drawer is pulled out, but another type, also side-mounted on the drawer, is not. The rollers are mounted on small plates that attach to the rear part of the drawer, and the drawer extends only to the roller plate. Thus, extension is a bit less than 6 inches less than the drawer length. Other types of steel side-mounted slides extend fully or somewhat more than fully, with extremely smooth and bump-free operation (ideal for stereo turntables), lock rigidly in the full-open position (good for kitchen cabinet cutting boards or computer workstations), and may have up to a 100-pound load rating. Some, made specifically for slide-out shelves, are very narrow, mounted on ¾-inch-thick edges; others are made just for computer keyboards.

Other designs are not ball-bearing types. There is a single track that mounts centered beneath the drawer and runs on nylon rollers. Another consists of a broad metal bracket that runs in a heavy plastic rail and mounts centered below the drawer.

Individual drawer rollers can be mounted in the bottom corners of the cabinet frame; the bottom edges of the drawer glide on them. Yet another variety is a *continuous hardwood dovetail slide* (FIG. 5-16) that mounts within the cabinet carcase and can be used singly or doubled on large, wide drawers.

One of the least expensive slide assemblies, nonetheless effective, is a rear-mounted plastic slide that runs along a T-shaped wood guide affixed to the drawer bottom, plus a pair of plastic side guides. The parts can be bought separately, so if you have some nice dry, straight hardwood, you can make your own center guides and save a bit more. With all of these slides, drawer extension is at least a few inches less than full.

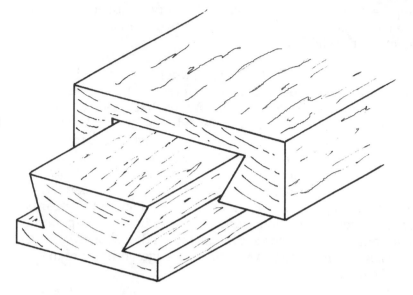

5-16
Dovetail drawer slide.

Tracks

Cabinets are often fitted with doors that slide rather than swing. The doors are in pairs, one bypassing the other. This makes for a neat installation with easy door adjustment and alignment and is often desirable where space is at a premium. The drawback is that only half of the cabinet interior is accessible at one time.

Sometimes the doors slide in grooves routed into the cabinet body proper, but in most cases a discrete track set and accompanying hardware makes the best installation, or at least the easiest. Several varieties are available. The ultimate choice depends largely upon the size and weight of the door and the material from which it is made.

Double track, shown in FIG. 5-17, the simplest and least expensive, it is installed on the surface at the top and bottom edges of the cabinet opening, either carcase or face frame. The track can stand free, or it can be recessed into a groove or hidden behind a molding or the face frame itself for deeply inset doors. Track pieces come in various lengths and in different sizes to accommodate door thicknesses of ¼, ½, and ¾ inch.

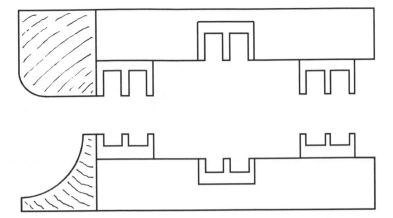

The track section installed at the top of the opening is deeper than the bottom one. The door panels must be cut to the proper height which allows them to be fully inserted into the upper track then swung in and dropped into the bottom one without coming free at the top. Apart from knobs or pulls on the door panels and fasteners for the track—sometimes only adhesive is used—no further hardware is required. This type of track may be made of molded plastic, hardwood, plated steel, or anodized aluminum. The door panels can be made of solid or composition wood, plywood, glass, or plastic.

Another simple kind of track for bypass sliding doors looks like a miniature railroad track. Two small rails extend upward, integrally molded into a base strip. The track is surface-mounted with screws; it may be set into matching top and bottom grooves in the cabinet body. Mating slots are cut in the top and bottom edges of the doors, deeper at the top, and the doors are set in place on the rails.

Large cabinetry, such as a full-height pantry- or bookshelf section, especially when built-in, may require a heavy-duty track for large, heavy bypass sliding doors. The most common method employs a support track affixed to the head jamb or top rail of the door opening to accommodate a set of rollers attached to the inner surface of the door and extending slightly above the top edge. The doors are thus suspended and free-rolling, and may or may not run in or against a bottom guide of some sort. The rollers are adjustable to some degree to ensure that the door can be hung straight.

There are several kinds of track assemblies for special applications. For example, *curved* or *curvable tracks* are mounted to the sides of certain kinds of cabinets fitted with tambour doors (like the sliding top on a rolltop desk) or similar flexible closures. Another track is a sturdy extruded aluminum rail and base assembly upon which special runners fitted with individual ball bearings travel. The runners are attached top and bottom to ¼-inch thick plate glass.

Pass tracks, used mostly on thick panels, are designed so that both panels lock into the same plane when closed, but as one panel opens, it cocks outward first, then slides across to clear the second panel. A cabinet pocket door installation can be made with special plastic L-shaped tracks that accept matching runner brackets; the door slides to the side, makes a right-angle turn, and disappears into the cabinet. Another special hardware set allows a front panel to pivot up to the horizontal position, then slide back inside the cabinet, barrister-bookcase-style. Yet another system allows a similar operation in either horizontal or vertical modes.

Fittings

The general term *fittings* covers a gamut of hardware and accessory items designed for particular purposes. Most of them are for kitchen cabinets, but some are designed for bathroom or closet installations. Many of these items can be employed for purposes or in locations not originally intended; a little imagination helps sometimes.

Kitchen-cabinet items include wastebasket shelves that pop out for easy access when you open the cabinet door, spice or knife racks designed to be built in, pullout pastry or cutting boards, and even a pullout extension table. There are slide-out steel-rod towel racks, cup racks, and wire basket units; stands and racks for storing cups, plates, platters, and cans of pop or soup—all intended for mounting in or on the cabinetry.

You can install swing-up appliance platforms that rise out of a base cabinet, swing-down knife or cookbook racks that appear from beneath the wall cabinets, or slide-in stemware racks. The list goes on and on; the purposes are to maximize available space and increase storage capacity and convenience.

There are many other items for various locations and uses, some worthwhile and some not. You will find closet-rod and organizer assemblies that can be installed in armoires; racks for belts, neckties, and jewelry; and so on. Similar doodads are available for baths, laundries, dining rooms, bars, rec rooms, and workshops.

A lot of these items come from small local manufacturers and are available in different forms. Hardware and housewares stores, many lumberyards, kitchen shops, and tool and hardware outlets carry a certain number of accessories. Mail-order catalogs are full of them, and there are endless advertisements for them in magazines dealing with household affairs. The field seems to be about equally divided into quality items and junk, worthwhile devices and gimcracks. Decide what might work for you, then purchase them before you build any special cabinetry to suit them. Designs and specifications change frequently, and a lot of this stuff is here today and gone tomorrow.

A wide assortment of specialty hardware is available, and most of these items allow you to build some function into your cabinetry that would otherwise be difficult or impossible. Many are not well known or available locally, and sometimes you have to search for them. But whatever your ideas or problems concerning a particular project, somewhere out there is a piece of hardware that will help you do the job.

Specialty items

For example, special leaf slides will allow you to add a pullout, pop-up extension leaf on a server cabinet. Tambour doors are not easy to build in the home shop, but they are easy to purchase ready-made in various sizes and styles.

Can't see the TV while it is tucked back in its cabinet? Add a swiveling extension pullout. A set of hinged brackets called *stay supports* will allow you to lift up and lock in an extra section of countertop. A double swivel plate separated by a row of ball bearings lets you build either a lazy susan or a rotating shelf set. Special pivot and shelf bracket sets are also made for this purpose.

Hardwood and other styles of grommets are available for routing wires of various sorts through cabinet walls. Audio- and videocassette and compact-disk trays and holders made of molded plastic are available for installation in custom cabinetry. Special heat-vent panels, as well as tiny "whisper" fans, are made to ventilate entertainment and computer station cabinetry.

You can purchase several different kinds of retainers designed to secure glass, plastic-sheet, brass woven wire, cane, and other kinds of panels in cabinet doorframes. If you want to install a clockface or decorative lighting in your cabinets, kits and components are available. The list seems never to end, and sometimes the biggest problem is finding a convenient source for the items you need. Having an array of mail-order catalogs at your fingertips helps a lot.

Fasteners & adhesives

CONSTRUCTING CABINETS involves cutting and fitting small pieces together to make a functional whole. This requires the use of fasteners and adhesives, sometimes alone and sometimes together, to secure the parts. These two aspects require considerable attention from the cabinetmaker if the project is to be successful.

Fasteners are the various devices used to join and secure the individual components of any cabinet assembly. Of the hundreds of different items made for hundreds of applications, several are important to the cabinetmaker. A good working knowledge of fastener items, their characteristics and functions, and their advantages and disadvantages for a given task ranks high on the list of the several elements of making top-quality cabinets of fine appearance. Using the right fastener in the right place makes the job easy and trouble-free. Using the wrong one, or using the right one incorrectly, leads to frustration and problems.

Often the decision to use one kind of fastener is a judgment call. Installing the best devices that money can buy is not always the best course, and overbuilding is an unnecessary waste of time, money, and effort. The selection process is best based upon a balanced assessment of service conditions, desired appearance, appropriate quality, final finish, building materials, location and surroundings of the finished cabinetry, and other pertinent factors.

The most commonly employed fastener in cabinetmaking has been the nail, and it still enjoys widespread use today. The first consideration is to select the right kind. There are six of particular interest to the cabinetmaker (FIG. 6-1).

Fasteners

Nails

6-1
Eight nails used in woodworking: left to right—brad (above), wire nail (below), 3d finish, 10d finish, 10d box, 10d common, 16d box, 16d casing.

Standard types. The *common nail* has the largest-diameter head and the largest shank diameter of the six and has greater head thickness. Thus, it is also the strongest, and is used in heavy-duty projects and where the head will be concealed or its appearance makes no difference. The *box nail* is similar but has a thinner and smaller head and a slimmer shank for any nail size. Unless strength is a factor, the box nail is usually chosen over the common nail.

Casing nails are used for finish work. The diameter of the head is not much greater than the shank, and that is equivalent to a box nail of comparable size. The gentle taper of the underside of the head allows a casing nail to be easily driven flush or countersunk without forcing wood fibers into a surrounding hump. Usually the nail is countersunk slightly, or "set," and concealed with filler.

A *finish* or *finishing nail* is similar, but somewhat thinner with a smaller, more rounded head. More readily available and more commonly used in cabinetwork and general woodwork than the casing nail, it is typically set and filled over. Although the two types are often used interchangeably, the casing nail is stronger, has greater holding power, and is less susceptible to pull-through.

Wire nails are similar to box nails but have short slender shanks and flat, thin heads. They are sometimes used for securing small pieces of material, especially if thin, where strength is not a factor and the exposed heads don't matter. *Brads* are small finish nails employed in attaching small moldings, thin pieces of stock, and similar applications.

The next step in selecting the right nail is to pick the right size. Common, box, casement, and finish nails are designated by an old standard called the *penny* system rather than by their length in inches, the symbol for penny written as *d*. A 10-penny nail, shown as 10d or 10-d, is always 3½ inches long. In cabinetwork, the most commonly used sizes are 3d, 4d, 6d, and 8d, usually in the finish style. The 2d, 5d, 7d, and 9d sizes are largely unavailable, but the others are easy to come by. The chart in FIG. 6-2 shows the sizes.

Nail sizes

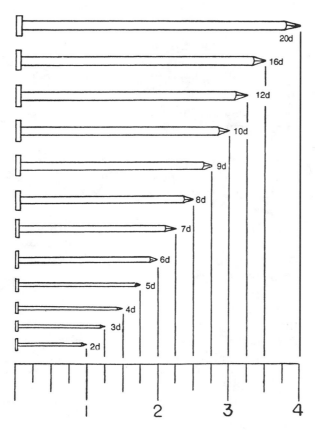

6-2
Nail sizes and lengths.

Nails are also made in standard diameters that depend upon their penny size and are stated as *gauge* numbers, referring to the size of the wire from which the nail was formed. An 8d common nail, for example, is 10¼ gauge. With these four kinds of nails, however, gauge is not of consequence for general usage.

The situation is different with wire nails and brads. Both are classified according to their length, in inches, and their wire gauge. Lengths range from ½ inch to 2 inches, gauges from 16 through 19.

While the most common finish for all six kinds of nails is plain steel, usually referred to as "bright finish," some are available in other finishes. Among the most common are *cold galvanized, hot-dip galvanized,* and *cement-coated.* You may need one of these coatings for a special application.

Specialty nails There are specialized nails you may require for some project. For example, you can purchase exact replicas of old *cut-nail* styles like *clinch, hinge, fine finish,* or *wrought-head* nails for antique reproduction or restoration work. *Ring-shanked nails* have shanks cut with sharp concentric rings for extra holding power.

Masonry nails in several styles and sizes are designed to be driven directly into masonry. They might be used when securing cabinet-mounting cleats to a concrete-block wall.

There are various tacks for general-purpose, upholstery, and decorative work. *Escutcheon pins*, usually made from brass, stainless steel, or nickel-plated steel, are also used mostly for decorative purposes.

Keep in mind that some kinds of nails are made of different materials. While steel is by far the most common, sometimes other materials serve (or look) better. You will find some choices in stainless steel, copper, brass, aluminum, bright or dull copper and brass finish, black finish, chrome or nickel plate; and blued, parkerized, or similar finishes.

Nailing techniques are not difficult, but as with any other procedure, some hints can help you do a better job with less effort. Make sure you have the right type and size of nail, neither too large nor too small. In most applications, penetration into the nailed member should be about ¾ inch, no less than ½ inch. The exception is driving into end grain; the penetration should be at least 1 inch and more if possible.

If you are working with a hard or splintery wood, or nailing close to an edge or at a sharp angle where the material might split, drill a *pilot hole* first. Make the hole slightly smaller than the nail shank and drill entirely through the first member. If the underlying piece is a relatively soft material or there is little danger of splitting and the nail should drive well, drilling into it may be unnecessary, perhaps inadvisable. Otherwise, make the hole through the first and into the second member equal in depth to about two-thirds the overall length of the nail.

There are two ways of nailing: *straight* or *face nailing*, and *toenailing*. Face nailing involves driving the nail straight through the surface of the first member and into the second. For best results, the nail should be canted just a bit in any direction where there is no danger of its breaking out through a lower surface, for better holding power.

In some materials you might have to tilt the nail a bit to clear a tough growth ring or a knot so that the nail will not deflect, bend around, and pop through a lower surface. Never try to nail through or directly adjacent to a knot. The material there might well be harder than the nail, and you will have no luck or bad luck, possibly a ruined workpiece.

Also, where you have enough room, stagger nail positions in a continuous W pattern rather than a straight line for better holding power. It is a good idea to refrain from driving two or more nails close together along the same grain line. This could promote a split; the nails tend to wedge the wood apart or at least weaken the piece materially.

Even the seemingly simple process of driving a nail has effective techniques. Size the hammer to the nail. Remember the old line about not driving tacks with a sledgehammer. The smaller the nail, the lighter the tap and the lighter the hammerhead.

Nails smaller than 6d bend easily if struck wrong. Hold the nail between your thumb and forefinger, set firmly at the desired angle, and tap it gently a time or two to get it started. Then get your thumb out of the way and drive the nail home by striking it squarely, not with glancing blows.

As you drive, make sure that the nail stays on course. That last healthy shot with the hammer is the one not to apply. That's the one that gets slightly misjudged and puts a dent in the workpiece—a minor disaster if the finish will be natural. Let all the nailheads stick up a bit and finish the job with a *nail set* of proper size. Care and patience with these procedures pay off in cabinetmaking.

But sometimes, despite your best efforts, a nail will not drive correctly. Removal is indicated. The trick is to do so without marring or damaging the surrounding surface and without pulling a chunk of wood free as the nail leaves the hole. If the nail has been only partly driven, you can grab it just beneath the head with the claws of a hammer, slip a piece of scrapwood beneath the hammerhead, and pull the nail free. The scrap protects the workpiece and allows added leverage for the claws.

If the nailhead is close to flush with the surface, you can use a piece of thin but rigid hardboard for surface protection. If the hammer claw is too thick, you can try a *flat-bar nail puller* or a prybar with a thin end. In any case, ease off on the pulling strain as the point of the nail nears the surface and work the nail free gently. This will help to prevent splinters from tearing free around the hole edge.

A pair of *electrician's diagonal cutters*, "dikes," will often work when nothing else will. Use a piece of scrap for surface protection and a screwdriver shank or similar object for a fulcrum if you need it. Take a good bite on the nailhead with the dikes and pry upward (FIG. 6-3) against the fulcrum. Repeat until you can get a grip with a hammer claw.

When all else fails, clip the nailhead off with the dikes (put your safety goggles on), then drive the nail in deep with a nail set and fill the hole.

Screws

Unless there is some compelling reason to use nails, cabinetmakers today are using screws as fasteners more than ever. Most freestanding cabinetry and top-quality constructions are best assembled with screws rather than nails. The reason is that despite the added cost, time, and difficulty, the finished product is stronger, more durable, and much less susceptible to loosening, wracking , or warping, or otherwise failing in service.

Applications

There are several situations where screws are the preferred fastener. Chief among them is preference. Today's new head and thread types and drive tools have made the job far more simple and efficient than was possible using just cabinet screwdrivers and slotted flat-head wood screws. Most workers, once properly equipped and having gained a bit of experience, are finding that in many cases by using screws they have better control over the joint-assembly processes with fewer problems and end up with a better job.

In addition, you should use screws in any application where maximum holding power is needed. Such situations might occur when a cabinet will carry a heavy load or concentrated weight or the joints must be solidly restrained from working loose under repeated vibration or strain. Ensuring complete stability of a cabinet assembly is another possibility, and screws should always be used to mount or secure any nonfreestanding cabinetry, such as a kitchen set, to the wall or floor.

Whenever the fastener must be left exposed or its exposure is desirable for decorative effect, screws are an obvious choice. You can obtain screws in several metals, finishes, and head designs, and various kinds of compatible finishing washers are available for decorative purposes.

Another instance when screws are almost mandatory is working in cramped quarters where driving nails would be awkward or impossible, with damage to the workpiece likely. A similar situation obtains when the workpieces are lightweight, perhaps a bit limber or flimsy, or don't have much support. Then assaulting the cabinet with a hammer is bound to cause damage, especially by loosening joints already made. Predrilling pilot holes and sinking a few screws, on the other hand, serves only to tighten the assembly, with little danger of damage if you are careful.

Another occasion when screws are helpful, or even of prime necessity, is when two components fail to mate, or spring apart after assembly, from warping or twisting. This problem can sometimes be rectified by driving the pieces back together under pressure. But nails usually do not have sufficient holding power for this chore. One or two screws driven in the right spots can often accomplish what nails cannot.

Finally, with rare exceptions, screws are employed to attach various kinds of hardware to the cabinet, such as hinges, knobs and pulls, and slides.

At one time, about the only kind of screws used in cabinetmaking were *straight-slotted flat-head wood screws* in plain or blued steel, latterly plated steel (typically cadmium). Occasionally *round-head screws* were used where they did not show; they are a bit easier to drive. *Oval-head screws* sometimes were installed for a decorative (or attractively functional) appearance, either alone or with finish or cup washers beneath the heads.

Brass screws of the same sort were driven in oak because a chemical reaction with steel leaves a growing dark stain on the wood. These same styles became increasingly available over the years with the *Phillips* configuration, which affords a better grip for the screwdriver blade. All of these screws continue in use today, except that plain steel has been entirely supplanted by plated steel.

Nowadays there are more choices (FIG. 6-4). In addition to straight and Phillips slots, there is the *Robertson* or *square drive*, which has recently become popular, and the *Posidrive* pattern (less common). Both allow easier driving with substantial torque.

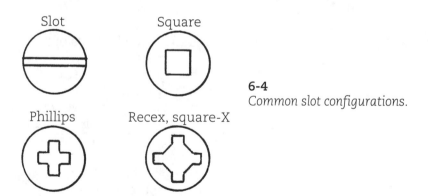

6-4
Common slot configurations.

While the standard variety of flathead wood screw with its tapered shank and cut-in thread is readily available, the *flat-head straight-shank wood screw* with a wide-spaced, spiral, extruded thread is rapidly becoming popular. This type is available in a complete range of sizes, in brass, stainless steel, or lubricated black carbon steel, and with square or Phillips slots. These are the best bet for general-purpose cabinetmaking because they have superior strength and drive extremely well in virtually all materials.

Specialty wood screws

Some special-use wood screws are valuable to the cabinetmaker. *Bugle-head* screws have wide-spaced spiral threads that extend clear to the head, unlike other screws, which have short, smooth shank sections. They drive very well in most materials and often do not need countersinking to lie flush with the surface, especially in soft woods.

Trim-head screws have small, unobtrusive heads that can be left visible; they usually do not require countersinking. Another style, similar but with a tighter spiral thread, is called a *tapping screw*. This style will thread its way into most woods without a pilot hole.

All three types come in steel or stainless steel, with square or Phillips slots. In addition, you might find *nibs screws* useful in some applications. Their shape is much like a conventional flathead screw, but the underside of the head is cut to produce a series of sharp little blades; the screw head cuts its own countersink in almost any material.

Two types of screws may be referred to as wood screws but really are different and designed for two particular purposes. Although not required, they serve those purposes better than any other types. One, called a *face-framing* screw, is made for securing face frames to carcases. The head is flat and very thin with a deep Phillips or square drive; the upper half of the shank is smooth, and the lower portion has a tight spiral thread. A special auger point plus a dry lubricant allows the screw to thread into the wood without drilling a pilot hole. There are two models for hard and soft woods. The other item is the *particleboard screw*, designed specifically to drive and hold well in that material. This is a bugle-head screw with a deep Phillips drive and a wide-spaced, steeply slanted thread.

All of these special screws are available in a limited range of sizes.

Wood-screw size designation has three parts: length, gauge number of the shank, and head configuration. A wood screw with a flat head and an 8-gauge shank 2½ inches long would be designated 8 × 2½ F.H. The drive-socket configuration is separately stated. Table 6-1 shows the most readily available combinations.

Table 6-1 The most readily available screw gauge/length combinations and screw gauge diameters

Screw #	¼	⅜	½	⅝	¾	⅞	1	1¼	1½	1¾	2	2¼	2½	2¾	3	3½	4	Dia.
1	X																	0.073
2	X	X	X															0.086
3	X	X	X	X														0.099
4		X	X	X	X	X	X											0.112
5		X	X	X	X	X	X											0.125
6		X	X	X	X	X	X		X									0.138
7		X	X	X	X	X	X	X	X									0.151
8	X	X	X	X	X	X	X	X	X	X		X		X				0.164
9			X	X	X	X	X	X	X	X	X	X	X					0.177
10			X	X	X	X	X	X	X	X	X	X	X		X	X		0.190
11				X	X	X	X	X	X	X	X							0.203
12					X	X	X	X	X	X	X	X			X	X		0.216
14						X	X	X	X	X	X	X	X	X	X	X	X	0.242
16							X	X	X	X	X	X	X	X	X	X		0.294
18								X	X	X	X	X	X	X	X	X	X	0.294
20									X	X	X	X	X	X	X	X	X	0.320

Wood-screw length is measured differently, depending on the head style. The length of a flathead screw is measured from the tip of the point to the top surface of the head. An oval-head screw is measured from the tip of the point to the greatest diameter of the head, the point where the underside taper stops and the rounded upper portion of the head begins. Round-head, pan-head, and fillister-head screws are measured along the shank from the underside of the head to the tip of the point. Head configurations are shown in FIG. 6-5. Screw lengths range from ¼ inch to 4 inches or more, depending upon gauge.

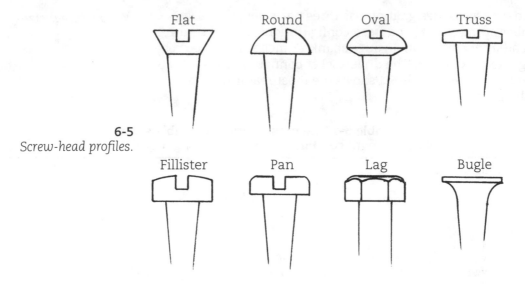

Flat   Round   Oval   Truss

6-5
Screw-head profiles.

Fillister   Pan   Lag   Bugle

The gauge number refers to the wire size from which the screw was fashioned, a specific diameter. The smaller the gauge number, the slimmer the screw shank. Gauges run from 0 to 20, but those commonly used in cabinetwork are 6, 8, 9, and 10, occasionally 4 and 12.

Sheet-metal screws Ranking next in importance to wood screws are the *sheet-metal* type. Originally designed for sheet-metal work, as the name implies, they are useful in many other applications because they drive and hold well and are readily available everywhere in several styles and many sizes.

The threads of sheet metal screws look much like wood-screw threads, but they are cut differently and run from tip to head. They are often generally called *self-tapping screws* because of their capability of cutting their own threads into the workpiece. Of the several different types of sheet-metal screws, only two are of particular interest to the cabinetmaker. Type A is the most familiar and common. The type F, made with an off-center chip-clearing slot, is called a *self-drilling sheet-metal screw*. There is no need for a pilot hole because the screw tip acts as a drill and the screw drills its own hole as it is driven.

Both Phillips and straight-slot drives are available, and there are usually five head configurations to select from. Flat, oval, and round heads have the same shape as their wood-screw counterparts. The *truss head* is similar to the round head but thinner and of greater diameter. The pan head, probably the most common, looks a little like a thin fillister head; this is a fine utility type.

The lengths and gauges of sheet-metal screws are the same as those for wood screws, but there is not as great a variety of sizes and types available.

The techniques of driving screws are simple enough, which is perhaps why one or another facet is so often ignored. The only way to get problem-free results is to do the job right.

Installation techniques

The first step is to drill a pilot hole, even if the material is soft. In cabinetwork there are not many situations where you can safely skip this step. A rough-and-ready set of storage cabinets for the garage banged together out of recycled boards might be one example. Standard wood screws have two diameters, one for the shank and the other for the full thread. When flathead or oval-head screws are used, the head diameter and underside taper must be considered.

Center-mark and drill the shank hole first. If you plan to cover the inset screw heads with wood plugs, drill the plug hole first to a depth just slightly less than the thickness of the plug. If the plugs are overlength, drill to about one-third the thickness of the upper workpiece (¼ inch for a ¾-inch-thick piece). The shank hole, centered in the plug hole, should just clear the smooth portion of the screw shank, and the depth should be just a bit more than the length of that smooth part.

Center a bit at the bottom of the shank hole (with the workpieces clamped or fastened together) and drill the pilot hole. This hole should be a little smaller in diameter than that of the full thread; sometimes this has to be adjusted somewhat, depending upon the hardness of the material. There is a danger in having the diameter too small; you might twist the screw off. On the other hand, if the pilot hole is too loose, you could have insufficient holding power. The pilot-hole depth should be about one-half as deep as the thread length in softwood, equal to thread length in hardwood. The total depth of the hole should be just a bit less than the length of the screw. If you are not using pilot-hole bits, select the correct bit sizes for normal purposes from TABLE 6-2.

Table 6-2 Clear and pilot hole drill sizes for screws

Screw #	1	2	3	4	5	6	7	8	9	10	11	12	14	16	18	20
Clear hole - Frac. drill	5/64	3/32	7/64	7/64	1/8	9/64	5/32	11/64	3/16	3/16	13/64	17/32	1/4	17/64	19/64	21/64
Clear hole - #drill	49	44	39	33	30	28	24	19	16	11	6	2	—	—	—	—
Pilot hole - Soft wood - Frac. drill	1/32	1/32	3/64	3/64	1/16	1/16	1/16	5/64	5/64	3/32	3/32	7/64	7/64	9/64	9/64	11/64
Pilot hole - Soft wood # drill	68	68	56	56	52	52	52	47	47	42	42	35	35	28	28	17
Pilot hole - Hard wood Frac. drill	1/32	3/64	1/16	1/16	5/64	5/64	3/32	3/32	7/64	7/64	1/8	1/8	9/64	5/32	3/16	13/64
Pilot hole - Hard wood	68	56	52	52	47	47	42	42	35	35	30	30	28	22	1	6

The next step, if oval-head or flathead screws are being used, is to countersink. An exception occurs, though, if finish or cup washers will be used; these rest upon the surface, and the hole depth should be lessened a bit to compensate. Use an 82-degree countersink for this, going slowly and checking the maximum diameter often. When that diameter is just a bit less than the head diameter (soft material) or exactly the same (hard material), quit.

One way to save time here and avoid potential problems with off-centered or slanted holes is to drill with one of the combination bits made for the purpose, as noted in chapter 2.

There are some old tricks that should never be used—for example, driving a screw most of the way with a hammer, then twisting the last turn flush. This speedy technique destroys the wood fibers around the screw and negates most of its holding power, not to mention deforming the screw head. Trying to force a screw into a too-small pilot hole is a mistake. Screw heads, especially brass, twist off with remarkable ease. Remove the screw and enlarge the pilot hole slightly.

Another old trick with hard-driving screws or hard material is to wipe soap onto the screw threads to make the driving easier. But this may cause a reaction with the wood fibers, and in time stains could appear or the screw become cemented into the hole. You can use beeswax or paraffin or a special product made for the purpose if there will be no interference with the proposed finish materials. This is not a bad idea when the screw material is soft relative to the workpiece material and maximum holding power is desired.

If you do twist a screw head off, there are three remedies. One is to forget it and fill the hole with putty. If the screw must be removed, there are two methods. One is to center a drill bit of somewhat smaller diameter exactly on the broken screw shank after prick-punching a good starter dot. Drill dead center through the screw shank, then pick out the remains. The replacement screw will then have to be at least one size larger to fill the hole and hold well. The other method is to drill a small hole in the center of the broken shank. Then insert a special tool called a *screw extractor* (commonly also known as an *easy-out*) and remove the screw by backing it out.

Many of the problems with screws come from selecting the wrong size. There is a rule of thumb that works for many applications: Whenever possible, all of the threaded part of the screw should be embedded in the "second" workpiece, the one being attached to. Obviously this is not always possible, especially when the newer styles of fully threaded screws are used, so another rule is to embed as much thread into the second workpiece as the thickness of the first, unless there is a danger of breaking through the back of the second piece. In that case, embed as much thread as possible, at least equal to two-thirds to three-quarters of the thickness of the second piece.

The foregoing applies when the screw thread is being driven into the second piece across the grain, as into the surface of a board. Screws driven into end grain, parallel with the grain, lose much of their holding power compared with an across-grain position. You can gain some strength by increasing screw length beyond normal and by increasing the screw gauge. You can also drill a smaller than usual pilot hole or none at all to gain a bit more holding power, but this runs the risk of splitting the wood.

Although time-consuming, there are a couple of techniques that will overcome this problem. Perhaps the best method is to bore a transverse hole through the workpiece from edge to edge, assuming it is small enough, a short way from the end-grain surface. Plug this hole with a hardwood dowel glued in place. Then drill pilot holes as usual, through the upper piece and into the doweled piece. When the screws are fully driven, they will bite into the cross-grain hardwood dowel instead of end grain and be solidly anchored (FIG. 6-6).

6-6

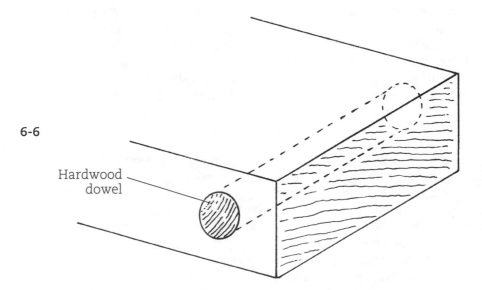

Hardwood
  dowel

If the second piece is too wide to bore through edge to edge, you can bore through it from top to bottom at appropriate screw locations just back from the end. Plug the holes with short lengths of dowel (FIG. 6-7). Cut and sand the ends flush to

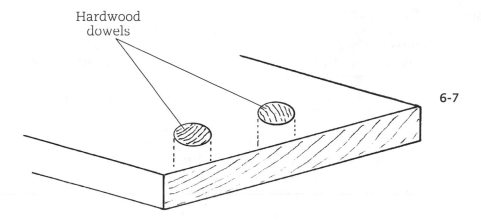

Hardwood
dowels

the surface. Install the screws as usual, driving them into the dowels.

Gauge selection is mostly a matter of common sense. The thicker and larger the workpieces, or the greater the stress and weight likely to be imposed upon the finished product, the larger the gauge should be. When there is a possibility of splitting the wood, stay with smaller gauges. Heavier gauges will afford greater rigidity; slimmer gauges will drive easier and cost less.

Finally, always use the proper size and type of screwdriver, with a blade in good shape, for the kind of screws you are using. Bad blades or power screwdriver bits can easily jack out of the screw-drive sockets and chew up the screw head or jump out completely and damage the workpiece surface or mar your nice new (expensive) hardware.

The softer the screw material, the more important it is to proceed with care, especially when you are driving with a power tool. For hand-driving exposed finish screws, the best tools are cabinetmaker's screwdrivers or gunsmith's screwdrivers (the patterns are somewhat different) with hollow-ground blades.

Machine screws   *Machine screws* are designed to be threaded into drilled and tapped holes or inserted into through-holes, then into special threaded retainers or secured with matching nuts. While they are used mostly for assembling metal parts, machinery and the like, you will probably need them in your cabinetmaking projects sooner or later. Knobs and pulls, for example, are frequently attached with them.

Machine screws are available with either slotted or Phillips slots, the latter being generally preferred because they drive more easily. The head styles typically available are pan, round, flat, oval, and less commonly, fillister. They are classified according to length in inches, gauge in the smaller sizes and diameter in the larger, and *thread pitch*, or number of threads per inch.

As with wood screws, the gauge refers to wire size and the diameter of the screw shank. Unlike wood screws, machine screws have flat tips, and in most sizes and types the threads run the entire length of the shank, or nearly so. Length is measured in the same way as for wood screws. Gauge numbers run from 1 through 12, then shift to the actual shank diameter in fractions of an inch.

Machine-screw threads are classified in two ways: *National Coarse* and *National Fine*, usually stated NC and NF. They differ in the number of threads per inch (TPI), which is referred to by specific number in the screw designation. Thus, a (gauge) number 6 screw might have 32 TPI (NC) or 40 TPI (NF). The NC varieties are in more common use for general-purpose applications.

Complete machine-screw designations might be 8-32 × ¾ F.H. or 6-40 × 2 R.H. These would refer to an 8-gauge screw with 32 threads per inch, ¾ inch long, with a flat head—a National Coarse configuration; or a 6-gauge screw with 40 threads per inch, 2 inches long, with a round head—a National Fine configuration. Following the designation there may be further reference to the kind of material (brass, stainless steel), the finish (chrome-plated, bright brass), or both.

The specific size of machine screws is important when it comes to drilling holes to receive them. They should be sized accurately, according to the figures listed in a tap-drill chart (TABLE 6-3). For any machine diameter, or gauge, and thread-pitch combination, there is one drill size for a through hole and another for a tapping hole, usually given for approximately 75 percent thread height. The through-hole size remains the same for any kind of material. The tapping-hole size might have to be varied slightly according to the nature of the material being tapped or if a different thread-height percentage is desired.

Table 6-3 Through-hole and tap drill chart for machine screws.

Screw size	Screw dia.	Clear drill	Tap drill
1-64	0.073	49	53
1-72	0.073	49	53
2-56	0.086	44	50
2-64	0.086	44	49
3-48	0.099	39	46
3-56	0.099	39	44
4-40	0.112	33	43
4-48	0.112	33	42
5-40	0.125	⅛	38
5-44	0.125	⅛	37
6-32	0.138	28	33
6-40	0.138	28	32
8-32	0.164	19	29
8-36	0.164	19	29
10-24	0.190	11	25
10-32	0.190	11	21
12-24	0.216	$\frac{7}{32}$	16
12-28	0.216	$\frac{7}{32}$	14
¼-20	0.250	¼	7
¼-28	0.250	¼	$\frac{7}{32}$
$\frac{5}{16}$-18	0.3125	$\frac{5}{16}$	F
$\frac{5}{16}$-24	0.3125	$\frac{5}{16}$	I
⅜-16	0.375	⅜	$\frac{5}{16}$
⅜-24	0.375	⅜	R

Lag screws Sometimes called *lag bolts*, which they are not, *lag screws* are not used in cabinet assembly but can be handy when a heavy or heavy-duty cabinet assembly must be securely anchored to a wall, floor, or ceiling. Lag screws are made with hexagonal heads (usually referred to as *hex heads*) and are driven with a socket, box-end, open-end, or similar wrench. A wide range of sizes is available, starting with ¼-inch shank diameter and 1-inch length. Threads are wide-spaced and deep. Always drill a clear hole through the first member and a pilot hole in the second.

Bolts Bolts are sometimes used in cabinetmaking. There are three kinds that you should be familiar with; stove, machine, and carriage (FIG. 6-8).

6-8
Representative bolt types: top—carriage bolt. Second row, left—hex-head machine bolt with hex nut; right— square nut and truss-head machine bolt. Third row, left—stove bolt and square nut; right—hex nut and hex-head machine bolt. Bottom—lag bolts or screws.

Stove bolts look much like machine screws, but the sizes are different. Those commonly available range in diameter from $\frac{5}{32}$ inch to ½ inch and in length from ⅜ inch to 6 inches. Drive slots and head shapes are the same as for machine screws, and except for some specialty items, they are made of plated steel. They can be used with either hex or square nuts but are frequently supplied with the latter. In most cases, the threads run the whole length of the shank, or nearly so. A good range of brass and stainless-steel screws is available.

Machine bolts are typically heavier and sturdier than stove bolts. Larger sizes have square or hex heads for wrench-driving.

Diameters from ¼ inch to 1 inch and more are available; lengths range from ¾ inch to 2 feet or more. Square or hex nuts can be used with them. They are made of various grades of steel, depending upon the strength required, and designated as SAE grades 0 (weakest, low-carbon steel) through 8.

Carriage bolts are made with broad round cap heads, with short, squared shoulders directly beneath, a little larger than the shank diameter. This type was originally designed for use in wood (in the carriage-building trade) so that the squared shoulder would seat firmly into the workpiece when the nut was drawn up snug but would not pull deep into the material because of the broad head. Carriage bolts are commonly available in diameters from ³⁄₁₆ to ¾ inch and lengths of ¾ inch up to 12 inches. The thread length is typically short, the plain shank proportionately long, and either square or hex nuts can be used.

Nuts

Standard sizes of nuts are made for use with machine screws and stove, carriage, and machine bolts. They are either square or hexagonal in shape and have NC or NF threads. Most are made of plated steel, usually zinc but sometimes nickel or chrome for special applications; brass and stainless steel are also available in some sizes. Size is designated not according to the outside dimension of the nut but by the shank diameter or gauge of the screw or bolt upon which it will be used, along with the required thread pitch. Thus, a ¼ × 20 nut for any length of "quarter-twenty" screw.

Washers

Washers of various sorts (FIG. 6-9) and in different combinations are frequently used in conjunction with nuts on screws and bolts. They can serve as a lock or anchor, or a bearing plate for the nut or another washer, or keep a screw head from pulling into the workpiece material, or slim down a hole inadvertantly drilled oversize. Which type you use depends upon the job at hand. Common *flat washers* are usually employed to provide support and a broader bearing surface beneath a bolt head or a nut. If the material is soft or the pressure must be spread over an even larger area, *fender washers* are the choice. *Lock washers* bite deep into whatever surfaces they bear on and seize tight; they come in nearly all gauge and fractional internal diameters.

6-9
Washers: clockwise from upper left—fender, cup or finish, flat or punched, shakeproof external or star, shakeproof internal lock.

Shakeproof or star washers are lighter-duty but effective and typically available up to ¼ inch (internal) in diameter. In all cases, washers are designated by the internal diameter of the hole, which is matched to the gauge or fractional diameter of the screw or bolt shank.

Anchors

Anchors (FIG. 6-10) can be separated into two general groups that have very little overlap: *masonry anchors* and *hollow-wall anchors*. Different terms are used in different parts of the country for these items. There are also numerous types of each, but usually only a few are available in any locale.

6-10
Anchors and shields: left-to-right—Molly bolt, plastic-plug anchor, drywall anchor, lag shield, machine-bolt anchor, rawl plug.

Hollow-wall anchors are known as *wallboard anchors, toggle bolts,* or *springhead toggle bolts, wing anchors, expansion bolts,* and other terms. Whatever the name or form, a hollow-wall anchor is inserted into a hole drilled through the wall sheathing and protrudes into the wall cavity. As a screw is driven into the anchor, it expands or otherwise changes shape to lock firmly into place.

In most designs, the screw can be removed and replaced at any time without disturbing the anchor. This is the system to use when mounting cabinets or shelving on the surface of any hollow wall (the presence of thermal insulation in the wall cavity does not matter). These anchors are rated for various loads in pounds, so be sure to select the correct size for the weight you will impose on them. Also, for many types, different lengths are available for different thicknesses of wall sheathing the anchor must pass through. Installation procedures vary considerably, so follow the manufacturer's instructions.

Masonry anchors include *nail anchors, machine-screw* and *machine-bolt* anchors, *lag-screw shields, lead-screw anchors,* and a wide range of neoprene, nylon, and plastic expansion-plug anchors. There is a wide assortment of sizes and lengths for various purposes and loads, and most are made to fit certain kinds and lengths of fasteners.

Masonry anchors are usually installed by drilling a hole of appropriate size in the masonry or concrete with a carbide-tipped masonry drill bit, cleaning the hole out thoroughly, and inserting the anchor. As the fastener is driven into the anchor body, it expands and grips the sides of the hole. Keeping the hole straight and round with no egging in the upper portion is crucial for maximum holding power.

These are the anchors to use when mounting cabinets on a concrete-block or poured concrete wall or securing base cabinets to a concrete floor. Be sure to select an appropriate load rating for wall work, and follow the manufacturer's instructions for installation. Note that some of these items can be used in materials other than concrete or masonry, although the holding power and load rating will likely be less.

Miscellaneous

There is no way to list everything that is available in miscellaneous hardware. However, a few items are especially useful and are found in most home shops. There are times when they are particularly valuable in cabinetmaking, and a knowledge of them could be important to your projects.

Hanger bolts

Hanger bolts (FIG. 6-11) are made in two ways. The most common is with a standard machine thread on one end and a tapered wood-screw thread on the other, with a short stretch of smooth shank between. The less common arrangement has a machine thread on each end. You can bolt them to or screw them into a wall or other section, either vertical or horizontal, then secure a cabinet to the protruding portion with washers and nuts. The sizes typically available are ¼-, ⁵⁄₁₆-, and ⅜-inch diameters; 16, 18, and 20 TPI, and lengths from 1 to 3 inches.

Hanger bolts   Dowel screen

6-11

Dowel screws

Dowel screws (FIG. 6-11) are similar to hanger bolts but have a tapered wood-screw thread at each end with a short length of plain shank between. Their principal use is to attach short legs to cabinet frames by first threading the screw into the frame, then threading the leg onto the exposed screw end. Installation can be a bit tricky because the pilot holes and screws must be perfectly straight and matched to one another. Prethreading both pilot holes with an ordinary wood screw of matching size helps. Sizes typically available are 1½- 2-, 2½-, and 3-inch lengths, ¼- and ⁵⁄₁₆-inch diameters.

Threaded rod is handy when you can't find a bolt of sufficient length or you need a really long fastener. Just lop a suitable section off a length of rod and add washers and nuts to each end. For example, you might make a butcher-block type of top for a barbecue cabinet or a kitchen island counter by through-boring a stack of 2-inch maple slats, then sandwich the pieces together with lengths of threaded rod, the nuts and washers hidden in deep counterbores and covered with wood plugs.

Threaded rod is available in stock lengths, often 3 feet, and several standard diameters and thread pitches, such as ¼-20 or ⅜-16.

An alternative to threaded rod is *plain rod* that you thread yourself. This would allow you to use brass or aluminum rod, which is not readily available as threaded rod.

The purpose of *escutcheon pins* is almost entirely decorative. They can be used to trace patterns or secure small decorative elements to cabinetry or furniture and are sometimes employed to attach metal plates. They are usually made of brass or plated steel. Common lengths are ⅜ and ½ inch, and diameters are ½₂, ³⁄₆₄, ¹⁄₁₆, ⁵⁄₆₄, and ⁷⁄₆₄ inch. Larger sizes can sometimes be found.

Small staples are often used with a staple gun to secure cabinet backs, thin wood sheets, vinyl coverings, upholstery materials, and the like. Larger staples can be used for heavier work, driven with a hammer or a pneumatic stapler. Several varieties in numerous sizes are available. However, they are more suited to production work than a home shop and are not generally found in high-quality cabinetry.

Inserts (FIG. 6-12) have the function of a nut embedded in one workpiece so that a second piece can be fastened to it with a machine screw or bolt. There are several types, all with great holding power. They are all installed by drilling a hole and threading the insert into it with a wrench or screwdriver. Inserts are made of brass (for oak) or steel and commonly come in ⅛-32, ¼-20, and ⁵⁄₁₆-18 internal thread sizes. The screw or bolt can be driven into the insert from either end with equal effectiveness.

A similar device, called a *T-nut*, has an internally threaded barrel in the same sizes, but instead of external threads, it has down-pointing teeth. Installation consists of drilling a

Fasteners & adhesives   143

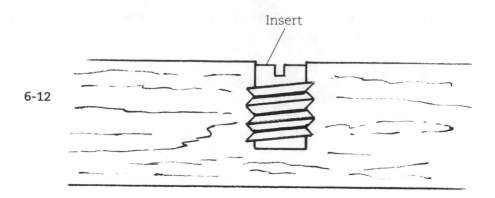

Insert

6-12

clearance hole for the barrel, then inserting it into the hole and hammering it down flush, driving the prongs deep into the wood. The screw or bolt must be threaded into the T-nut on the barrel end so that the strain will act to pull the T-nut into the wood rather than out.

All of these devices are excellent where plenty of strength is required. Joints or attachments must be made particularly tight. The cabinet must be capable of being disassembled easily and reassembled with no damage and good fit at the joints.

Joint sets   There are several kinds of *joint sets* (FIG. 6-13) on the market. One consists of a zinc insert much like the ones discussed above, along with matching steel connector bolts. Cross-dowel joint sets consist of a steel dowel drilled and tapped crosswise and a matching special bolt with a thin, flathead and Allen (hex) drive. The dowel is inserted in one piece at right angles; the bolt runs through the second piece and into the dowel.

Joint connectors come in two principal designs. One is for holding two pieces together face-to-face. Each connector is made of two parts—a bolt (¼-20 is common) with a flathead, a drive socket, and a special long-barrelled cap nut that when installed looks just like the bolt head. One size is made specifically for joining two ¾-inch-thick pieces; other lengths when the two parts are combined are 2, 2¾, 3½, and 4¾ inches.

The second design, typified by a device called a *Tite Joint fastener*, is made for securing two pieces of any ordinary

Mechanical connector sets

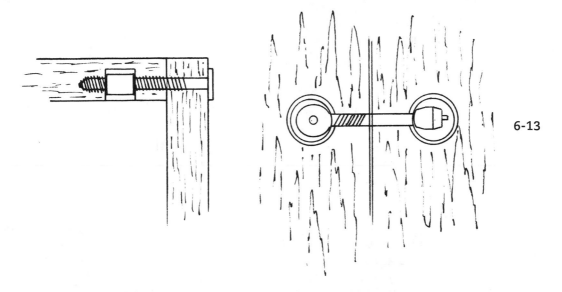

6-13

thickness together edge-to-edge. These are ideal for making any kind of edge joint in plywood or solid lumber on large cabinet tops or broad solid-wood sides and are especially valuable in constructing countertops. It is wise to use the special drill guide and drill offered with this hardware. These fasteners can also be used where disassembly is required.

Drive fasteners

There are several kinds of simple stamped-metal drive *fasteners* (FIG. 6-14) designed to be driven home with a hammer. They must be used where their appearance does not matter and typically are handy on the backs of flat miter and flat butt joints for extra strength and rigidity. They can be used parallel with or at angles to the grain with little danger of splits and are driven down flush with the surface.

Chevron fasteners work well on flat miter joints. *Corrugated fasteners* come in several sizes, drive well in soft wood but with increasing difficulty as the hardness factor rises, and work well on any flat joints.

Drive fasteners

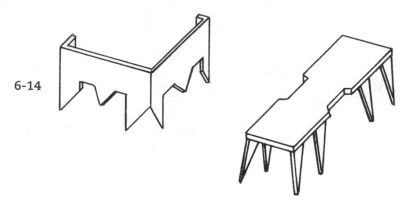

6-14

Skotch fasteners consist of a strip of metal with four long sharp prongs extending downward at each end. As the prongs drive into the wood, their shape tends to draw the two workpieces together. Clamp nails must be driven into thin matching slots cut in the two workpieces. Although more difficult to install, they also draw the pieces tightly together and hold very firmly.

Dowel pins
You can make your own *dowel pins* by cutting them from dowel rod, but buying them ready-made is easier, and you will get a better product; the cost is low. Plain straight-sided pins work all right, but the best have chamfered edges, spiraled full-length glue grooves to allow air and excess glue to escape as the pin is tapped home, and are made of a good hardwood such as birch or maple. You can buy them in individual sizes of ¼- to ½-inch diameters and lengths from 1½ to 2½ inches, or you can get assortment packages with a little of everything.

For unusual diameters or lengths, or when the dowel ends will remain exposed and a contrasting or matching color or grain is desired, making your own pins will be necessary. Use quality dowel rod, which is available in several diameters and wood species. If you cannot find the required dowel rod, you can make your own dowels from square stock with a dowel-making tool or shape them on a wood-turning lathe.

Wood *plugs* are installed in counterbores to cover countersunk screws, disguising them or adding a contrasting note with a different color of wood in a natural finish. Buying them is easier than making them yourself, and there is a good variety available. They are flat-topped with tapered sides and usually come in diameters of ⅜ and ½ inch. The woods typically offered are birch, oak, cherry, and walnut, and both face and end grains are available.

Often, especially when the grain, color, and figure of the workpiece must be matched as closely as possible under a natural finish, making your own plugs is necessary. You can do this by cutting the plugs from the same stock that the workpiece was fashioned from, using an appropriate size plug cutter. The result is a face-grain plug. This is most easily done with a drill press, but a hand electric drill and a vertical alignment jig will work too. An alternative is to cut lengths of dowel rod, which results in an exposed end grain.

Wood buttons are plugs with small mushroom-shaped heads. They are used in the same way as plugs, but only when a decorative effect is desired because they extend above the surrounding surface. They are made to fit hole diameters of ⅜, ½, and ¾ inch and come in walnut, birch, cherry, and oak. They can be press-fitted for easy removal or glued permanently in place.

The type of spline that has become popularly known as a *biscuit* (probably because of its appearance) since the recent advent of low-cost plate-joining machines for the home shop, has been around for years as a plate, lemon, or Lamello spline.

Biscuits are made of compressed and crosshatched beech in a particular shape to match the joiner blades, the grain running diagonally. Once glue contacts the wood, it swells almost immediately, locking into place in the mating grooves cut into the workpieces.

There are three sizes available, designated 0 (⅝ × 1¾ inches), 10 (¾ × 2⅛ inches), and 20 (1 × 2⅜ inches). The more biscuits used in each joint, the stronger the joint. The rule of thumb is to keep a separation of about 5 inches between centerlines and to use the largest size without the cut breaking through on the back.

Bonding agents

Several substances commonly used in woodworking and associated fields have bonding properties to attach two materials or workpieces together. The traditional bonding agents are *glues*, made of natural materials like animal hide. They have been largely supplanted in recent years by the generally more effective and easier-to-use synthetic material combinations, categorized as *adhesives*.

Rubber-based bonding agents are usually regarded as *cements*, but in practice, any agent that bonds wood to wood is generally called a glue, and one that bonds wood to something else is called a cement; an adhesive, by definition, is a substance that with the right formulation will bond anything to anything.

Usually you will probably use only one, maybe two, kinds of bonding agents in your cabinetmaking projects, but you will find a passing familiarity with all of them helpful. Use TABLE 6-4 as a quick reference guide.

Table 6-4 Types, characteristics, and uses of bonding agents

Glue	Uses	Temp. °F	Clamp	Strength	Mois. resis.	Workability
ACC	Interior Exterior Nonporous surfaces Repair	40°+	n/a	High	Excellent	Poor
Aliphatic Resin	Interior Veneering Cabinetry Furniture General	45°+	1 hr.	High	Poor	Very good Fills well
Animal	Interior Furniture Cabinetry Restorations General	70°+	2-3 hrs	V. high	Poor	Excellent Fills v. well
Casein	Interior Protected Ext. Oily woods Laminating	32°+	2-3 hrs. +	High	Fair	Good Fills well

Contact Cement	End joints
	General
	Bonding of
	  veneers,
	  laminates,
	  etc. to wood
		70°+	Instant bond	V. high	Excellent	None

Epoxy	Interior Exterior Bonds nearly all materials Fast assembly	Any	None reg.	V. high	Waterproof	V. good Machinable Excellent filler
Hot melt	Interior Fast assembly Temp. tacking	70°+	None reg.	Moderate	Fair	Poor
Polyvinyl	Interior Cabinetry Veneering General	60°+	1-2 hrs.	High	Fair	V. Good Fair filler
Resorcinol	Exterior General	70°+	16-24 hrs.	V. high	Waterproof	Good Fills well
Urea- formaldehyde	Interior Protected ext. General	70°+	16+ hrs.	High	Good	Good Poor filler

Aliphatic resin, a *thermoplastic adhesive*, the strongest and best of the *polyvinyl* glues, is best known as *yellow glue* because of its characteristic (and unique) color. This is a particularly good choice for edge-gluing and is the best all-around glue for general home cabinetmaking and woodworking. It is a liquid, has good gap-filling properties, is fairly heat-resistant, dries hard, sands well, and works easily.

The glue-line color is cream, and is almost indistinguishable in many woods. Finishes, including lacquers, do not bother it, and it has a long shelf life. If separation of the glue and vehicle occurs, they can be quickly remixed. The only drawback is that it has poor water resistance, but this is not a problem in most cabinetmaking projects. It is available in a variety of quantities, from small applicator squeeze bottles to bulk.

This glue can be used at temperatures above 45 degrees F but tends to set fast at temperatures over 80 degrees F, especially in low humidity. Keep the glue well mixed and spread it evenly

Aliphatic resin adhesive

on one mating surface in a moderately thick coat, heavy on end grain. Mate the pieces as soon as possible and clamp them at once. Use moderate pressure and clamp for about 1 hour.

Polyvinyl adhesive

Polyvinyl adhesive is another of the thermoplastics, second best to aliphatic resin, very popular, and recognizable as familiar white glue. It is a good choice for all-around woodworking, cabinetry, and casework, and is excellent for gluing paper goods. It is liquid, somewhat moisture-resistant, does not fill gaps especially well, cures reasonably hard, and makes a joint somewhat less strong than yellow glue does.

It cures by loss of moisture into the wood, so the moisture content of the workpieces should be on the order of 12 percent maximum for a good bond. It is only moderately heat-resistant and does not sand well, clogging the paper.

The glue line color is a translucent white, sometimes with a yellowish tinge. It will soften under some solvent-based finishes, especially lacquer. Shelf life is good. Quantity sizes available are comparable to those of yellow glue.

White glue is easy to use, nonstaining, and has good open time. Application should not be made at less than 60 degrees F, and the glue works better as the temperature rises. However, it sets up rapidly in low-humidity conditions.

All the workpieces should be lined up and ready to assemble with no wasted time. Spread an even, medium-thick layer on one mating surface and join them immediately. Clamp at once, and be sure to scrape off any excess glue that squeezes out. Clamping time should be at least 1 hour if there is no stress on the joint and the temperature is 70 degrees F, longer otherwise.

Animal glue

Animal glues are the traditional bonding agents that have been in use for many decades. They are still readily available and still used by many artisans, especially those who prefer to emulate the old ways or are restoring or replicating antique cabinetry or furniture with full authenticity. There are two kinds.

Liquid hide glue, the ready-mixed variety for easy application, comes in several container sizes. It is not at all moisture-resistant and will soften even in high-humidity conditions. It fills gaps extremely well and can also be used to fill out chips and cracks. It makes a tough, very strong joint, cures hard, and can be sanded; it works more easily than white or yellow glue and has an open time of an hour or more. The glue-line color is usually dark brown, so it is especially useful in gluing dark woods like walnut or mahogany. Finishes do not bother it if they are not water-based, and it has a decent shelf life.

Hide glue should be applied when the air temperature is 70 degrees F or higher; low humidity may cause skimming, but the working time is good. You can use this glue at lower temperatures if you keep the supply warm. Spread a thin even coat over both workpiece surfaces, leaving no bare spots. Wait until the glue is just tacky, then mate the pieces with a slight sliding motion. Clamp with even, moderate pressure for at least 2 hours at 75 degrees F or higher, increasingly longer in cooler conditions.

The second variety is called *hot glue* or *hot animal glue*. It comes in powder or flake form by the pound. It must be mixed with water in specific proportions in a glue pot—electric today, and thermostatically controlled—heated to about 140 degrees F, and stirred until it becomes a smooth liquid. Application is made with a special glue brush with just the right stiffness. The glue must be fully hot when applied and the joint clamped immediately before the glue has a chance to cool. The ambient temperature should be at least 70 degrees F, the clamping time at least 2 hours.

Casein glue, another traditional type, is made from dried milk curd and available in powder form in cans of various weights. It is prepared by mixing with water, then letting it stand for several minutes before applying. Casein powder has a long shelf life if kept dry and tightly contained but a short pot life; it should be mixed only in small quantities and applied immediately. As soon as it thickens in the mixing container, throw it away and mix a fresh batch.

Casein glue

Casein is a strong glue with good moisture resistance and good gap-filling properties. It can be applied in any temperature above freezing but cures faster in warmer temperatures. It is useful in all general cabinetmaking jobs, including outdoor cabinetry, such as a barbecue unit, not exposed directly to the weather. It is also the glue of choice for oily woods like yew, teak, or pitch pine. Casein sands satisfactorily, has a dark glue line, and works readily if kept fresh.

Apply a thin, even coat to each surface and mate the parts immediately. For gap filling, let a small amount thicken and pack the cavity, repacking if the glue tends to flow out. Clamp the parts under moderate pressure for at least 2 hours. Curing time varies considerably with temperature, humidity, and the materials being glued and can be several hours.

Hot melt glue

Hot melt glue is a relatively recent innovation. It comes in solid cylindrical-stick form, with different formulations for different bonding purposes. Selecting the correct variety is crucial for a successful job. The glue is applied by running the stick through a special electric applicator called a *glue gun* that melts the glue and drives the liquid through a nozzle onto the workpiece as a beadline.

Hot melt is a bit tricky to use and is not satisfactory for most cabinetmaking purposes. The glue must be as liquid as possible as it is applied to wet the surfaces being bonded. Ambient temperature, as well as that of the workpieces, should be at least 70 degrees F, preferably more. The glue bead should be applied rapidly and the glue spread by the pressure of the parts being mated; this must be done quickly. The resulting bond, not especially strong under the best circumstances, is intended for light-duty indoor service only. Clamping is not needed, and strong hand pressure is usually sufficient to make the bond.

This glue shines in making temporary tacks between pieces that will later be separated, as in some kinds of wood turning and applying overlay moldings and decorative pieces to cabinet doors, drawer fronts, and face frames. It is also fine for applying small decorative items made of materials other than wood, porous or not. The advantage is that hot melt is easy, fast, and clean to use.

Although *contact cement* can be used in many applications, one is particularly important to cabinetmakers: bonding plastic, plastic laminate, or veneer to a wood substrate. Putting on a plastic laminate countertop is the most common chore; veneer is usually applied with other glues, and plain plastics have limited presence in custom cabinetry.

Contact cement is made from a synthetic rubber base. There are two types. One is highly flammable and explosive and has a deserved reputation for being not only toxic but highly dangerous to use. Avoid it.

Select the nonflammable variety, which can be cleaned up with water and has no volatile solvents in it. Although the bond is not quite as strong as that of the flammable type, when properly done, it is more than sufficient for any household countertop service.

Contact cement is tricky to use. Doing a practice run or two with scraps or on a project of little consequence is a good idea if you are unfamiliar with the process. Applying the glue is easy, but mating the parts must be done exactly the first time because there is no second chance. There is no slippage, and the parts become immediately immobile. Clamping is not needed, but pressure should be applied to the laminate surface with a special heavy roller or by solidly thumping a carpet-padded chunk of 2-x-4 with a hammer, covering the entire surface.

The cement is ready to use direct from the can. The usual procedure is to brush or roll a fairly thick coat onto the surface of the substrate and the back of the laminate, then let it dry until the milky color disappears and the coating is shiny clear. If any areas appear dry, uneven, or too thin, a second coat can be applied and let dry. When a piece of brown wrapping paper or shopping bag does not adhere to the surface when pressed down gently, the cement is ready; it should not be left overlong.

Contact cement

There are various approaches to joining the materials. You can cover the substrate surface with a layer of brown paper or strips of waxed paper laid front to back and overlapping at the sides. Some workers prefer a series of slender wood dowels spaced about a foot apart. The laminate is placed on top, aligned exactly and often starting at one end or the back with much of the sheet raised a bit, and the paper or dowels successively removed as the sheet is lowered. Bonding is almost instantaneous. All work should be done at 70 degrees F or more.

Other bonding agents

There are a few other bonding agents that it is well to know about because you might need them all in due course.

Alpha-cyanoacrylate is most familiar as "Superglue" and is also called ACC. This is a quick-tacking, quick-drying, and strong-adhering glue meant for use on nonporous materials. It is useless on wood or other porous surfaces. It has some applications where few or no other agents will do the job as in making a practically invisible mend on a broken porcelain cabinet knob. The solvent, should you get some on your fingers, is acetone or ordinary fingernail polish remover.

Resorcinol resin is a thermoset plastic bonding agent that comes in two parts: resin and catalyst. It must be mixed as needed for application within about 8 hours, then clamped for 16 to 24 hours. Its important feature is that it is fully waterproof. A cabinetry application might be something built into an open-decked boat, such as a driver's console.

Epoxy is another thermoset that comes in two parts, a liquid resin and a liquid hardener or catalyst, mixed equally as needed. It will bond practically anything and has great strength but is not easy to use and is very expensive. Cabinetry applications would be few, as when great strength is necessary or a joint or some hardware item needs repairing.

Urea-formaldehyde is a powder thermoset that is mixed with water as needed—usually known as *plastic resin glue*. It does not fill gaps well and can be used only in tight joints with 16 hours of clamping under moderate pressure at 70 degrees F or more.

But it is moisture-resistant, makes a very strong joint, is good for general woodworking, and is readily available.

Mastics come in a variety of forms and are made of numerous substances for numerous purposes. These are thick adhesives that may come in tubes or bulk containers. Those that might be used in some woodworking and cabinetmaking or cabinet installation chores are commonly called *construction adhesive* or *panel adhesive* and are applied in beads with a caulking gun.

Gluing & clamping

The first step in achieving a good glue joint is to select the right kind of glue for the job. Beyond that, there are some simple points to keep in mind. Foremost is the fact that a good glue joint depends upon good alignment and fit of the joint parts. Never depend upon gap-filling properties or mechanical fasteners to compensate for a poorly cut joint because problems will surely occur.

Spread the glue as evenly as possible. When you mate flat surfaces, spreading too much glue means that a lot will be squeezed out at the edges and have to be cleaned up later. Or you might get trapped air bubbles that could weaken the joint. Pour too much into a dowel-pin hole, and the wood might split when you drive the pin in because the extra glue can't escape (one reason for using spiral-grooved pins). On the other hand, if you use too little glue, you will have a "starved joint" with little strength.

The surface porosity of the wood has an effect on the joint. Porous surfaces need more glue; tight-grained surfaces need less. Edge gluing usually requires the least amount of glue or the thinnest coating, while face-to-face gluing needs a bit more, and end-grain gluing needs the most. The density of the wood also plays a part. A light, soft, porous wood requires a thinner glue (not a thinner coating) because it will absorb some of the moisture in the glue and thicken it. A hard, smooth, dense wood needs a thicker glue.

Surfaces to be glued must be clean, even, smooth, and free of dust or other contaminants. Anything that might mix or interfere with the glue will weaken the joint. Wood surfaces oxidize, so best results are obtained when the joint surfaces are cut, sanded, planed, or edged to expose fresh, unoxidized material just prior to gluing. If the wood is naturally oily, use a glue suitable for that condition.

The integrity of a glue joint also depends upon the moisture content of the workpieces. Ideally, that should be around 10 percent. A high moisture content weakens glue joints by adding moisture and interfering with proper curing; a very low one draws excessive moisture out.

Thus, always use top-quality, kiln-dried, or long-term air-dried stock, preferably wood that has acclimated for at least several weeks in the area where it will be used. Checking the moisture content of your cabinetmaking stock with a *moisture meter* is a good idea despite the fairly high cost of the instrument.

When assembling glue joints, you must be aware of the *pot life* of the glue, the time span during which the glue stays good. You must also be able to assemble the joint and set the clamps within the characteristic *open time* of the glue, the time during which it remains workable after being spread.

At some point after being exposed to the air the properties of a glue will begin to change. It must be spread, the joint parts adjusted, and clamped before this occurs if the joint is to achieve full strength. The pot life of premixed liquid glues is long, nearly the same as shelf life, but those you must mix fresh should be mixed only in quantities for immediate use.

This means that you need to have all your tools, equipment, and supplies laid out and ready so that you can apply glue, mate parts, clamp, and set fasteners quickly. To ensure correct assembly, dry-fit the joint parts and check for correct assembly and proper clearances. Make sure that no more work needs to be done.

Mark the pieces with light pencil lines to show which part goes where and in what direction if the joint is a complex one. You might also crosshatch the surfaces upon which glue must be spread.

Drying or curing rates of glue joints will vary widely, depending upon several factors like ambient temperature, relative humidity, viscosity and type of glue, and characteristics of the wood. It is important that no joint be loaded or subjected to any pressure before it is fully cured lest the bond be weakened.

Early surfacing or other working of the assembled piece in the joint areas is not a good idea either. The wood adjacent to the glue line swells somewhat from moisture. Premature surfacing leaves a sunken area along the glue line when the wood dries completely.

When you set clamps, do so rapidly and in logical order, tightening each one in succession in two or three rounds. Spread the clamp pressure with blocks or pads and keep it as even as you can. As you set and adjust the clamps, be sure to check the workpieces for squareness, plumb, and alignment, so that nothing goes permanently awry.

Leave the clamps in place for at least the recommended clamp time, longer if you can or conditions warrant. The joint must be fully closed, with perhaps just a bit of glue squeezed out along the glue line. Thin glues or coatings require relatively light pressure; thick glues or coatings need more. Not enough results in an uneven, weak, or even useless glue joint that depends mostly on the hardened glue interface rather than a bond between the parts. But too much squeezes the glue out so that little or no bond can occur—the starved joint.

If fasteners are to be used in conjunction with glue, drive those at whatever time is convenient but preferably early on if you can do so without disturbing the clamp or the joint alignment. Driving fasteners after the glue joint has cured runs the risk of breaking the bond.

Woodworking joints

JOINERY IS the process of constructing articles, especially furniture and cabinets, by joining pieces of wood together. There was a time when joinery was a well-recognized trade, a combination of manual art and craft, and a master joiner was an artisan worthy of great respect among his peers. Much experience and a thorough knowledge of the methods and techniques of cutting and assembling appropriate joints, as well as an understanding of the woods being worked, was required—no small chore when you consider that there are over 100 kinds of woodworking joints and a huge array of wood species that might be used.

The home cabinetmaker today is in a different position, however, and need not achieve such exalted status to do a creditable job of building cabinetry of perfectly acceptable quality. On the other hand, there is no way to avoid absorbing some knowledge about the process. You can't build cabinets without doing so. A cabinet is no better than its poorest joint. The quality and serviceability of the cabinetry you construct will depend to a considerable degree on the selection and quality of the joints you make.

The following pages treat the more common kinds of woodworking joints and some of the general principles of joinery. Consideration is given to modern machine-aided procedures and techniques that are suited to amateur shopwork as opposed to the more complex ones of traditional handcrafting.

Edge joints

The *edge* of a piece of stock means the narrow plane or side at an angle to the top and bottom surfaces, running parallel with the grain, usually but not always the "long" dimension. Edge joints are about the simplest to make and are widely used in all kinds of woodworking. The purpose may be to build a wider surface from two or more narrow pieces laid edge-to-edge in a series with the grain running parallel.

In this case, if the stock is plainsawn (hardwood) or flat-grained (softwood), alternate the orientation of each piece successively from heart side up to heart side down (FIG. 7-1). This positions the growth rings in opposite directions from piece to piece and results in a workpiece that is more stable dimensionally and is easier and more satisfactory to work.

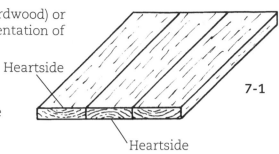

Heartside

7-1

Heartside

Edge joints also come into play when two or more pieces are joined at angles. If the position is edge-to-edge, as for a 45-degree form, reversing the heart-side positions is worthwhile if possible. If the position is edge-to-face, as in a right-angle joint, relative position seldom matters.

Edge joints in rough work can be made using fasteners like clamp nails or Skotch fasteners. For cabinetry and most woodworking projects, glue is used. If the joint is properly made, with the edges freshly surfaced, square, and plane with full surface contact, the joint will be stronger than the wood itself.

To make a joint stronger than plane flat edges would produce, the edges may be machined into a different and perhaps interlocking configuration, adding some mechanical strength and increasing the surface area to be bonded by the glue. Where even more strength is needed, the joint can be reinforced with a spline, biscuit, dowel pins, or metal fasteners.

The simplest edge joint is called a *plain edge* (FIG. 7-2). If the edges are plane and even, as when ripped on a table saw with a fine-toothed blade, they can be joined with mechanical fasteners, with or without glue, depending upon intended service and quality. But for a visible glued joint with a fine glue line, all mating edges should be smooth. Coat the edges with an appropriate glue, join, and clamp, using blocks to make sure the pieces do not separate or buckle.

Plain edge

7-2

Plain edge joint

Rabbeted edge

An easy and effective way to make a more stable edge joint of greater strength, also making the joint easier to align and assemble, is to cut matching

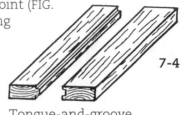

7-3

Rabbet edge joint

rabbets into mating edges (FIG.7-3). You can do this with a table or radial arm saw and a dado head, on a jointer or shaper, with a router or a power plane, or even with a hand rabbet plane.

Tongue-and-groove edge

The *tongue-and-groove* (T&G) edge joint (FIG. 7-4) makes use of a standard milling pattern commonly found even at small lumberyards. You can make your own on a table saw or with a molding head.

7-4

Tongue-and-groove edge joint

Milled edge

7-5

Milled edge joint

A *milled edge* joint (FIG. 7-5) has a bit more complex shape, both edges mating exactly. Specific configurations may vary a bit, which is immaterial. The surface area of the joint is maximized, but not that much extra strength is gained for the extra work involved.

Doweled edge

For more strength, in the *doweled edge*, the mating edges are first planed, then aligned for a series of dowel pins (FIG. 7-6). The pin diameter in most cases should be half the thickness of the piece into which it will be set. In very thick pieces, diameter is a judgment call.

7-6

Doweled edge joint

Dowel spacing is typically every 6 inches. Penetration into each workpiece is usually about two and one half times the dowel diameter. Once the matching dowel holes are bored, glue is applied, the dowels set in one edge, the edges glue-coated along with the protruding dowel-pin halves, and the pieces joined. Proper alignment is crucial and can be difficult. Good jigs are almost essential in most cases.

Splined edge

Another method of joining is to employ a *spline* set into close-fitting grooves in each edge (FIG. 7-7)—a full-length spline, exposed at the ends. It can be hidden by stopping it and the grooves short of the ends of the workpieces; this is called a *stopped spline*.

7-7

Splined edge joint

Or two or more shorter sections of spline can be set in. Be sure to leave enough extra groove depth and length to allow excess glue to escape without disturbing the joint integrity.

Much the same arrangement can be achieved, usually with greater ease and effectiveness, using a plate joiner and biscuits. These are nothing more than sophisticated splines that can be set quickly as needed.

Butt joints

Butt joints; also called *plain joints*, along with edge joints are probably the most commonly used joints in woodworking. Except perhaps for the plain edge joint, they are the simplest to make, but they are also the weakest and can be exasperatingly difficult to asssemble properly.

Because one of the mating surfaces is always end grain, glue has little effectiveness, and nails and screws have seriously reduced holding power. This means that to attain reasonable strength, the joint has to be bolstered with some sort of reinforcement. There are two general kinds of butt joint. One is the *flat butt*: Both pieces lie flat, and an end is joined to an edge, as in most picture frames. The other is the *edge butt*: An end is joined to a surface with both pieces standing on edge, as in a drawer.

Plain flat butt

Figure 7-8 shows a *plain flat butt* with no reinforcing. The only way this can be effectively made is when both pieces are attached to a substrate, like moldings on a door face, or as pieces of a face frame secured to the edges of a carcase or some similar arrangement. It is not a stand-alone joint.

Reinforcement can be added by driving long nails or screws through one edge into the end of the second piece or securing the two with corrugated or Skotch fasteners. Even so, this makes a weak joint subject to separation.

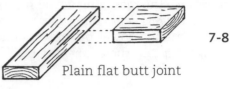

7-8

Plain flat butt joint

Frame butt   A *frame butt joint* (FIG. 7-9), considerably stronger than its plain counterpart, is made by adding a pair of dowel pins. It is sometimes called a *doweled flat butt joint*. This joint will stand alone and is effective provided the application is light-duty. Biscuits or other splines can be substituted for the dowel pins to make a *splined frame butt joint*.

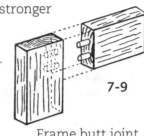

7-9

Frame butt joint

Corner butt   When two members are stood on edge and joined to make a corner, the joint is called a *corner butt joint* or an *edge butt joint* (FIG. 7-10). A common construction found in many box designs, it is typically made with nails or screws, along with glue, to secure the pieces. As with flat joints, dowel pins can be substituted for more strength (*doweled corner butt*), or splines or biscuits can be installed (*splined or plated corner butt*).

7-10

Corner butt joint

Middle-rail butt   A middle-rail butt joint (FIG. 7-11) can be made either on-edge or flat, end-to-surface or end-to-edge. An effective joint cannot be made without mechanical aid, and again, nails and screws are commonly employed in this construction. If

7-11

Middle-rail butt joint

dowel pins are set, the joint is a *doweled middle-rail butt*. Biscuits or splines can also be installed. The arrangement is common to shelving sets.

Another very common arrangement is a *glue-block corner butt joint* (FIG. 7-12). It is widely employed in cabinets, countertop frames, furniture, and general woodworking because it is simple to make but reasonably strong and effective. The corner-butt joint is made in the usual way, with fasteners or splines, and the glue block is then added to fill out the corner. Depending on the size of the pieces, the block may be mechanically fastened to the corner members (or vice versa) along with glue. The block is usually sized to cover the entire corner.

Glue-block corner butt

7-12

Glue-block corner butt

In some cases where a glue-block corner butt joint might be advantageous, a *gusset corner butt joint* (FIG. 7-13) is employed instead. This works especially well where space is limited or more extensive support or greater strength is desired. The gusset is a flat triangular piece usually cut from plywood or board stock. It is glued and secured with nails or screws into the corner, usually flush with the upper edges of the cornered pieces, and typically extends farther along those pieces than a glue block would. The gussets also afford added support and anchoring points for a top piece.

Gusset corner butt

7-13

Gusset corner butt joint

A *dado* is a square-sided slot cut into a workpiece across the grain of the wood. If the slot is cut with the grain, it is not a dado but a *groove*.

Dado joints have the advantage of considerable strength for little added work. There are many variations. They are relatively easy to make and are probably the most useful joints

Dado joints

for home cabinetmaking projects. They are at their best wherever edge support is required, as in bookshelving or cupboard shelves. Even a shallow dado provides added holding surface and automatically aligns and retains cabinet components, restraining them from warping or wracking.

You can readily cut most dadoes on a table saw fitted with a dado-blade set, and they are even easier to make on a radial arm saw because you can see exactly what you are doing. They can be cut with a router and sometimes are best done that way.

Similarly, mating pieces may be trimmed with a saw or cut with a router, depending upon the shape required. When cutting dadoes in solid wood, make the cut depth one-half the total thickness of the stock. In plywood, reduce the depth to one-quarter the thickness to avoid weakening the material.

Plain dado

The *plain* or *simple dado joint* (FIG. 7-14) is the easiest to make and is widely used in shelving constructions. Just dado the supporting piece all the way across, a tiny bit wider than the thickness of the mating piece. Insert the butt end of the mating piece into the dado and secure it with glue and nails or screws.

7-14

Plain dado joint

This arrangement is also sometimes employed in adjustable shelving sets with a series of dadoes and no glue or fasteners. The shelf spacing can be altered or the shelves removed to suit varying needs.

Blind dado

When you assemble a plain dado, the end of the joint is visible and depending upon the nature of the cabinetry, may be considered unattractive. The edge could be covered with a trim molding to hide the joint, of course, but there is a better approach. Cut a dado into the supporting piece, ending the cut an inch or two from the opposite edge of the piece. This is called a *blind* or *stopped* (sometimes just *stop*) *dado* (FIG. 7-15).

The blind end of the cut will be curved, and the butt end of the mating piece will have to be cut on a matching curve; this is a *curved-shoulder blind dado joint*. Or you can cut the end of the dado square with a chisel, making for an easy square cut on the butt end of the mating piece; this is a *square-shoulder blind dado*.

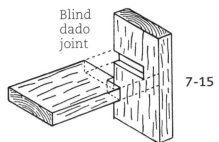

Blind dado joint

7-15

Either way affords maximum strength in the joint, and the finished appearance is that of an extremely tight-fitting butt joint. The sloppy method, admittedly easier, is to leave the dado end curved and the mating butt end squared.

A *shouldered dado* (FIG. 7-16), also called a *rabbeted dado*, is sometimes employed just for a different appearance. It is weaker and requires more work than a plain dado. The dado is cut fully across the workpiece, usually in a width just a tiny bit greater than half the thickness of the mating piece. The butt end of the mating piece is rabbeted to half thickness, and the width of the rabbet should be just a bit less than the depth of the dado. This joint can also be made in stopped form.

Shouldered dado

7-16

Shouldered dado joint

A potential problem with the dado joints just discussed is that they are relatively easy to separate with lateral force. A *half-dovetail dado* (FIG. 7-17) addresses that problem by creating a lock against pullout. The joint must be assembled by sliding the mating pieces together.

Half-dovetail dado

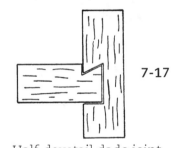

7-17

The joining can be done with glue alone or with nails or screws as an aid. The dado must be cut with a router. The half dovetail on the mating piece could be cut with a saw, but is best done with a router. The cuts should be precise and the fit tight—just loose enough to allow a decent glue coating. A stopped form is possible but tricky to do with precision.

Half-dovetail dado joint

If maximum resistance against pullout of the joint is desired, make a *full-dovetail dado* (FIG. 7-18). The dado must be cut with a router, usually to a depth of one-half the thickness of the stock.

Full-dovetail dado

The mating butt end can be saw-cut, but using a router or shaper makes more sense and affords a better, cleaner cut. Clearances should be just sufficient to allow assembly without binding and a good glue bond.

7-18

Full-dovetail dado joint

Corner dado

The *corner dado* (FIG. 7-19) is not often used but is handy for open-ended shelf sets and similar constructions. The length and depth of the dado can be varied, and the mating shelf corners cut to match.

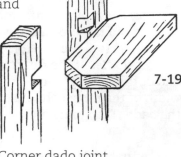

7-19

Corner dado joint

Groove joint

A *groove* is a square-sided cut parallel with the grain. If the groove is close to an edge and force is exerted toward that edge, the joint is inherently weak because the remaining wood has a tendency to split away. In most cases, a minimum ¼ inch of full-thickness stock should remain between the groove's outer edge and the edge of the workpiece. The groove depth is usually equal to one-half the thickness of the workpiece, and the width is just slightly greater than the thickness of the mating piece.

The most common application for a *groove joint* (FIG. 7-20) in cabinetry is in drawer bottoms. The drawer sides are grooved on a table or radial arm saw, and the front is dadoed at a matching location; the drawer back may or may not be dadoed. The drawer bottom is inserted into the grooves and dadoes. It is not glued and may be fastened only at the back, so the joint must be made with care.

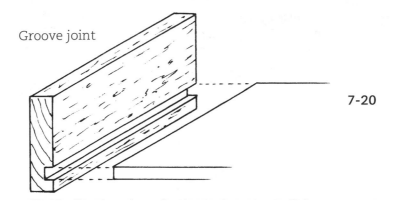

Groove joint

7-20

Rabbet joints

Rabbet (sometimes *rebate*) cuts are common in all kinds of woodworking and are often made as one or more steps in different joints. Four rabbet joints are useful in cabinetry in particular. None are especially strong, and they are generally assembled with glue and nails or screws, sometimes glue blocks or backings as well.

Rabbet joints are simple to make and often helpful in squaring up an assembly as it is put together. Depending upon the visual effect and strength required, the rabbet may be cut to a depth equal to anywhere from one-quarter to two-thirds the thickness of the stock.

Simple rabbet

The *simple rabbet joint* (FIG. 7-21), a good one to use in constructing cabinet frames or base frames, consists of a lengthwise notch in one workpiece to accomodate the full-thickness edge of the mating piece. The rabbet can be made with a hand or power plane, more easily with a table or radial arm saw or a router or shaper. Whatever the process, the mating surfaces must be square, plane, and smooth.

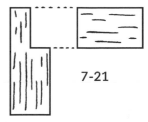

7-21

Simple rabbet joint

Double rabbet

A *double rabbet joint* (FIG. 7-22) is stronger than the simple rabbet and takes just twice as long to make. Matching rabbets are cut into the edges of both workpieces. The rabbets should be sized to allow just a slight clearance for glue.

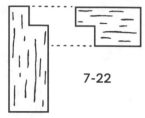

7-22

Double rabbet joint

Edge rabbet

An *edge rabbet joint* (FIG. 7-23) is a form of double rabbet where the joint is made lengthwise and usually parallel with the grain of the wood. This is common to box and case construction, and the process is the same as for a double rabbet.

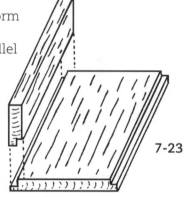

7-23

Edge rabbet joint

Back-panel rabbet

When a cabinet or case requires a back panel, mounting the panel directly on the rear edges of the case leaves the raw edges of the back panel visible as a rim. Even when finished, they may be unsightly. But if a *back-panel rabbet* (FIG. 7-24) is cut into the rear edges of the case before assembly, the back panel is hidden from view.

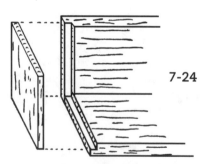

7-24

Back-panel rabbet joint

This construction adds considerable strength and wracking resistance to a cabinet and helps square it during assembly.

Often the rabbet depth is made slightly greater than the back-panel thickness to ensure that the panel will not be visible.

Miter joints

Miter joints are made of two workpieces, the ends or edges cut at matching angles. They are joined so that the cut surfaces of both pieces are hidden but otherwise are much like butt joints. They are weak joints, needing reinforcement, and may be made either flat or on-edge. *Simple miters* join in the same plane; *compound miters* join in two planes and are more complex.

Assembling most miter joints can be tricky, especially when glue is used, because the parts tend to slip apart while being worked. Whenever possible, appropriate clamps or vises should be used. Miter joints are not difficult to make, usually using a table or radial arm saw.

Plain miter

A *plain flat miter joint* (FIG. 7-25) is made when two pieces are assembled with their wider surfaces at top and bottom. A *plain edge miter joint* is made when the pieces are standing on edge.

The flat miter can be secured with nails or Skotch or corrugated fasteners. An edge miter typically has room for at least two nails or screws, which can be driven into both pieces for added strength. The flat miter is very weak unless both pieces are attached to a subsurface, as in a molding on a door face. The edge miter is stronger and can stand alone provided the duty is not too rigorous.

Plain miter joint

7-25

Half-lap flat miter

The strength of a flat miter joint can be increased considerably by cutting *half laps* on the mating pieces (FIG. 7-26). The appearance is that of a plain flat miter, but there is substantial face-grain area in the lap faces that can be successfully glued. Mechanical fasteners can be added, too. There would be no point in constructing a half-lap edge miter.

7-26

Half-lap flat miter joint

Offset miter

The *offset flat miter joint* (FIG. 7-27) has strength somewhat greater than a plain flat miter because of the larger gluing surface and the presence of some face grain. But its main advantage lies in allowing two pieces of different widths to be mated in a miter joint, hiding all end grain.

An offset edge miter is easy to cut and is stronger than its plain counterpart. Its advantage is that the joint is much less susceptible to sliding apart as it is assembled and is somewhat more stable. Nails or screws are needed for good strength.

7-27

Offset miter joint

Rabbeted miter

The *rabbeted miter joint* (FIG. 7-28) is the edge-joint counterpart of the offset flat miter. The cut conformation looks the same, but the cuts are made in a different plane for on-edge box-type construction. Because of the increased glue surface and added strength, as well as greater ease of assembly, this is a good edge joint for cabinetwork. Nails or screws must be driven to secure the joint fully.

7-28

Rabbeted miter joint

Doweled miter

The *doweled flat miter* (FIG. 7-29) is a traditional joint of substantial strength. With proper jigging, it is not difficult to make but does take some time and patience. It is more suitable to wide workpieces to allow plenty of room for at least two dowel pins. A doweled-edge miter is not practical.

7-29

Doweled miter joint

To gain more strength than a doweled flat miter with less effort, make a *splined flat miter* (FIG. 7-30). Cut matching dadoes in the mitered ends of the workpieces and insert a spline of whatever width seems appropriate.

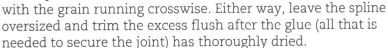

7-30

Splined miter joint

A common spline material is hardboard ¼ inch thick set in a just slightly oversize dado. If the fit is too tight, there is a risk of splitting the workpieces. If a wood spline is desired, use hardwood with the grain running crosswise. Either way, leave the spline oversized and trim the excess flush after the glue (all that is needed to secure the joint) has thoroughly dried.

You can make a *splined edge miter* using the same techniques, inserting a thin strip of wood in dadoes running the full length of the miter cuts. Glue alone will secure the joint, and no mechanical fasteners (and subsequent hole filling) are needed. The dadoes must be perfectly aligned.

With the splined flat miter, the spline edges are visible and may be unattractive. You can avoid this on outer or inner edges (but not both) by making a *blind-splined flat miter joint* (FIG. 7-31). Stop the dadoes short of the face of one edge and cut the head of the spline to fit the curved (or squared) ends of the dadoes.

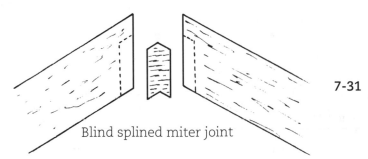

7-31

Blind splined miter joint

The spline ends are also visible in splined edge miter joints. Because of their relatively small size, they are unobtrusive, but there may be a need to hide one end. In that case, a blind-splined-edge miter joint will do the job.

Feathered miter

A *feathered flat miter* (FIG. 7-32) is a very strong and stable construction. The dadoes are cut across the points of the miter. The spline is typically not visible at the inner faces of the edges. Along the outer edges it is very prominent.

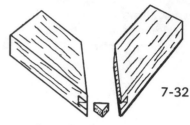

7-32

Feathered miter joint

Wood is used, often in a contrasting color for decorative emphasis. Because the grain should run across the spline, the exposed edges are end grain and will have a different appearance even if made of matching wood. All of this is immaterial, of course, if the finish is paint.

This construction could also be used in an edge joint, as in a case, for an interesting visual effect. A series or stack of spline inserts of contrasting wood across an edge joint could be an emphatic design feature.

Plated miter

7-33

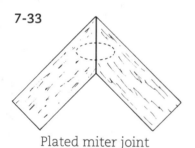

Plated miter joint

A *plated* or *biscuit miter joint* (FIG. 7-33) is probably the strongest miter-joint construction you can make. In a flat joint, if the stock is ¾ inch thick or more, two biscuits can be inserted in the joint after cutting the slots with a plate joiner.

In an edge joint, you can insert as many biscuits end-to-end as the length of the joint will allow, leaving a short space between them. Because of the strength, rigidity, and precision of this type of edge joint, it is ideal for all angles and lengths of miter joints that would otherwise be difficult to fit cleanly.

Lock miter

The *lock miter joint* (FIG. 7-34) has long been used in quality cabinet construction. It is very strong, locks together solidly, allows in-square assembly, and requires no mechanical fasteners to secure it. Hence, the surfaces of the workpieces remain unblemished.

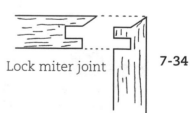

Lock miter joint

7-34

However, the joint can be difficult to make and takes some time and patience. You can do it with a series of cuts on a table or radial arm saw, but the dimensions and cuts have to be perfect or the pieces will not mate properly. The best approach is to use a set of matching lock-miter cutters on a shaper or router.

Any edge miter joint, regardless of the specific shape of the mating joint surfaces, can be made into a *glue-block miter joint*. Cut a wood block to match the miter angles and glue it to the inside of the joint. Orientation of the grain of the glue block is not crucial, especially if it is a hardwood. Secure the block with nails, or better, screws.

Glue-block miter

A gusset in an edge miter joint performs the same function as a glue block by reinforcing the corner. A gusset is very simple to make, using any scrap or plywood and cutting it to match the joint angle. Install the gusset with glue and screws or nails; usually it is positioned flush with the upper or outer edges of the workpieces.

Gusset miter

In a *compound miter joint* (FIG. 7-35), the mating surfaces of the workpieces are angled in two planes. Compound miters are not common in cabinetwork but can occur. A simple example of compound miter construction is a square planter with tapered sides, requiring four compound edge miters cut to 45 degrees across each mating edge and a design angle lengthwise of each edge.

Compound miter

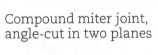

Compound miter joint, angle-cut in two planes

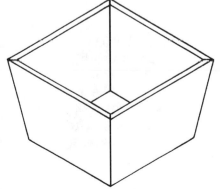

7-35

Woodworking joints   173

Lap joints

Lap joints are simple, strong, rigid, and easy to make, and come in many variations. Whenever one workpiece meets or crosses over another and the surfaces must remain flush with each other, a lap joint is formed. They are usually but not always glued, and secured with screws or nails.

Cross lap

One of the most common lap joints is made when two pieces lie across one another flatwise with all surfaces flush—a *cross lap joint* (FIG. 7-36). This requires cutting away matching notches to one-half the thickness of each piece. The pieces need not be of the same width.

7-36

Cross lap joint

Edge lap

The *edge lap* or *edge cross lap* (FIG. 7-37) is the on-edge counterpart of the cross lap. The thickness or height of each piece must be the same, and the notches are cut to half thickness, but the widths can be different. Often this joint is left unsecured for ready disassembly, and usually securing it with fasteners is difficult or impractical.

7-37

Edge lap joint

Middle lap

A *middle lap joint* (FIG. 7-38), also called a *T-lap*, is a good choice to use instead of a simple flat T-butt joint, since it has far more strength and rigidity. It works well, for example, in a face frame. The workpieces must be of the same thickness, but the widths can be different. Securing it from the back with screws, along with glue, makes a strong joint.

7-38

T or middle lap joint

The *end lap joint* (FIG. 7-39) is the same as a T-lap but located at the ends of the workpieces. This joint is sometimes used in cabinet face frames and especially door frames, exhibiting half end grain and half face grain in each direction on each corner. As with other flat lap joints, it can be secured with both glue and screws driven from the back for considerable strength.

End lap

7-39

End lap joint

Also called a *keyed lap*, the *dovetail lap* (FIG. 7-40) might be employed for extra strength and resistance against pull-apart or simply for decorative effect in stained or natural-finished cabinetry. In the latter case, a heart, club, or any other geometric form could be used in place of the simple dovetail, with an inlay effect.

Dovetail lap

7-40

Dovetail lap joint

A *splice* occurs when two pieces of stock of the same width and thickness are joined end-to-end. This is sometimes necessary when long lengths are unavailable—not uncommon, especially with exotic woods. A typical use for a splice joint in cabinetry would be continuation of a piece of applied molding or making a long piece such as a face rail or counter edging from two or more pieces. There are several useful splices that are easy to make (FIG. 7-41).

Splices

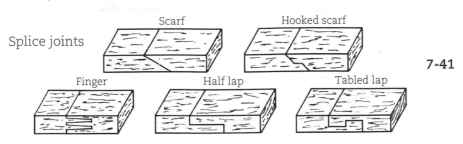

Splice joints

Scarf   Hooked scarf

Finger   Half lap   Tabled lap

7-41

Woodworking joints   175

Scarf The *scarf splice joint* consists simply of matching angle cuts, usually 45 degrees or more to provide maximum gluing surface. In thicker pieces, the joint may be reinforced with dowel pins, and nails or brads might also be driven in stock of any thickness. Care must be taken to avoid splitting.

Hooked scarf If the parts of a plain scarf slip past one another just a bit during assembly, the result is a joint of poor appearance that must be worked further. The *hooked scarf* gets around this problem. Because of the shape of the cuts, the two parts of the assembly can be pushed tightly together without bypassing, making a splice with a clean joint line. It does take longer to make, however.

Finger The *finger splice joint* can be used to join any number of like pieces of stock end to end, and in most cases the finished product is stronger than its individual components. This joint used to be found only in commercially processed lumber or products, but now finger-joint cutter sets allow you to make precision finger joints in your shop. These router bits can be used to make remarkably strong edge joints as well as splices.

Half lap The *half lap splice* is easy to make and effective. Just cut away matching half thicknesses at the end of each workpiece and mate them. You can provide substantial glue surface, and there is ample material, except in very thin stock, to drive nails or screws for added resistance to pull-apart or pivoting.

Tabled lap The *tabled lap splice* resists forces about equally well in all directions, especially against pull- or push-apart and pivoting. The length of the lap can be as great as you wish, and the notches are easily cut on a table or radial arm saw. The notch size is not crucial, but the workpieces should mate well and present flush surfaces.

Mortise-and-tenon joints A *mortise* is a slot or opening cut into the workpiece; a *tenon* is a tongue fashioned on the mating workpiece, sized to fit the mortise exactly. When joined, the two parts are mated in a mortise-and-tenon joint.

Although they require care and patience, these joints are employed in top-grade cabinetry. They produce strong, rigid articles capable of long service even under rigorous conditions. They are usually made with all corners squared, but occasionally one sees rounded mortises and tenons. Either kind can be made with hand tools, a steady hand, and lots of time, but the easiest and generally more accurate methods for the home artisan utilize jigs and power tools.

There are some rule-of-thumb numbers to keep in mind for most applications. Any mortise should be kept at least ½ inch from an end or ⁵⁄₁₆ inch from the face of a workpiece, and those distances should be made greater if possible. Tenon thickness should be half or more the thickness of the piece on which it is formed, and about two and a half times its thickness in length. The mortise should be ⅛ inch deeper than the tenon length, to form a glue pocket. All of these dimensions are judgmental, depending upon the workpieces; the bigger the tenon and the smaller the mortise in comparison with their workpieces, the better. A balance must be struck, and there are many variations where the dimensional specifics are not crucial.

Open

The simplest of these joints is the *open mortise-and-tenon* (FIG. 7-42), often used on cabinet-door frames. The mortise is easily cut on a table saw, using appropriate fixtures to clamp and guide the workpiece. The mating tenon can also be cut on the table saw or by making repeated passes with a radial arm saw. The tenon can be made somewhat longer than the mortise depth and trimmed and sanded flush after assembly. Note that this arrangement can make a right-angle corner joint or an end-to-end joint.

7-42

Open mortise-and-tenon joint

Stub

The *stub mortise-and-tenon joint* (FIG. 7-43) is also easy to make. Again, the cuts can be made on a table saw or a radial arm saw. The tenon is shorter than normal and fits into a groove. This is often a stile-rail joint, the remainder of the

7-43

Stub mortise-and-tenon joint

groove filled with a thin panel. It can also be made with the groove stopped at the inner end, in which case the dimensions must be accurate so that the stub width is an exact fit.

Blind　When visible end grain in the joint is objectionable, craft a *blind mortise-and-tenon* (FIG. 7-44). There are three common ways of making this joint, the mortise shaped and located to mate exactly with the tenon. A *shouldered blind mortise-and-tenon joint* has a square or rectangular tenon where stock has been cut away on all sides. In a *full blind mortise-and-tenon joint*, the tenon is cut fully across the workpiece on two opposite surfaces. In a *rounded blind mortise-and-tenon*, the two parts are cut wholly round or with rounded corners.

7-44

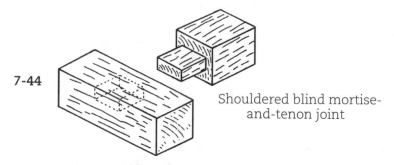

Shouldered blind mortise-
and-tenon joint

In addition, all three can be constructed with one or even two hidden wedges in them, which effectively locks the joint tight. They must be nicely calculated for size to avoid splitting. When so made, they are termed *blind-wedged, shouldered*, and so on.

Through　A *through mortise-and-tenon* (FIG. 7-45) is fashioned with a shouldered tenon (with stock cut away on all four sides) that extends entirely through the mortise in the mating piece. The end grain of the tenon is visible; it should fill the mortise completely and be left overlong, then trimmed and sanded flush after assembly.

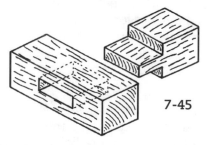

7-45

Through mortise-and-tenon
joint

178　Custom Cabinets

Often a wedge, perhaps of contrasting color, is driven into a precut slot in the tenon from the open side of the joint, locking the pieces firmly together. When this is done for decorative purposes, the wedge should fill the entire slot in the tenon for the sake of appearance. This joint is called a *wedged mortise-and-tenon*.

Barefaced

A *barefaced tenon* looks like a half lap, with stock cut away only on one side or shoulder (sometimes top and/or bottom as well). If the mortise in the mating piece is open on one side and the outside face of the tenon lies flush with that of the mortised piece, the joint is a *barefaced mortise-and-tenon joint*. The mortise in the mating piece may be positioned so that the tenon is to the inside, fully inset with the outside surfaces of both pieces, either flush or offset; this is a *blind barefaced mortise-and-tenon joint* (FIG. 7-46).

Barefaced

Blind barefaced

7-46
Mortise-and-tenon joints.

Haunched

When a mortise-and-tenon joint is used in a frame that surrounds a thinner panel, often a part of the tenon must be cut away in a modified shoulder form to clear the panel. This is called a *haunched mortise-and-tenon* when all or part of the shoulder is visible after the joint is assembled. If the haunch is hidden within a matching mortise in the mating workpiece, it is a *blind* or *concealed haunched mortise-and-tenon joint* (FIG. 7-47).

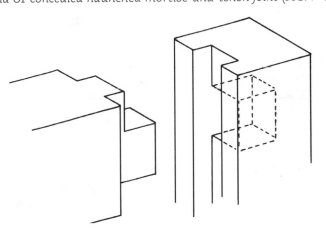

7-47
Haunched mortise-and-tenon joint.

Dovetail joints

Dovetail joints are made of two alternating and mating parts: pins and the notches into which they fit. They are difficult to build by hand, requiring skill, patience, and a lot of time. Nonetheless, they have long been great favorites with cabinetmakers and turn up in top-quality cabinetry. They are sometimes employed primarily for their decorative impact, especially when contrasting woods and a natural finish are part of the design.

But they have great holding power, assuming they are tightly fitted and properly glued; additional fasteners are superfluous. Dovetails are lock-type joints, rugged, stable, and inflexible. They are often considered the finest joints for drawers, box forms, and almost any kind of casework. Fortunately for today's amateur cabinetmaker, a wide array of jigs and power equipment has greatly simplified dovetail construction. Patience and care are still a requirement, but the equipment allows the necessary precision while reducing the time and skill factors.

Through

The *through dovetail joint* (FIG. 7-48) is the easiest to make. All notches and pins are cut entirely through the workpieces, with alternating end and face grains visible. They are best started with a half notch and mating half pin at the top and preferably should end the same way at the bottom. Pin and notch size depends upon the jigs employed unless hand-cut. Then the maximum width is typically the same as the thickness of the stock.

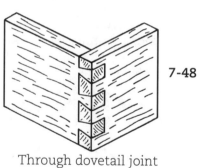

7-48

Through dovetail joint

Half blind

When a dovetail joint is desired for its strength and locking qualities but the visible end grain of the pins must be hidden on one surface, use a *half-blind* or *lapped dovetail joint* (FIG. 7-49). The pins are cut fully through one workpiece, but the matching notches are cut only partway into the mating workpiece, typically to about two-thirds to three-quarters thickness. The

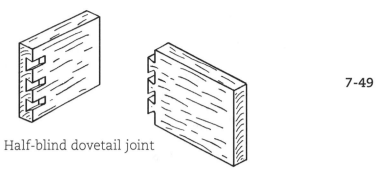

Half-blind dovetail joint

7-49

only end grain visible is at the end of the notched piece. For a perfect flush fit, the notches may be cut a hair deep and the notch ends sanded flush after the joint is assembled.

Blind

When a dovetail joint is employed solely for strength and it is desirable to conceal as much of the joint lines as possible, a *blind* or *stop-lapped dovetail joint* (FIG. 7-50) can be made. The pins and notches are cut so that when the parts are assembled, only a thin strip of end grain, the width of which is variable and can be made almost paper-thin, remains visible.

7-50

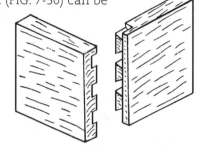

Blind dovetail joint

Box joint

The *box joint* (FIG. 7-51) is the simplest of the complex joints to make, yet it has considerable strength and can be employed as a decorative element in cabinetmaking. At one time this joint appeared in all manner of prosaic items, such as dynamite and ammunition crates and salt codfish boxes. Nowadays, while it sometimes still appears in commercial boxes, the main application lies in drawer, case, and chest corners.

7-51

Box joint

Woodworking joints   181

If you use a guide or jig and a router to make a box joint, the size of the pins and notches will be predetermined. However, you can readily make the required cuts on a table or radial arm saw with appropriate fixtures. In that case, you can make the pins and notches whatever size you wish and lay them out in whatever frequency seems appealing. The usual arrangement is to start with a full-size notch at the top of one workpiece and a matching pin on the other, then alternate in equal sizes to the bottom. But you can also vary the widths or frequency of occurrence in whatever way suits your fancy.

As with dovetail joints, box joints can be made in half-blind or blind fashion, although they seldom are.

Lock joint

One of the ruggedest joints you can make, ideal for drawer corners front or back, is the *lock joint* (FIG. 7-52). Five passes on a radial arm or table saw will do the job, producing a solid joint with little work. The cuts must be accurate, or the parts will not mate properly.

Lock joint   7-52

First, select appropriate dimensions for the cuts, depending upon the thickness of the workpieces. Start by making the wide cut into the end of piece A. Next, make the narrow cut across the inner surface of piece A, leaving the better part of the end as waste. Make the third cut on piece B, the narrow dado. The fourth cut is the same depth as the dado, across the inner end surface of piece B, and the last cut is the deep crosscut that leaves the small tenon on the end of the piece. If you have made your measurements, saw setups, and cuts with precision, the two pieces will slip together easily, and a thin coating of glue will ensure a tough joint.

Coped joints (FIG. 7-53) are seldom used in cabinetry but can come in handy at times. They are used to join two like pieces, such as moldings, at an inside corner, right-angle or otherwise. If a miter joint might open up, the angles are difficult to cut, or a troublesome compound angle is encountered, a coped joint is often the answer.

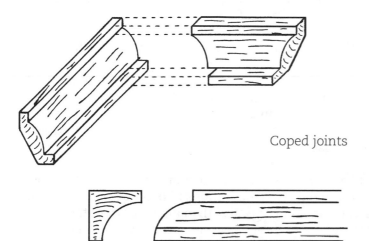

Coped joints

To make a *right-angle coped joint*, the end of the first piece is cut off square. Then the profile of the first piece must be cut into the end of the second piece, so that a perfect end butt joint can be made that follows the profile faithfully, leaving no gaps.

This can be done by scribing the profile with a pair of dividers, tracing along the profile with one leg and duplicating it on the second workpiece with the other. Or you can use a template former, then trace around the form. Once the outline is made on the second piece, cut the excess wood away with a coping saw. Instead of making the cut square across the workpiece, however, angle the saw blade back a little—2 or 3 degrees is sufficient. This will ensure a tight fit along the visible joint line.

Joinery tips

Fabricating joints of good quality suitable for the applications at hand is largely a matter of common sense and careful crafting. If you keep a few principles in mind, you should have little difficulty.

The first step is to decide which joint, or combination of joints, will be best for your project. Consider strength: Some joints are stronger than others. None should have even the possibility of failing under their intended service. Consider appearance: Some joints look better than others; some can be decorative or part of the design; others may be hidden. Consider difficulty: Many joints are hard to make and may not be worth the effort, given the project design and use.

Consider ease of assembly: Some joint assembly is difficult. Consider quality: Cabinetry comes in all levels for many purposes, from toolshed to living room. Consider required skill: Stick with joints you can fabricate well and select the simplest joint that will get the job done satisfactorily. Consider your equipment: Some joints are best made with sophisticated gear you may not have.

If you make all the joints in a project of one or two kinds, you can perform the required operations in production-line fashion. Make all the dadoes of one size, then all of another; then set up for rabbets, followed by shelf peg holes, followed by tenons, and so on. Precise measurements are absolutely crucial, so use the proper devices of top quality and double-check everything, especially when transferring measurements.

You must have a clean, precise fit throughout a joint: All the surfaces must mate well, and the contact areas must be smooth and plane for the glue to bond properly. All cuts have to be made with care and accuracy, which means that all cutting edges must be kept supersharp if you are to expect good results.

Remember that maximum edge- and face-grain surfaces in the joints make for the strongest construction; end grain is weak. When you need added strength, often the best answer is to use a simple joint and beef it up with a spline, mechanical fastener, glue block, or some other aid. Complexity does not necessarily equate with quality.

Doors

ALTHOUGH THEY are not part of every cabinet project, doors are prevalent enough that their design and construction are one important aspect of cabinetmaking. Doors are the most visible part of a cabinet, a vital component of the overall design and decor and a sure indicator of the quality of the cabinetry. They are often the focal point for the artistry and craftsmanship of the maker.

At the same time, doors must be fully functional. Every door is a separate piece of cabinetwork in itself and has to be solidly made to withstand the strains of constant service that can be severe at times. Each door must be well fitted and properly aligned, and cannot rely upon any part of the cabinetry except itself for strength and rigidity. There are several types of doors to consider as well as a number of standard construction techniques.

Door types

There are probably hundreds of variations on door designs. Many are plain, straightforward, and easy to build. Others are ornate and complex, requiring considerable time and expertise. In cabinetwork, however, there are only three basic types.

Hinged doors

By far the most common kind of cabinet door is the *side-swinging hinged door*. Most have a pair of hinges mounted on one side to swing out to the left or right. In some cases, a single length of continuous or piano hinge is installed instead. Hinged cabinet doors always open outward. There are many styles and finishes of hinges available to produce just about any appearance you desire.

Hinged doors of this sort are denoted in two ways: by the "hand" and by the way they fill or cover the cabinet opening. With respect to cupboards, cabinets, bookcases, and similar items, if the hinges are on your left when you face the door, it is a *left-hand door*; on the right, a *right-hand door* (FIG. 8-1). In theory, the locks or latches should also be so termed, but because the hand of entry and passageway doors is denoted somewhat differently, you may encounter some confusion. Be sure to select hardware for the correct hand, or the universal variety that can be mounted either way.

Left-hand

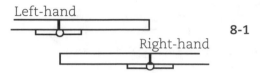

8-1

Right-hand

There are several door designations that depend on the way they are mounted. Figure 8-2 shows a *flush door*. The outer surface of the door lies flush with the stiles of the face frame or flush with the outer edges of the carcass where there is no face frame. For the sake of appearance, the crack around the edges of the door should be uniform and the fit close. If any great swelling or shrinking occurs or the door cracks or warps, the door may appear out of true or may bind.

Flush with face frame

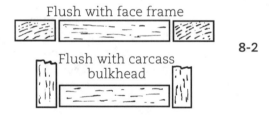

8-2

Flush with carcass bulkhead

A *flush overlay door* (FIG. 8-3), often termed by the amount of overlay (typically ¾ or ½ inch), lies entirely outside the cabinet face frame, overlapping it on each side, and usually top and bottom as well, by a specified amount. The door hides the whole opening so need not be fitted as exactly as a flush door, and a little warping or unsquareness often goes unnoticed.

However, in many installations, such as the European style, this system calls for the doors to be aligned with each other; the amount of overlay varies with the design; and there is only a small crack between adjacent doors; the entire cabinet is hidden. Thus, the alignment must be well-nigh perfect (but the hinges usually employed allow for adjustment of the door position).

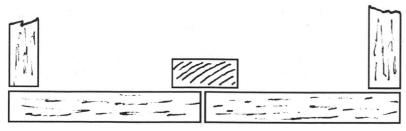

8-3 *Flush overlay doors.*

The *reveal overlay door* (FIG. 8-4) is a bit different. The overlap is variable, covering only part of the face-frame members or bulkhead or end-panel edges. Especially in cabinets with wide face frames, a large part of the face-frame or panel-edge area is visible, and there is a strong shadow line. The overlap is typically ¾ inch on face-frame cabinetry, but as little as ³⁄₁₆ inch where two doors meet at a bulkhead edge.

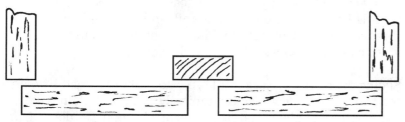

8-4 *Reveal overlay doors.*

The *lip* or *offset door* (FIG. 8-5) is a perennial favorite. It has a narrow rabbet cut around the entire inside perimeter of the door. The resulting outer lip covers a small part of the face frame or much of the end- or bulkhead-panel edges, concealing the entire opening. This is a "forgiving" type of door. The inside clearances can be quite loose, exact fitting is not essential, and any slight unsquareness of the cabinet can usually be concealed.

8-5 *Lipped door.*

A *drop door* is hinged at the bottom to swing downward and either pivots slightly past the upright vertical to rest or has a top-mounted latch. The door can be arranged to swing 180 degrees or more and hang straight down, or drop to the horizontal like the tailgate of a pickup truck. In that case, light decorative chain, elbow supports, or slide-out support rails are installed to position and hold the door. This allows the inside of the door to be used as a work surface.

A *swing-up door* is just that, hinged at the top so that it can be lifted upward out of the way in the same fashion as the compartments above the seats in commercial airliners. This is a useful arrangement in some high-storage cabinets or where movement of side-swinging doors may be restricted. Special support hardware is needed to keep the door open.

Sliding doors

Sliding doors are nearly always installed in matched pairs, two to any cabinet opening. On rare occasions, two pairs are installed with no center meeting rail, and a three-door arrangement is also possible. They are often used in stereo-video cabinetry, bookshelves, and display cabinets.

Sliding doors; the easiest of all types to make and install when made in the simplest fashion, typically consist of plain panels cut to size from sheet material such as plywood, hardboard, or glass and set in either saw-cut grooves in the cabinet body or separately mounted plastic or metal tracks made for the purpose. But sliders can also be ornate and heavy.

The chief advantage of sliding doors is that they can be installed where space is tight and where hinged swinging doors would be awkward or interfere with other cabinetry or furniture. Other advantages are low cost (depending upon design), ease of construction, and ease of fitting and installation. The biggest disadvantage is that only half of the cabinet space is accessible at a time. In addition, the bottom track tends to accumulate dust and dirt, and warped panels can cause problems.

There are several ways to make the tracks to guide the door panels. The simplest is to cut grooves in the cabinet floor or bottom rail and in the rail above the doors with a saw or router during cabinet construction. For thin panels, the grooves are made somewhat wider than the full panel thickness; ample clearance is needed for each panel and for the panels to pass one another. For thicker panels, rather than cutting a full-width groove, the panel edges are rabbeted to about half thickness, and grooves are cut to match.

If cutting grooves is not in order, another method is to mount three small strips of wood to the cabinet surfaces to form channels. A good source for ready-made strips of this sort in numerous sizes is the basswood stripwood sold by hobby shops. Another possibility is to install ready-made tracks of aluminum or plastic. They can be surface-mounted or set into grooves. Yet another method is to cut single grooves in the bottom and top of each door and mount matching rails in cabinet grooves. The rails can be of metal, wood, or plastic. Figure 8-6 shows some of these arrangements.

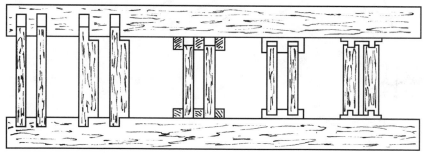

8-6 *In cross section, five ways of installing bypass sliding doors.*

Rolling doors

Rolling doors, a variation of sliding doors, are so large and heavy that they do not slide well unless roller-mounted. In cabinetry, the most common applications are in large wood panels that cover cabinets 3 to 7 feet or so in height and in cabinets employing thick glass panels as doors.

Arrangements for hanging rolling doors vary. Some systems use base or floor tracks, usually of aluminum, to guide ball-bearing wheels or rollers mounted in the panel bottom. Sliding patio doors are a common example. Another system uses an overhead track, with adjustable ball-bearing rollers mounted to the panel top; the panel is suspended from the track. Another arrangement, used with glass panels, consists of mating channels fitted with ball bearings in rows—no rollers or wheels.

Tambour doors

Until a few years ago, *tambour doors* (FIG. 8-7) were seldom seen on anything but antique rolltop desks. Now they are regaining some popularity and can be effectively employed in many kinds of cabinets. They have two important advantages. First, when opened, they disappear completely into the cabinet leaving the interior fully accessible. Second, they will operate around curves and corners, even the compound variety.

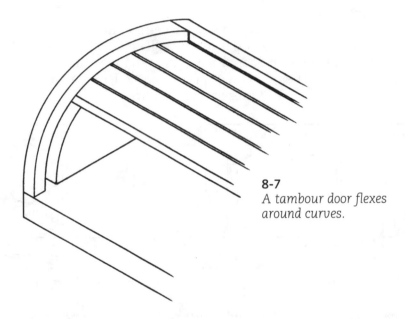

8-7
A tambour door flexes around curves.

Tambour doors can be purchased in several sizes. They can be shop-built; patience is required. The door consists of a series of wood slats—any dimensionally stable variety can be used— glued individually, if you use the old method, to a canvas backing. The modern alternative is to join the slats with special plastic hinges that slip into saw kerfs cut in the edges of each slat or (simpler) with those that simply slip onto the slats.

These doors can be operated either vertically or horizontally. In the vertical mode (slats horizontal), they run in fairly deep grooves cut into the cabinet body (FIG. 8-8).

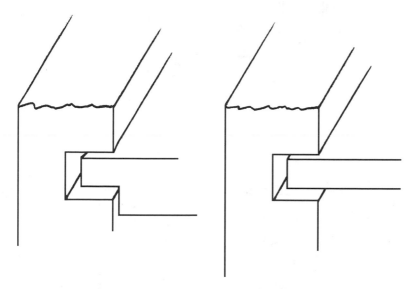

8-8 *The slats of a thick tambour door can be rabbeted to run in a narrow groove (left); thin slats are left at full thickness (right).*

Thin doors are usually set in full-width grooves. Thicker ones are usually made of slats with rabbeted ends to reduce the required width of the grooves. Either way, groove width is important to smooth operation. Too narrow, and the door will bind; too wide, and it will cock and jam. In the horizontal mode (slats vertical), the usual arrangement is to cut grooves in the slat ends to run on matching metal or plastic single rails set into the cabinet body, top and bottom (FIG. 8-9).

Semifixed doors

Semifixed doors are more commonly called *access panels* or *hatches.* They are not usually installed with hinges and often not with any type of hardware that is visible, and they are fixed so that they must be removed entirely to provide access. They should be used only where removal is an infrequent necessity, space is at a premium, and a facade uncluttered with hardware is a part of the design. This is also a good arrangement to avoid unauthorized access.

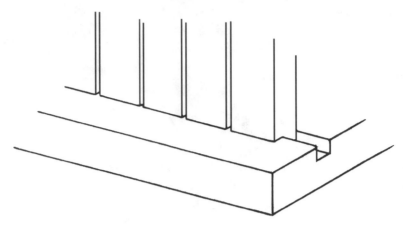

The purpose of such doors might be to hide equipment from view, such as an undercounter hot-water tank, or to make machinery, plumbing fittings, and similar items accessible for inspection, service, or repair. The door panels are typically made to match other doors, drawers, and blank panels in the cabinet assembly. The may be held in place by means of spring clips, cupboard door catches, concealed latches, a support groove-and-catch arrangement, or hidden wood screws.

Door construction

Doors can be classified according to their general construction method—some widely used and some less so, some practical in certain applications but not in others. Although some construction methods are easier than others, all can be handled in a well-equipped shop; the degree of expertise needed ranges from modest to considerable.

Often the best course is to purchase some kinds of doors, especially when the degree of construction difficulty is high or the shop equipment is only basic. And sometimes you can buy nice factory-made doors for less than you can build them. But if you opt for that course, be sure to select the appropriate sizes and styles and have them on hand before you design and build the cabinetry.

Solid-wood doors

The simplest doors to make are plain solid wood—the easiest merely a length cut from a board. There are obvious limitations here. The door opening can be no wider than the plank width, so only narrow doors can be made.

Also, solid sections are likely to warp and will also shrink a certain amount depending upon the species. This problem can be minimized by selecting good-quality, clear, defect-free, well-seasoned stock and allowing it to season further for two or three months on the jobsite.

Lay in more stock than is required and select the best portions to use. If a piece is flat and true when you begin to work it, it will probably remain so. A slight warp or cup can usually be smoothed out with a planer, and careful fitting can disguise minor out-of-true problems. Using either quartersawn or edge-grain stock will help because it is less susceptible than other cuts to cupping and shrinking.

When one board is not wide enough, two or more can be joined edge-to-edge to make glued-up solid panels. The result is a heavy, solid, sturdy door, especially if made with reinforced edge joints. However, this kind of door is also prone to warping, and the fit, even if carefully made, may shift around somewhat over time and under varying atmospheric conditions.

The larger the door, the greater the expansion and contraction problems. Solid wood is never still. You can minimize the problem by adding cross pieces to the top and bottom ends (FIG. 8-10). If used in a relatively stable environment and well made with top-grade materials and careful craftsmanship, glued-up doors can be effective, extremely serviceable, and handsome.

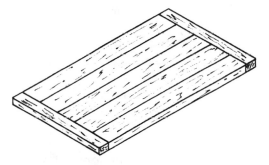

8-10
Transverse end pieces help to stabilize solid-wood panels made from strips.

Braced solid doors (FIG. 8-11) are also built up from a number of narrow strips. This popular method is often used in making natural-finish doors of knotty pine and other rustic designs. The usual procedure is to cut several pieces of kiln-dried and site-cured paneling plank to identical lengths, then set them together edge-to-edge (the tongue-and-groove pattern is preferred) and facedown.

8-11
Typical braced door made of solid oak strips.

With the pieces pulled tightly together, back braces are fastened crosswise, one near the top and another near the bottom. Depending upon door size, a third brace may be centered between the first two or run diagonally between them to form a Z. Usually a few nails secure the parts, then screws are set to secure everything tightly together. Glue is not generally used but can be, especially on the back braces.

When the assembly is complete, the final trimming and fitting can be done. The back braces must be positioned and fitted so that they do not interfere with the cabinet rails or shelf edges. This method produces doors of fine quality and appearance when properly made, but they have the same disadvantages as other solid doors.

Batten construction can be used for larger cabinet or cupboard doors but is usually confined to pieces that require large, heavy doors. *Continuous batten doors* are made by cutting several pieces to match the door height and another series to match the door width. The vertical pieces are pushed tightly together and clamped, then the horizontal ones are fastened to them with wood screws in a continuous cover. The edge joints can be squared but are much better as tongue-and-groove or rabbet patterns.

The resulting two-layer door is very strong and sturdy and less susceptible to warping, shrinkage, and expansion-contraction problems than other solid doors. But they are heavy, bulky, and expensive.

The tambour construction method mentioned earlier might also be considered a solid type of door. But because of the way it is made and the relatively small size of the slats, problems such as warping and shrinking are seldom bothersome if the door is well made.

Regardless of construction, solid doors can be made in flush, lipped, or overlay styles. They can be side-hinged, top-hinged, or bottom-hinged, and they can be installed as sliding or rolling doors. The tambour style has a unique installation arrangement.

Panel doors

Panel doors (FIG. 8-12) are easy to make and widely used in all sorts of cabinetwork. Plywood is probably the most popular material because the doors can be quickly cut to one-piece size and are readily fitted. No additional work is really required, although usually some sort of edge treatment and perhaps some decorative touches are desirable.

If the finish is to be opaque, softwood plywood in a cabinet grade is the common choice, mostly because the cost is relatively low, availability is good, and the material is fairly easy to work with. Softwood plywood will also take a fine semitransparent or transparent finish, but this does not usually present a suitable appearance in furniture-grade cabinetry.

In that capacity, a hardwood plywood is the better material and is used almost exclusively where the finish is to be natural or semitransparent. Much of the decorative effect is provided by the inherent characteristics of the surface veneer rather than an applied finish. Other embellishments such as carving, moldings, panel shaping, or routing of patterns may be added.

8-12
Flat-panel door (particleboard).

Either hardwood or softwood plywood has the advantage of affording discrete panels of large size while retaining very good dimensional stability. Plywoods change little in that respect and are not particularly susceptible to warp, especially in thicknesses over ½ inch. Plywood is also stiff; even a large door will not have a limber or flimsy feel. It is much stronger than necessary for this application and retains hardware well.

Hardboard is another stable material that is often used for panel doors. Thin stock, ⅛-inch and ¼-inch, is not suitable for hinged doors except in small sizes because it is not stiff enough and hardware attachment can cause problems. The greater thicknesses can be used with reasonable success, but weight is a problem; hardboard is quite heavy. Also, availability may be difficult. The most practical application is in relatively small sliding doors. The perforated variety can be used where ventilation is a desirable feature.

Particleboard, especially in the heavier densities, is fairly good for panel doors in cabinetry that will be painted or used for utilitarian purposes. This material is stable, not likely to warp, and solid and sturdy. It is also heavy, must be well supported, and is susceptible to water damage. But with proper edge treatment and finishing it can be used in practically all circumstances where its final appearance is acceptable. Although usually covered with an opaque finish, particle-board will accept stains, although patchily, and can be clear-finished. The minimum thickness for doors should be ⅝ inch, and ¾-inch affords the best results.

Laminate-panel doors can be installed as sliding or hinged doors and can use either plywood, hardboard, particleboard, or glued-up solid wood strips as a core. A decorative plastic laminate is applied to the core face, followed by an edge treatment.

The best-quality door uses a laminate applied to both core surfaces for a balanced construction. A standard grade of laminate is applied to the face, a backer grade to the reverse. With a ⅝-inch thick core, the resulting panel is about ¾ inch thick and uses standard hardware. The edge treatment varies depending upon how the door is to be fitted, but often a band of matching laminate is applied.

Glass-panel doors used to be installed mostly as sliders on ball-bearing roller guides, but some new designs of hardware now allow discrete all-glass panels to be hinged and latched. Several types of glass, both clear and tinted, can be used, some of which is available in standard sizes.

These panes can be bought off the shelf, and you can size the cabinet openings to suit. But you can also have plate or float glass cut to order at any glass shop and have the sharp edges and corners ground smooth as well. Some shops sell used glass salvaged from broken storefront windows at an advantageous price. Note that tempered glass and some other specialty types are available only in certain sizes and cannot be cut to fit.

Sheets of clear, semiopaque, opaque, and patterned plastic can be used in much the same way as glass, although special ball-bearing tracks are not needed. You can buy these materials in several stock sizes and cut them to size in your shop. You can bevel the edges and round the corners for easy sliding in plain tracks or grooves, or you can adapt glass-panel hinges and latches to the panels. Plastic doors can also be fitted with standard hardware used on wood doors; some modification is often required but is not problematic.

Louver doors

Louver doors (FIG. 8-13) are much easier to buy than to build. Numerous stock sizes are available. They can be shop-built, but the job entails fashioning joints for the rails and stiles and inletting the slats into the stiles. Making all those thin slats with the rounded edges is no easy task.

8-13
Louver door (clear Ponderosa pine).

There are some variations in louver-door design. The full-louver type features a rank of louvers from top to bottom. The two-section variety has a rail separating the louvers into two sets. A half-louver door has louvers in the upper portion and a solid panel below the rail; this arrangement is usually found only in relatively tall doors.

The louvers may be fixed in place or may be movable on pivot pins by means of a center adjusting bar that operates all the louvers simultaneously. That type is generally used for window coverings. There are three types of louvers. One is narrow, one wide, the third a chevron pattern. The louvers may be set in the open style, where there is space between the slats, or tight together. Chevron louvers are often stacked tightly, forming an essentially solid panel.

As the name implies, a *frame-and-panel door* (FIG. 8-14) is made by setting a panel into a frame. There are many ways of doing so, a wide range of materials that can be used, and innumerable decorative variations. The frames are most often made of solid wood; hardwood is preferred, but softwoods are frequently used. Plywood will do the job with some advantages but with more difficulty and usually less pleasing results.

8-14
Frame-and-panel door with raised panel (knotty eastern white pine).

The panels set into the frames can be made from glued-up solid wood, softwood or hardwood plywood, or hardboard. Glass is often used, and so is plastic. Metal screening, decorative metal grillwork, and caning are also fairly common and easy to work with.

The panels may be a combination of materials. Vertical-grade plastic laminate can be applied to a hardboard or plywood backer, for example, either as a uniform sheet or in a mosaic or other design. You can apply wallpaper, sheet vinyl, or fabrics to a backer in similar fashion. There are lots of possibilities for imaginative treatments.

Frame-and-panel doors lend themselves nicely to almost any kind of installation and have the advantages of excellent appearance, stability of shape and dimensions, and limitless flexibility of design and finish combinations. Although more difficult to make than some other types, they can be turned out in the home shop with excellent results. While they are mostly set up as hinged doors, they can be installed as drop, tip-up, and sliding doors. They also work well as semifixed doors, made to match the drawer fronts and hinged doors in the cabinet. They can easily be fitted in flush, lipped, or overlay modes.

Building doors

There are a number of major steps in constructing cabinet doors plus a few minor ones that depend on the complexity of the design. Some of the steps are interchangeable among types and designs, and some will vary slightly depending upon those factors, the material and hardware, the sophistication of shop equipment and tools, and the expertise and ideas of the user. The steps can be modified to suit your circumstances, and you should not hesitate to do so. Solid, panel, and frame-and-panel doors are covered, since these are the most popular types for home construction.

Step 1 The first step is to determine the dimensions of the door. They may be given on your plan; if so, check them to make sure there are no discrepancies. If you are planning to build the cabinet face frame to fit a preselected door size, calculate the overall finished width and height of the door openings.

If the cabinet carcase is already built, measure the width and the height of the door opening at several points. If each set of dimensions is the same, plus or minus about 1/64 inch for furniture-grade cabinetry (a bit less for utility cabinets), just make a note of the two greatest figures. If there is much variation, jot all the measurements down on a sketch so you can program the variations, or clearances for them, into the door construction. Take the two maximum dimensions of height and width as your starting point.

Step 2 Now you can lay out the door to rough size. Start with your maximum height and width dimensions of the door opening as the overall dimensions of the door. From these figures, subtract the proper clearances or add the desired overlap. For the moment, assume that the door opening is true and in square, with no serious dimensional variations. Note that in many designs the door bottoms extend below the cabinet bottom and align with each other or the face-frame lower edges—an open-ended arrangement. Thus, the clearance factor applies only at the top of the door in such instances, not the bottom.

For a flush door, a clearance of $\frac{1}{16}$ inch around the perimeter is satisfactory for most cabinets. A little more is all right for utility-grade cabinets, a bit less perhaps for fine casework. In most instances, the door will be $\frac{1}{8}$ inch narrower and $\frac{1}{8}$ inch shorter than its opening.

For lipped doors, first decide upon the width of the rabbet cut around the inside perimeter of the door, A $\frac{3}{8}$-inch or $\frac{1}{2}$-inch cut is usual. Again, a $\frac{1}{16}$-inch clearance is satisfactory, but this time it will be around the rabbet perimeter. This means that the remainder of the lip formed by the rabbet cut will extend beyond the door opening by the width of the rabbet minus the clearance of $\frac{1}{16}$ inch—$\frac{7}{16}$ inch for a $\frac{1}{2}$-inch rabbet, for example. In that case the door would measure $\frac{7}{8}$ inch taller and $\frac{7}{8}$ inch wider than the opening.

If the door is an overlay design, the overlap can be any dimension that seems appropriate or is allowable for the hinges you have selected. A lap of $\frac{1}{2}$ or $\frac{3}{4}$ inch is common and may be held on all edges or just the two sides. Or you can choose a figure that allows the overlaps to hide the face frame or just barely cover the opening and expose most of the face frame. Clearance does not come into play, so all you need to do is add the desired side, top, and bottom (if needed) overlaps to the door-opening dimensions to come up with the overall dimensions for the door.

Now you need to look ahead. Some dimension allowances may be necessary, depending on how the door will be made and finished. If only some light finish sanding will be needed, leave the dimensions as they are. If the door will be primed and painted or get two or three coats of varnish, reducing the height and width of flush doors and widening the rabbet of lipped doors by $\frac{1}{32}$ inch or so is in order.

If you plan to use an edge treatment such as a band or molding that will add to the overall dimensions, you will need to subtract that thickness from the panel dimensions. This is especially important with flush doors but of consequence on overlay doors only when the edging material is rather thick or two doors are to meet with a minimum vertical closure crack.

If the opening is not square or the dimensions do not run true, you will have to make whatever allowances are necessary for the door to fill or cover the opening, then do the required adjusting as the door is fitted. This could involve cutting shy on one edge and full on another, cutting edges on a slight taper, or leaving extra material that can be hand-shaped later.

There is no way to outline the procedures because problem possibilities are endless. Solutions vary, and often patience and ingenuity are needed. But if the situation is particularly confusing, one method that saves much time and effort is to make a pattern. Secure a sheet of fairly stiff cardboard or posterboard over the opening, flat and plane against the face frame or carcase edges. Trace the outline, cut along the line with scissors, and you have an accurate template to work from.

Step 3   With the dimension sorted out, you can begin to construct the door. This step is divided into three parts: solid, panel, and frame-and-panel doors.

Solid doors   For a one-piece door, select a suitable length of stock. For a glued-up door, glue and surface a sheet of material slightly larger than the overall door dimensions. Reinforcing the edge joints is a good idea. Then trim the workpiece to size. If any machining of the rough edges will be done, such as trimming with a plane or a disk sander, be sure to allow for that; otherwise the process could remove enough material to leave you with an undersized door.

If you are making a braced door, cut the pieces of board to length—door height for a vertical arrangement, door width for horizontal stacking. Lay the pieces facedown on a clean flat surface, align the edges, and draw them up snugly with bar clamps.

Cut the back braces to size. These are usually 3 to 4 inches wide at least and all of the same material. They must be sized to stay well clear of any interior components of the cabinet. Tack the upper and lower braces in place 2 or 3 inches from the door edges with a couple of nails, or clamp them in place, and fit the diagonal brace between them.

With all the parts correctly aligned and fixed, drill and countersink a series of holes and drive wood screws home. The result should look something like FIG. 8-15. For added strength and rigidity, you can add a second diagonal brace, fitting it across the first with a cross-lap joint.

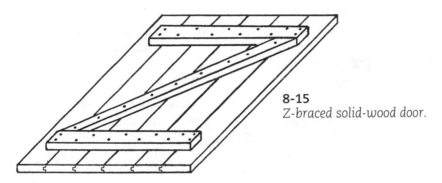

8-15
Z-braced solid-wood door.

At this point your job may be done, save for a bit of trimming or sanding, if the door is a utility or rustic type. Often, though, an edge treatment is desirable on the exposed end-grain areas. There are several ways to accomplish this (FIG. 8-16). Apply a thin edge-band strip of wood with glue. This is sometimes chancy because glue adherence to end grain is not especially good.

Another method is to attach a rectangular rail of the same material across the end grain. In fact, doors can be made this way, using top and bottom rails fastened to each piece in lieu of back braces. The rail can be flat, or T-shaped and set into a dado.

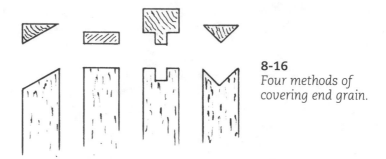

8-16
Four methods of covering end grain.

Another possibility is to make a 45-degree miter cut across the end grain with the cut angle facing inward. Then fit a triangular strip across the face of the cut, squaring off the edge again with face-grain material that will not show from the outside.

A more difficult arrangement that leaves the door grain pattern undisturbed on both faces is to cut or rout a deep V across the end grain. Fit a triangular strip into the V. Except for two bits of end grain, the piece is invisible.

Panel doors   To cut a panel door from sheet material like plywood, all you need do is transfer the proper measurements (or trace your pattern) to the stock and make the required cuts. If your cutting equipment or method is likely to leave some rough edges or wander a bit when you cut from a large sheet, make oversize rough cuts to get a manageable workpiece that can be accurately and smoothly trimmed to the necessary size.

Be sure to place the "good" side of the workpiece up or down in relation to the cutting action of the saw to prevent visible splintering, and use a fine-toothed blade for the smoothest cut.

Laminate-covered panel doors are made in the same way, except that there are two or maybe three pieces to cut. Start by making the core; plywood or particleboard is the usual choice. Then cut a piece of vertical-grade laminate just slightly larger all around than the core piece. This will allow for clean edge trimming later. If the core will be edged, be sure to allow for that and determine whether the edging will be best applied before or after the facing. Often a third piece is used as well, a sheet of backer laminate applied to the inner door face. Cut this piece the same size as the outer facing. Do not bond the pieces together until you have determined that the door will fit properly; that subject will be covered later.

When you fabricate doors from sheet plastic, make the initial cuts as accurately and smoothly as you can and as close to the finished dimensions as possible. This will save time and effort during the fitting process and reduce the chances of damage from excess handling. But take great care not to remove too much material or cut shy because there is no way to compensate with these materials. Always work plastics with the protective paper covering in place. If the covering is missing take extra care because scratches appear easily.

Most relatively small frame-and-panel doors consist of a center panel surrounded by a frame made of rails at top and bottom and and a stile on each side. Larger doors may include a middle rail or two separating panels. If there are several panels, they may be separated by one or more mullions, vertical members running from rail to rail (FIG. 8-17).

Frame-and-panel doors

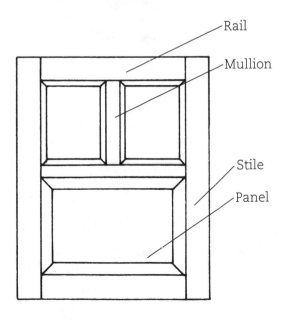

Rail

Mullion

Stile

Panel

8-17
Parts of frame-and-panel door.

The outer edge of the frame may be plain and square or may be shaped in some decorative fashion. The inside edge of the frame is shaped in one of several profiles in order to hold the panel in place. There are several ways to accomplish this and at the same time make sturdy corner joints.

The panel also has certain forms (FIG. 8-18). If it is flat on both sides, it may be called a *plain* or *plane panel*, sometimes a *straight panel*. An *overlay panel* consists of a plain panel with a smaller, decoratively shaped panel centered and glued to it, creating a *raised-panel* effect.

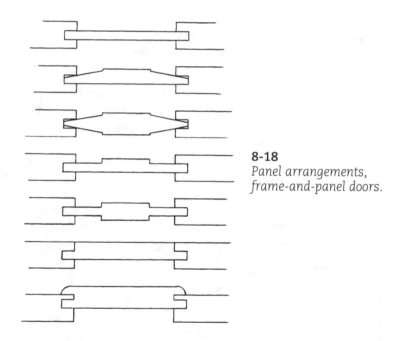

8-18
Panel arrangements, frame-and-panel doors.

A true raised panel, the class act of frame-and-panel doors, is made by shaping the perimeter of a full solid-wood panel. A wide, shallow bevel is often used, and if the bevel is on only one face of the panel, it is called *beveled one side*, if on both faces, *beveled two sides*. If the shaping is a wide but shallow rabbet cut, the panel may be called *shoulder—raised one side*, or *shoulder—raised two sides*.

A *flush panel* is set with the panel face flush with either the back or the front face of the frame, while an *elevated panel* extends beyond the frame face. In most cases, however, the panel is centered within the frame.

The first step in making a frame-and-panel door is to select the corner joint. It must be strong because even normal service for a door involves stresses and strains. The usual practice is to place the rails between the stiles, which always leaves exposed end grain on the stiles. The simplest construction dictates squared inner edges of the frame, with a groove to retain the panel or a rabbet into which a panel can be set after the frame is assembled, to be restrained by strips of narrow molding.

In that case, the stub tenon joint is about the easiest to make, with the stub slipping into the panel groove (FIG. 8-19). A haunched mortise-and-tenon is a bit harder but stronger, and the open mortise-and-tenon is another good choice; both can be pinned with dowel pegs set through the joint front to back and trimmed off Shaker-fashion.

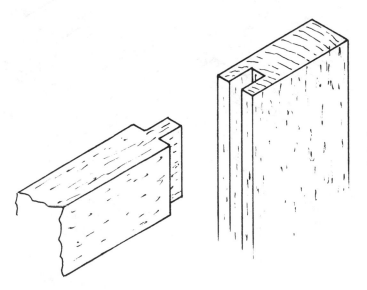

8-19
Stub tenon makes a good corner joint for doorframes.

Another option, depending on whether the joint is large enough, is to make a stub tenon reinforced with dowel pins or plates. You could also build the door just as you would a picture frame, with mitered corners reinforced with splines or plates. With this arrangement, all end grain is concealed, and the result is reasonably sturdy. Another possibility is the end-lap joint, but it should be pegged through, front to back, for added strength.

If you prefer the more fashionable shaped inner frame edges, a different plan is required. This involves a kind of construction called *cope and stick*, using a stuck joint (FIG. 8-20). The stick cut, which can be in any of several profiles, is made along the inside edges of the stiles and rails, full-length; it includes the groove needed for the panel. The mating cope cut is typically made on the ends of the rails only, although no rule says that it cannot be made on the ends of the stiles only. That arrangement would place the stiles between the rails.

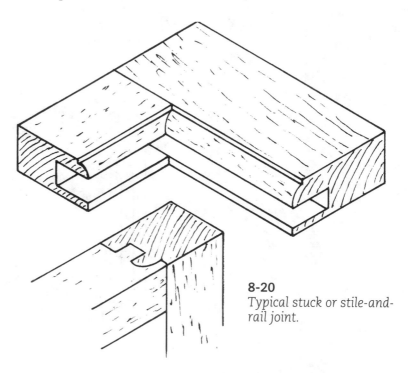

8-20
Typical stuck or stile-and-rail joint.

Fashioning a stuck joint used to require a heavy-duty shaper, a lot of time and patience, and considerable expertise to make everything come out right. Nowadays you can do this job without much trouble in your shop with a heavy-duty router, a router table, and a set of matched cope-and-stick or stile and rail cutters (FIG. 8-21). Because the cutters are matched, the coped ends slip right into the sticking to make a perfect stuck joint at each frame corner. The arrangement is sturdy enough for most ordinary applications.

With the joining method selected, cut the rails and stiles to proper width and length. Take care of whatever dressing is needed to clean the pieces up so that they are square, flat, and smooth on all surfaces.

If the panel will be set in grooves or rabbets in a square-edged frame (FIG. 8-22), take care of that chore next. A panel groove is typically ⁵⁄₁₆ or ⅜ inch deep and just a bit wider than the panel thickness at its edges. The same is satisfactory for a rabbet width, which is usually cut to about half the thickness of the stock—⅜ inch for standard ¾-inch frames. With that done, fashion your chosen corner joints, assemble them dry, and check for correct fit.

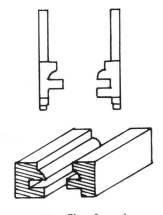

8-21 *Profile of stuck-joint cutter set.*

8-22
Grooved rails (above) or rabbeted rails (below) work well in frame-and-panel doors.

For the cope-and-stick arrangement, start with the sticking. Set up the router with a 4-inch or higher fence with as small an opening at the cutter head as possible for maximum backup of the workpiece. This reduces chipping and increases safety. The cutters are designed for ¾-inch stock thickness; adjust the bit height so that it centers on the workpiece edge.

Using a piece of same-size scrap, set up at least two, preferably three or four, featherboards or other restraints to keep the workpieces tight against the fence and tabletop as you make the cuts. Safety is the main consideration, but for good cuts it is essential to keep the pieces from chattering. Do a trial run with a scrap piece, make any necessary adjustments, then run the stickings on both stiles and rails.

To complete the stuck joint, you now have to make the cope cuts. Change your router setup to the cope bit. If your router table accomodates a miter gauge (like a table saw) you are all set. Run a piece of scrap through, positioned with the grain, to make sure the bit height is correct and the resulting cope exactly fits the sticking you have just completed. Fit the scrap piece into the rail sticking with the ends flush and cope the ends of both. The scrap will back the rail and prevent splintering as it clears the cutter.

If your router table does not accept a miter gauge, you will need a push block. As previously outlined, cut a cope profile into the edge of a piece of scrap a couple of inches wide and about a foot long for a backer that you can easily hold on to. Square up another piece of flat scrap 5 or 6 inches wide and long enough to extend from the cutter bit off the end of the router table a few inches where you can get a grip on it. Line all the pieces up (FIG. 8-23) and push them along slowly and evenly until the rail is past the cutter.

When all the pieces are cut, check them for fit and alignment. Save all the scrap pieces; they will allow you to set the cutter bit heights for the next job easily, and can also be reused as backings.

Making the panel is the next step. Irrespective of style or material, the common procedure is to fit the panel a bit loosely in its groove to allow for expansion and contraction. Dimensions ¹⁄₁₆ inch less in width and height than those of the perimeter of the groove bottom will do the job. The panel is not secured tightly with glue or fasteners but restrained only by the groove sides or a molding strip for a rabbeted frame.

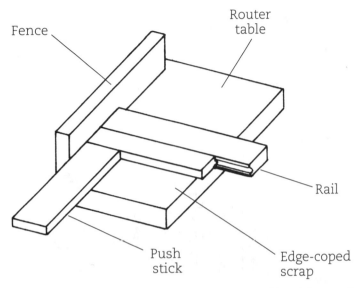

8-23 *This system of coping rail ends on a router table with a push stick and rail backer is safe and effective.*

To make a plain panel, just cut sheet stock to the proper size, making sure that it is true and square, or make a glued-up panel and trim and surface it. Smooth any rough edges.

To make an overlay panel, follow the same procedure to make the door panel. You can cut the overlay panel at the same time or after the door has been completed. This panel can be of the same shape as the door panel or done in some decorative layout.

The parts for a laminate-covered panel should be cut and assembled now, using the standard application procedures. If the panel is to be covered with caning, wall covering, fabric, or some other material, be sure to make dimensional allowances in the frame groove width or depth or in the panel itself.

It is often best to fit and apply such materials when the panel is made rather than after the door is assembled, but a lot depends on the frame's finish. You may find it best to set the covered panel into a rabbet rather than a groove and secure it after the frame has been completed and finished.

There are several ways to make a raised panel. One is to set up a table saw to cut bevels on a panel run vertically past the blade (FIG. 8-24), using a very slight tilt for a shallow bevel or about 16 degrees for a steep, short one. Bevels can also be cut on a radial arm saw by laying the panel faceup on the table and swinging the saw head down almost parallel with the panel face.

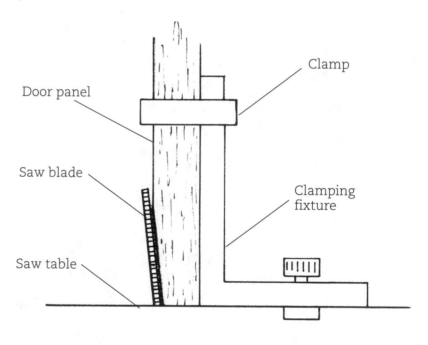

8-24 *Making raised panels with a table saw.*

In either case, best results are obtained by using a fine-toothed blade and cutting the end grain first, then the face grain. Smoothing the saw cuts can be done with a sander or a power plane. Another method is to make flat-bottomed shoulders all around the panel by making repeated passes over a dado head with the panel laid flat on the saw table. An alternative is to rout wide rabbets. Yet another is to clamp the panel down flat and make repeated passes with a power plane or a hand rabbet plane.

A more satisfactory method than any of those is one newly available to home workers. Set up the router table with an appropriate cutter, fixtures, and hold-downs. This arrangement will allow you to select any of several cutter patterns that will produce handsome shaped panels (FIG. 8-25). An even better arrangement is the professional method employing a large spindle shaper.

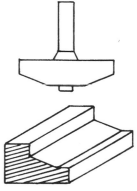

8-25 *Profile of raised panel cutter.*

Now make a dry run for the final assembly. Snug all of the pieces together, using clamps where necessary. Check all the joints for proper fit, make sure the panel seats correctly, and make sure that the frame is in square. Disassemble to make necessary adjustments.

If the door is to be lipped, you can do this now to the individual pieces or earlier when the groove or rabbet was cut, or you can wait until the assembly is complete. The same is true if the frame edges are to be beveled or rounded or decorative cutting is to be done to the frame or the panel. Choose whatever course is easiest for you. Once everything is done, apply glue to the joints, assemble the parts again, and clamp firmly for the required time. Take care not to clamp too hard; this can cause a starved or skewed joint.

Meeting doors are two adjacent doors, one hinged on the left, the other on the right, so that when they close, they meet in the middle. When a single flush door closes, the ⅟₁₆-inch crack that is visible is not usually considered objectionable. But when two door edges meet, whether flush or overlay, the appearance of that slight crack between the two may be undesirable. Also, sometimes the cabinet design calls for one door, usually the left-hand one, to be held closed by the right-hand door when it latches.

Meeting doors

Both situations are taken care of by attaching an astragal molding to the inner meeting edge of the door that will restrain the other, or a strip of molding to the face so that it overlaps the meeting edge. If the visible crack is not objectionable, a double rabbet will do the job nicely and can be fashioned to fit closely. If the idea is simply to change the appearance of the crack, the door edges can be beveled; this is especially effective if the door panels are vertically grooved for decorative effect (see FIG. 8-26).

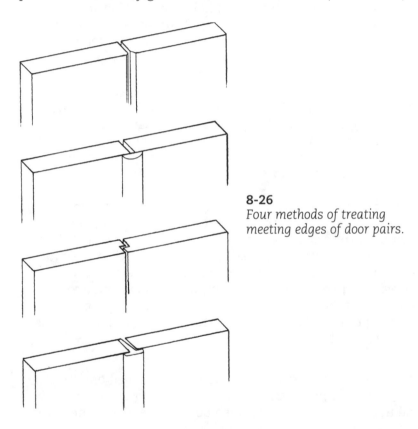

8-26
Four methods of treating meeting edges of door pairs.

Fitting doors When the door has been assembled (before the finishing process), the next step is fitting the door into the cabinet. This applies to all doors, commercially made or home built, regardless of type. Of course, if you have purchased prefinished doors, you must adjust the cabinet opening.

If the door is flush-fit, set it into place in the cabinet opening. If the fit is faulty or the door will not slip easily into place, trim as necessary but be careful not to remove too much material. Match any unevenness in the face frame or cabinet edges with the door frame, or taper the edges to match out-of-squareness.

Judicious use of planes, files, sander, and similar finishing equipment will do the job. You can insert pieces of thin cardboard or folded paper to wedge the door in place evenly. Try for a uniform clearance of about $\frac{1}{16}$ inch or a bit less, depending upon the final finish, at all meeting edges of door and cabinet. You can get away with a bit less on the hinge side.

If the door is the lipped type, the job is a little harder because you can't see what you are doing. First make sure that the rabbet is cut deep enough to allow the interior face of the door to sit freely in the opening, no binding anywhere. Then see if the lines of the door edges are parallel with the lines of the cabinet or face frame that are visible. If the lines are not parallel and the door sits crookedly you may have to make the rabbet wider. This will result in greater clearance so that the door edges can be shifted parallel with the cabinet lines.

With the overlay door, the main consideration is that the lines of the door match the lines of the cabinet and that where there are two or more doors, they all align correctly with one another and maintain their proper relationship with the visible parts of the cabinet body. All edges should at least appear to be plumb and level, although sometimes a little compromise is necessary.

Another step sometimes taken where a very close fit is desired between the door edge and the meeting rail of the cabinet is to bevel the inside corner slightly. An alternative is to cut the entire door edge on a slight angle—2 or 3 degrees is enough—so that the door will swing in without binding. The meeting crack can be made almost invisible.

This completes the gross fitting process. Now is the time to take care of any additional treatments you might have in mind for the door. One touch used on lipped or overlay doors is to fashion a curved edge around the outer door surface. This can be done with a router, a shaper, or a molding head in a table saw.

A partial-depth arc is common; the curve covers only a portion of the edge, but you can as easily shape the entire thickness of the material. You need not be confined to a curved shape because cutting a bevel, chamfer, rabbet, ogee, bead, or some other profile is just as easy (FIG. 8-27).

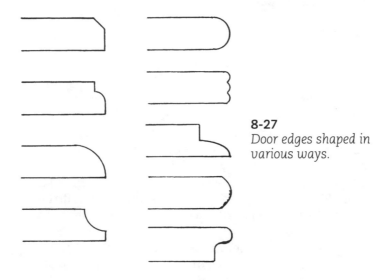

8-27
Door edges shaped in various ways.

Nor need these decorative cuts be confined to the edges of the door. You can lay out a pattern on the door face and make shallow cuts with a router fitted with a rabbeting, veining, or V-groove bit. This is not a difficult chore, although it does require a bit of practice and a steady hand.

Another possibility for trimming a door is to apply pieces of molding directly to the finished face (FIG. 8-28). Select or make a flat-bottomed type such as half-round, nose-and-cove, stop, or screen molding. Cut mitered joints at the corners and glue the strips to the door.

You can purchase specialty moldings made in inside and outside curves, as well as machine-carved wood blocks for similar application. The moldings can be permanently affixed now if you wish, but often a better procedure is to do all the

216   Custom Cabinets

necessary cutting and fitting now and set the pieces aside for later application. After the door has been sanded and prepared for its finish coatings, and sometimes even after all the finishing is done, the molding can be assembled, making the process a bit easier.

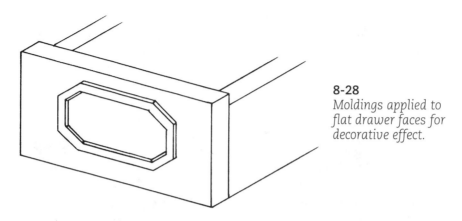

8-28
Moldings applied to flat drawer faces for decorative effect.

The last steps in making a cabinet door involve mounting the hardware, doing the final fitting and trimming, and installing the door. How well and how carefully this is done is a major factor in how well the door will function over time. The exact details of the process vary with the kind of door and the type of hardware.

First, the hinges. For a door less than 3 feet high and 2 feet wide in ¾-inch thickness and of standard materials and construction, a single pair of hinges should be sufficient. For larger or exceptionally heavy doors, add a third hinge (*called a pair-and-a-half*). A 1½- or 2-inch size is adequate in most instances, but for large or heavy doors, opt for a 2½-inch or even 3-inch set.

The exact procedure for installing the hinges varies. If there are instructions on the package, follow them exactly. Otherwise, follow these general steps. Measure a short distance up from the door bottom and down from the top on the hinge side. The exact dimension is up to you—2 to 3 inches is common—and does not matter so long as the measurements stay the same for all the doors in matching cabinet sections and the spacings are in proportion to the door height.

Hanging doors

Mark the door edge and set the hinges in place. Line them up so that they are squared to the door in proper relationship with the door edge and the pins and barrels line up exactly with one another. If there is any misalignment, the door is apt to bind or catch, and there will be excessive wear on the hinges.

Hold each hinge firmly in place. If no mortise is needed, mark the center of one screw hole; a centering punch is good for this chore. If a mortise is required, trace the position of the hinge leaf, measure the leaf thickness, and make the mortise cut with a router or chisel. Set the hinge back in place—the leaf surface should be flush with the door edge—and mark the hole position.

Drill a pilot hole for one screw at each hinge. The hole should be sized to the screw and must be straight and in the dead center of the hole in the leaf. Otherwise the screw could drive at an angle or go off-center, which will draw the hinge out of line when the screw is tightened.

Attach the hinges to the door with one screw per leaf. Drive the screws carefully, making sure that they stay straight and centered. If the wood is grainy, the screw may try to follow the softer fibers and cant off. If this happens, remove the screw and reset it. If need be, you can insert a sliver of wood into the hole to help force the screw into the correct position.

Set the door in position in the cabinet and check the clearances, making sure that the door is accurately placed. Mark the center of one screw hole in each cabinet-to-frame leaf and remove the door. Drill a single pilot hole for each hinge, reset the door, and drive one screw per leaf (FIG. 8-29).

Swing the door slowly through its entire opening arc and check for binding or wracking and proper fit all around the edges. If all is well, drill the remaining pilot holes and drive the rest of the screws.

If the fit is not just right, now is the time to fix it because the problems are likely to get worse rather than better with time. If the door does not have enough clearance or sticks, mark the bothersome areas, remove the door if necessary, and shave or sand small amounts of material off. Remove only small amounts and check often so that there is little chance of ruining the door by removing too much.

8-29 *Driving the first screw when hanging a cabinet door.*

If alignment is the problem, you might have to place a slip of paper or thin cardboard under one hinge leaf or mortise one leaf just a fraction deeper to reposition the door. Surface-mounted hinges can be treated the same way, shimming or mortising as needed.

This will probably throw the clearances off, necessitating some further work in that department. If the hinges are cockeyed, you will have to adjust their position accordingly, perhaps shifting the mounting screws by stuffing splinters into the holes to move their centers.

As for the hinges themselves, the surface-mounted variety is easiest and quickest to install. For that reason, mortised butt and European hinges are installed less frequently on cabinet doors than pivot or decorative surface-mounted hinges.

When you install butt hinges, you can make the mortise cut, also called the *gain*, in either of two ways (FIG. 8-30). Make one cut equal in depth to the thickness of one hinge leaf in the cabinet face-frame edge and another in the door edge. Or make a double-depth gain cut in the door edge alone. The fit will be the same, but the former procedure is usually favored.

Double gain   Single gain

8-30

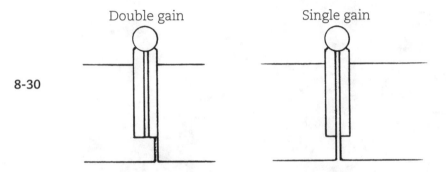

Occasionally butt hinges are mounted with only one leaf mortised, the other surface mounted. The leaf thickness determines the hinge-side door clearance.

Once the door is fitted and operating smoothly, you can install the remaining hardware. Set the knobs or pulls in place and secure them, and mount and adjust the catches inside the cabinet. Or install latch asssemblies according to the manufacturer's directions.

Fitting a sliding door is a bit simpler than a swinging door. If you are using manufactured tracks, set them in place and anchor them to the cabinet. The deeper track goes at the top, the shallower one at the bottom, The two must be exactly aligned top-to-bottom and side-to-side. The distance between the two should also be the same at all points, give or take a small fraction. If there is any appreciable variance, the doors will not slide properly.

Set the panels in place and check the fit. They should slide freely and pass with no problem; the outer edges should line up with the cabinet sides without gapping. Gaps mean the doors or the cabinet opening, or all of them, are out of square. If the fit is off, make any necessary corrections.

Round and smooth the bottom running edges of the doors, round the bottom corners so they will not catch, and smooth the upper edges. A bit of paraffin or beeswax usually makes the sliding a bit smoother but should be administered after all the finishing has been completed. Finally, mount pulls or knobs and catches or locks.

Glass doors are handled a little differently (and carefully). The clearances are typically looser, and the doors never fit tightly. The hinged type may be flush or overlay, depending upon the hardware used, and bypass sliding doors are installed on ball-bearing tracks that typically position the glass a little bit to the inside of the cabinet outer edges.

If the cabinet opening is exactly in square, as it should be, the glass can be cut exactly square to the same dimensions as the opening less the clearance allowance and an edge-grinding allowance for flush doors, oversize for overlay doors. Certain dimensional allowances might have to be made for the mounting hardware too. The best bet is to work closely with your glass supplier. If possible, have them make the measurements and determine the required panel size. Then if there is an error, it's on them.

The cabinet door is now complete except for the final finishing process. If necessary, mark the door in some unobtrusive but positive way so that you can tell after finishing which opening it fits. Remove the door and strip off all the hardware. Set the door aside to be finished along with the rest of the cabinetry.

CHAPTER 9

Drawers

IN BASIC FORM, a drawer is nothing but an open-topped box made to slide in and out of an enclosed cabinet. But drawers are seldom simple. There are many levels of quality, from quick and cheap through heavy-duty utility to custom showcase furniture, and there are many ways to construct drawers. In addition, drawers or drawerlike constructions are often fitted or intended for purposes other than storage.

Drawers lead the hardest life of any part of a cabinet assembly, regardless of the service conditions imposed. They are forever being yanked and pulled on, leaned against, jerked sideways, jiggled about, and slammed shut. They are routinely overloaded, sometimes fall out of their tracks, and are subject to varying degrees of wear and tear. Because of the way their several parts are arranged, they are susceptible to expansion and contraction, wracking, warping, and various kinds of mechanical damage. Yet a drawer—any drawer—is expected to slide in and out freely, carry a heavy load, close tightly and stay that way, and otherwise perform faultlessly forever.

The interesting thing is that drawers will do just that. All you have to do is plan their construction well for their intended purposes, build them well and a bit more ruggedly than seems required, and install them properly.

Drawer construction

There are several different kinds of drawers, depending upon the way the drawer front, or face, fits in the cabinet (FIG. 9-1). A *flush* drawer front fits flush with the face frame. A flush drawer may also be used in a frameless cabinet, fitted flush with the cabinet edges, but usually the construction is slightly different. Like its door counterpart, the flush drawer is the most difficult to fit accurately.

A *lipped* drawer is made so that the drawer face sets partly within the opening and the lip covers a portion of the face frame surrounding the opening. The lip is formed by making a rabbet cut around the inner perimeter of the drawer face,

222   *Custom Cabinets*

hiding the clearance crack around the edge. This kind of drawer does not lend itself well to installation in frameless cabinetry, although it can be done.

Flush   Lipped

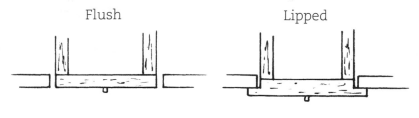

Reveal overlay   Flush overlay

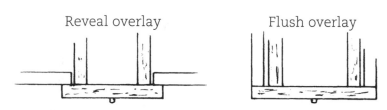

The front of a *reveal overlay* drawer lies entirely outside the cabinet face frame. The extent of the overlay may be equal around the opening but often is greater at the sides than at top or bottom. Part of the face frame (the exact amount varies with design) is exposed. This type of drawer can also be used with frameless cabinetry.

The *flush overlay* drawer does away with the need for a face frame and is made to conceal the case edges. This design is often used where there are several drawers stacked or ranged alongside one another to present a smooth, unbroken cabinet-section face.

Another kind of drawer arrangement is sometimes used as a decorative device—the *inset* drawer. The sides of the drawer extend outward slightly beyond the face, usually to an extent that makes the face of the pull or knob about even with the ends of the drawer sides. Those in turn typically lie flush with the face-frame surface. The rail below the drawer must be double thick or have a finished filler plate attached to it to fill the gap that results from the setback of the drawer front.

Most drawers consist of five parts: the *front* or *face*, right and left *sides*, *back*, and *bottom*. Additional parts may include a *subface*, *dividers*, *trays* with or without *slide rails*, and various kinds of *guides* or *runners* on which the drawer slides in and out. In some constructions, the latter may be a part of the cabinet casework or part of both cabinet and drawer.

The drawer front, or face, is usually made of plywood or solid wood, a softwood or a hardwood. The preferred stock thickness is ¾ inch, but this can be varied. Thinner stock, however, is practical only in small drawers. Side pieces are typically made from ½-inch-thick stock, which reduces cost but provides adequate strength and increases drawer volume and workability.

A clear hardwood is the choice for top-quality construction, but plywood is commonly used. You can choose thicker stock in solid wood or plywood, especially for heavy-duty construction such as shop or hardware storage drawers. For small drawers that will carry little weight, ⅜-inch plywood or hardwood is adequate and allows a bit of extra usable room in the drawer.

The back is usually cut from the same material as the sides. The most commonly used materials for drawer bottoms is ¼-inch plywood or hardboard, the former preferred. Both are tough and solid with little propensity for expanding or contracting. For smaller drawers, a thinner stock can be used, and for large utility drawers that might be heavily loaded, select an appropriately thick plywood.

Solid wood is a good choice for drawer faces, sides, and backs because you can work it easily and usually it requires no further edge treatment, as plywood does. White pine is an old favorite, and edge-grain fir or another softwood can be used. In the hardwoods, maple is a leading choice, especially for sides and backs. Cherry, oak, and mahogany or lauan are popular, and walnut, butternut, pecan, and several other species see frequent use.

The chief disadvantage in using solid-wood stock, especially a softwood, is the possibility of warping—to a lesser degree, shrinkage, expansion, and contraction. Selection of prime stock can mitigate all of these troubles. Another difficulty is that if the drawers are large, the stock might have to be glued up from several smaller pieces and then surfaced, a considerable amount of extra work.

Drawer size is not a problem when you use plywood because the parts for any practical drawer size can be cut from plywood sheets. Warping, shrinking, and expansion-contraction are not usually problems of consequence with plywood because it is a relatively stable material. On the other hand it is more difficult than solid wood to work with, the joinery is trickier, and exposed edges usually require some sort of treatment in the interest of appearance. Other concessions may have to be made when the material, at least the face, must match other visible parts of the cabinetry.

Particleboard is occasionally selected for drawer parts, but it is not a good choice. Although it is useful in some phases of moderate-quality cabinetry, it is heavy, harder to work, and less serviceable and dependable than solid wood or plywood.

The strength, rigidity, serviceability, and overall quality of a drawer, not to mention its appearance, depends mostly upon how well it is put together. A drawer face takes a lot of punishment during its lifetime as the drawer is jerked open and slammed shut, especially if it is large and heavy. The back is subject to many stresses as it restrains the drawer contents. The sides do too, and have to hold the drawer together and perhaps support the slide or guide system. The bottom obviously takes a lot of punishment. The better the material quality, joinery, and overall craftsmanship, the more durable and trouble-free the drawer is likely to be.

The easiest way to build a drawer is to assemble a box from four pieces of stock butted together at the corners. Drive a few nails through the butt joints and nail a piece of hardboard to the bottom edges. Cheap and quick—also pretty ineffective: It will come apart faster than you can build it. Even substituting screws and glue for the nails won't help much. There are better designs.

There are several ways to join the front to the sides. A locking joint works best because it affords the front little opportunity to separate from the sides under the strain of repeated opening and closing. Dado and rabbet joints can be used, especially in the smaller drawer sizes intended for no more than moderately heavy duty.

The easiest procedure is to cut a rabbet down the inside edge of each side of the drawer front. The cut depth is usually about half the thickness of the stock, the width of the cut equal to the thickness of the side pieces. Called a *simple rabbet* or *flush rabbet joint* (FIG. 9-2), it works nicely for flush-type drawers.

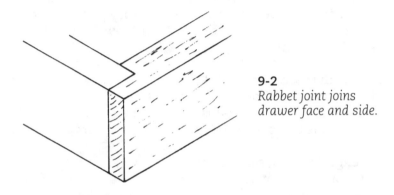

9-2
Rabbet joint joins drawer face and side.

You can get better results, though, from a *beveled rabbet joint* (FIG. 9-3). The width of the rabbet cut is about 1/16 inch wider than the thickness of the sides. The exposed edge of the rabbet cut on the front is tapered inward slightly, which allows good clearance for the side pieces and shows only a small clearance crack between the front and the cabinet face frame. If the drawer is to be lipped, the width of the rabbet cut should equal the thickness of the side piece plus the desired amount of lip, and the depth of the rabbet cut should equal the thickness of the drawer front minus the thickness of the lip.

The treatment is a little different for overlay drawers. The easiest joint to use is a *dado overlap* (FIG. 9-4). Cut a dado down the inside surface of the front a short distance from each end. The distance from the front ends inward to the dadoes should equal the desired overlap plus about 1/16 inch for clearance. The dado width should be equal (plus a tiny bit) to the thickness of the side pieces, and the depth is typically about half the thickness of the front piece. Note, however, that this joint does not lock and is weak in a direct pull; it depends largely on screws and glue for its strength.

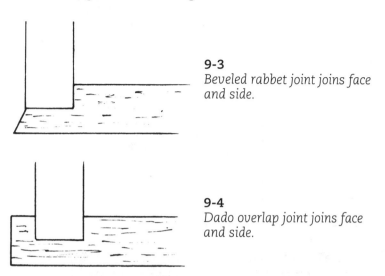

9-3
Beveled rabbet joint joins face and side.

9-4
Dado overlap joint joins face and side.

For a stronger joint, use a *dovetail dado*, which locks the two pieces solidly together; a *half dovetail* is also a good choice (FIG. 9-5). There are several other strong locking joints that can be used on either flush or lipped drawers. The *double dado* is effective and simple to cut, and lends itself equally well to either type of drawer.

Full dovetail   Half dovetail

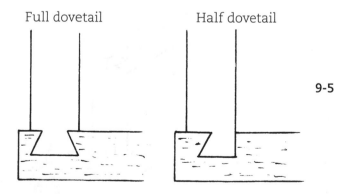

9-5

The *lock joint* (FIG. 9-6) is harder to cut but is also stronger, and the *milled shaper joint* is also effective, providing matching cutters are employed so that the two profiles are exact mates. Another joint widely used in top-quality drawer construction is the *multiple dovetail*, in *half-blind* or *through* form. For decorative effect, the dovetails can be left exposed on the drawer faces, the woods of the sides and the face of contrasting color.

Double dado   Lock

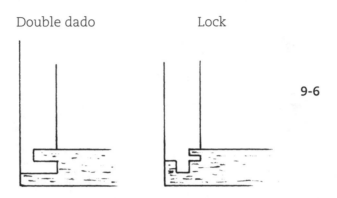

9-6

In many cases you can construct a drawer more easily, although with somewhat greater cost and labor, by using a *subface*. Join the subface to the drawer sides as usual, then apply a face later with glue and screws driven from the inside through the subface (FIG. 9-7).

9-7
Drawer box can be made with a subface, the finish face added in any style.

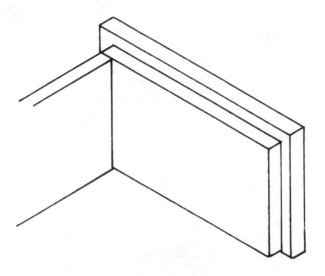

This makes it easy to make a set of drawer boxes that are to be painted, for example, and after finishing and fitting them apply separately made faces with a natural finish that matches the remainder of the cabinet exterior. This is most commonly done with overlay or lipped drawers but will work with flush drawers as well.

Fitting the drawer back to the sides can also be done in a number of ways (FIG. 9-8). A simple *butt joint* is often used here, especially in small and lightweight drawers; if secured with screws and glue, it is an amply strong construction. An ordinary *dado joint* is perhaps the most common arrangement; considering the strength gained for the simplicity of the joint, it is very effective.

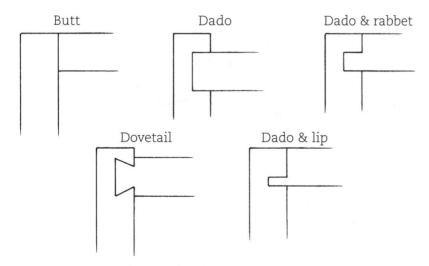

9-8
Drawer sides joined to backs with these joints.

A slight variation, somewhat stronger, is a *dado-and-rabbet (shouldered dado)* joint. This involves more operations—a dado on each side and matching rabbet cuts on the back—but the extra effort is worthwhile.

For a locking joint, the *full dovetail dado*, also called a *French dado*, is an excellent choice. This can also be done in half-dado fashion. A joint frequently found in high-grade construction is the *multiple dovetail*, half-blind or through. And if a complex joint is the challenge, this is a logical spot for a *box joint*. Other complex joints could be used, but there isn't much point.

Nailing the drawer bottom to the lower edges of the box is not a good idea; it will work loose in short order. Screws will work better, but not much. In most cases, the bottom is set in a groove cut close to the bottom edges of the inside surfaces of the front and side pieces. This gives the bottom ample support around three edges.

Sometimes the bottom is also fitted into a fourth groove in the back piece, but this is usually an unnecessary complication, since assembling the drawer is a tricky bit of business. Typically, the bottom of the drawer back rests upon the bottom piece, and two or three fasteners are driven through the bottom into the back (FIG. 9-9).

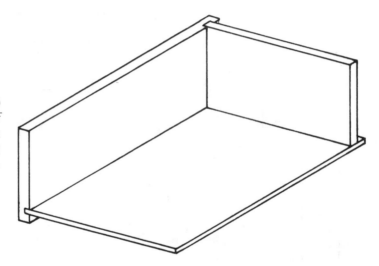

9-9
Typical method of installing drawer bottom in grooves, back resting on bottom.

For added support, a rail can be run underneath the bottom at its midpoint, front to back and slotted into the drawer front. This arrangement can also constitute part of the guide system.

Setting the bottom in grooves is usually done with plywood or hardboard ⅛ or more often ¼ inch thick in medium-duty or lighter drawers. But in heavy-duty or utility drawers that require more strength, the bottom stock is more apt to be ⅜ or even ½ inch thick. Here, a combination of dado and butt joints can be used along with the bottom groove system. Picking the right combination is important; if you don't, you cannot assemble the drawer. An alternative method is to support the bottom on narrow cleats screwed and glued to the front, back, and sides (FIG. 9-10).

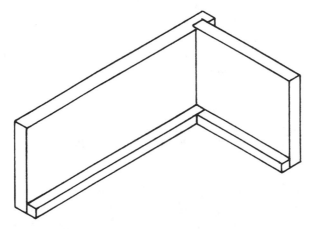

9-10
*Bottoms of heavy-duty utility
drawers supported
by cleats.*

The fact that a joined drawer is generally considered a mark of quality construction does not mean that you can't build one any other way. If you do not have the necessary equipment or skills (or inclination) for that kind of joinery, there isn't much choice.

One way around the problem, especially useful for heavy-duty utility and storage drawers that assemble quickly and easily, is to make a *double box* (construction details are covered later). This consists of one box within another, assembled with alternating butt joints. Hold the bottom in place with cleats. Using plywood ⅜ inch thick will result in a sturdy ¾-inch construction.

Another method is to build a simple box frame and assemble it with butt or miter joints at the corners reinforced with dowel pins, splines, plates (biscuits), and/or glue blocks. Install glued support strips to hold the bottom piece, and fit gussets underneath at the corners to keep the drawer from wracking.

Building drawers is not hard but does take time and patience. Attention to detail is what spells the difference between a good job and a poor one. Constructing several drawers at once is

Building drawers

often advantageous since this reduces the time involved per unit. By setting up a little assembly line, you can do the job more quickly and easily and enjoy better and more uniform results. The drawback is that errors or mediocre construction practices, if not corrected, will be uniformly displayed in the finished products. But whether done well or poorly, there are only a few steps to the process of drawer construction. The following will cover both joined and double-box drawers.

Step 1   First make plans and decisions if you have not already done so. You need to decide how the drawer front will fit; flush, lipped, and so on. The arrangement usually matches that of the doors but does not have to.

Determine what materials you prefer to use and make sure that you have enough of everything on hand to cut all the pieces. Decide upon the final finish, and if it will be clear or natural, determine the most desirable grain orientation for the face—horizontal or vertical. Will there be decorative moldings, carving, inlays, routing?

Decide exactly what hardware you want to use and purchase it. This is especially important if something special is involved or the hardware design and the cabinet design are interdependent. Select the kind of guide or slide hardware you want and purchase that. If you decide to make your own guide system, work out the details and make sure you have the right materials.

Finally, decide upon the joinery. Use the simplest joints that are adequate and appropriate for the size, materials, and projected service conditions of the drawer.

Step 2   Check the drawer opening to make sure that the stiles and rails or carcase edges are level and plumb and that all the corners are square. Measure the height and width of the opening. If there are problems with the opening dimensions, you may have to build the drawer to suit or make adjustments during the final fitting.

Determine the overall depth of the cabinet, which will determine the maximum length of the drawer. The usual practice is to make the drawer as long as will readily fit in place, but there may be some reason to build a shorter one. Sometimes the drawer sides are extended so that they touch the back wall of the cabinet just as the face comes to rest in exactly the right closed position. This requires accurate measurements and construction.

Now relate all of the dimensional information to the drawer size, the guide system, the joint types, and the hardware. For a flush drawer, allow ¹⁄₁₆-inch clearance between the face perimeter and the cabinet members. This can be a bit less at the sides if beveled rabbet joints are used. If the final finish will be paint, make an allowance for the coatings. Work out clearances and other dimensional input for the guide system.

It is a good idea to make notes and sketches of all this as you go along. Then you don't have to rely on memory, and errors are likely to turn up while they can be easily erased. In this kind of job, a mistake in construction can mean starting all over again.

You can take care of this step now or later, depending upon your preference and the dictates of the materials being used. Installing cabinet-mounted parts of the guide or slide system now instead of later can save some effort and aggravation later. Also, working on a drawer parked on the workbench is usually easier than working inside a cabinet. So any adjustments or alterations that have to be made in the system can be done more easily in the early stages of construction than on or in the cabinet after the assembly is complete.

Step 3

If you have selected commercial hardware for the guide system, follow the manufacturer's instructions and install the cabinet-mounted parts. Depending upon the cabinet design, this may entail putting in some extra rails, support blocks, or shims to align the pieces properly. If some of this can be accomplished by modifying the drawer shape, that may be the easier course.

Make doubly sure that all tracks and rails are level and square to the opening, parallel as necessary, and otherwise correctly aligned. If they are not, you will have no end of trouble with drawer fit and operation. If you are making your own system, cut and fit the cabinet parts and install them.

When everything is in place, take another series of measurements, remembering to allow for all clearances, and check them against your earlier notes and sketches. You may find that some slight corrections or modifications will have to be made to your plan. You may discover that for some reason you cannot install the guide system just as you had planned, so the drawer construction must be altered a bit. If there are problems, make the necessary adjustments now.

Step 4 Lay out and cut the five principal parts of the drawer, choosing the best or most appropriate parts of your stock. Double-check to make sure all the parts have squared corners and clean edges and are flat and true. Any problems of this sort will be much magnified later when you begin to join the parts, so if you feel any part is unacceptable for the quality you have in mind, make corrections or cut a new piece now.

Step 5 Now comes the cutting and fitting of joints and the assembly of the parts. To show you how this goes, the following steps will cover two construction methods. The first uses simple joinery and results in a drawer that is satisfactory for just about any kind of home cabinetry. This process can be modified to include increasingly complex joinery and ornamentation to produce quality levels up to and including fine furniture. Note that there are many ways to build such a drawer and almost infinite variation in the exact details of equipment setup, tool use, and construction procedures; other methods and procedure sequences can be quite different.

The second kind of construction requires a bit more material but less effort for any size and uses only the simplest of all joints, the butt joint. This kind of drawer can be built on the back porch with no special equipment—in fact, with no power tools. The result is more than adequate for utility and storage purposes, and with some extra care, good materials and hardware, and a nice finish, can serve well in a kitchen or living room.

To establish the design characteristics of this drawer, assume that it is a flush type using double dado joints to join the face to the sides and simple dadoes to join the sides to the back. Those four pieces will be made of solid ¾-inch Philippine mahogany. The bottom piece will be ¼-inch hardboard set in grooves in the side and front pieces. The guide system will be side-mounted ball-bearing slides.

The projected use is in the pedestal cabinet of a desk. The joinery will be done on a table saw fitted with a dado head. The same operations could be done with a molding head or by making repeated passes with an ordinary cabinet blade. Other equipment can also be employed, such as a router, radial arm saw, router table, shaper, or hand tools.

To begin, set the dado blade height to just a bit more than half the thickness of the side-piece stock. In this case, a ⅜-inch-deep dado is needed. Set the dado width at ¼ inch. Decide which surface of each side piece will be the inside and which the outside, and mark them. (Often there is little if any difference in appearance and quality, and it doesn't matter.)

Set one side piece into a clamping miter gauge and align the piece so that the outside edge of the dado cut will lie ¼ inch inboard from the end of the piece. With everything lined up and secured, run the cut (FIG. 9-11). Repeat the process with the second side, and set both aside for the moment.

Now leave the dado blade set at the ¼-inch width but crank the height up to equal the thickness of the side pieces plus a clearance allowance of ¹⁄₁₆ inch; the total is ¹³⁄₁₆ inch. Stand the front piece on end and secure it in a jig or clamping fixture, aligned so that the centerline of this dado will fall exactly along the centerline of the piece.

This will result in a centered dado ¼ inch wide and a strip of material on each side ¼ inch wide. Double-check the

measurements and setup, and cut the dado (FIG. 9-12). Turn the piece over and repeat the process on the other end.

Decide which surface will be the show face of the piece. In present form, this piece has two tongues at each end, inner and outer. Those on the inner side are tenons because in due course they will fit in the dadoes you have just cut in the side pieces.

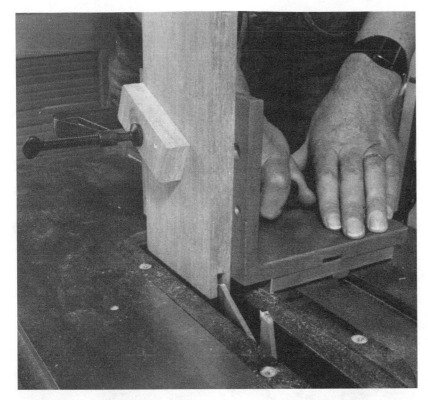

Both of these tenons must now be cut shorter so that they will fit snugly into the side-piece dadoes. The tongues on the outside will remain as is, completely hiding the end grain of the side pieces. In this case, the tenons must be ⅜ inch long, so you must trim off ⁷⁄₁₆ inch of material from each one. You can do this with the dado blade, or better, with a fine-toothed cabinet blade fitted in the saw.

Clamp the front, faceup, in a miter gauge, align the piece with the saw blade to remove ⁷⁄₁₆ inch exactly, and make the cut (FIG. 9-13). Be sure that the blade is not set too high—no more than ½ inch.

Turn the piece around (don't flip it over!) and make the same cut on the other end. Now check the parts for fit. If you have made the cuts accurately, the side pieces should slip into the

9-13
Trimming tenons on front piece.

front piece easily and squarely, each end of the front extending beyond the side-piece ends by ¹⁄₁₆ inch.

Next, cut the dadoes in the ends of the side pieces to accept the back piece. The cuts should be the same width as the thickness of the back-piece stock. The depth should be no more than half of the side-piece thickness. The dadoes will each be ¾ inch wide, plus just a whisker to allow for an easy fit without jamming, and ⅜ inch deep. Set the dado blade accordingly and make the cuts on the inside face of each side piece. The outer edge of each dado is ½ inch in from the side piece end and parallel with it.

Now lay out the dimensions of the bottom piece on a sheet of
¼-inch hardboard. The usual practice is to allow at least a
¼-inch rim (but no more than ⅜ inch) to set into the retaining
grooves in the sides and face.

An expansion allowance of ⅟₁₆ inch all around should be figured
in. In this case, then, the width of the bottom piece should be
equal to the inside width of the drawer plus ½ inch for a ¼-inch-
deep groove, less ⅛ inch. The length is equal to the inside
length (or depth) of the drawer plus ¼ inch, less ⅟₁₆ inch.

Cut the bottom piece, check for squareness, and smooth off
any rough edges. Rounding them slightly makes assembly
easier.

Lay out the front and side pieces for the bottom-piece retaining
grooves. The groove depth is typically ¼ inch, and the width is
just a fraction more than the bottom-piece thickness to allow a
free slip fit. The bottom edge of the groove is usually set at ⁵⁄₁₆ to
⅜ inch up from the bottom edges of the side and front pieces.

Set the dado blade and rip fence on the saw accordingly, check
for alignment and accuracy, and cut the grooves (FIG. 9-14).

9-14
*Cutting grooves in side pieces
to hold bottom piece.*

That leaves the back piece. The width (height when in place) should be equal to the distance from the top edge of each side down to the top edge of the groove for the bottom piece. In this arrangement, the bottom piece is set in place first; then the back slips down in its dadoes and rests upon the bottom piece.

The length of the back (width when installed) is equal to the distance between the bottom of the two dadoes in the ends of the side pieces less just a bit for fitting clearance. Often the best procedure is to rough-size the back piece a little large when all the pieces are cut at the outset of the project, then trim it to exact size during assembly. This can save trying to fit a piece that isn't quite the right size or having to cut a new one.

Now comes the assembly, when you discover how good your work has been so far. Set the sides on edge on a flat clean surface and slide the front piece into place. Slide the bottom into its grooves, then the back piece into the rear dadoes (FIG. 9-15).

9-15
Assembling drawer.

Check each joint for a tight fit, and make sure all corners are squared up. You may find it easier to hold everything in place with corner clamps, a band clamp, or whatever suits while you make sure everything is just right. Disassemble the drawer and make adjustments.

Reassemble the drawer sides and front, this time with glue and fasteners. Select fasteners of adequate length, and drill pilot holes and countersink as necessary. If the finish will be clear or natural, omit visible fasteners or counterbore for plugs.

Slide the bottom into place, unsecured; it should "float." Insert the back into its dadoes and secure it with glue and fasteners. This is an end-grain orientation, so use fasteners longer than usual. Turn the drawer over and fasten the bottom to the lower edge of the back with short fasteners.

The double-box drawer is made without joinery more complex than simple butt joints. In this example, all the parts are made of ½-inch softwood plywood to form a heavy-duty storage drawer.

Double-box drawer

Pieces of scrap construction-grade plywood are satisfactory because appearance does not count. However, using a better-grade stock would result in a presentable drawer that could be used anywhere. The guiding system will be the corners formed by the cabinet sides and bottom.

First, establish the overall outside dimensions of the drawer—height, width, and length. Assume the height to be 8 inches, the width 16 inches, and the length (depth) 20 inches.

Cut the pieces of stock for the inner box of the drawer, the face grain of the plywood running lengthwise on each piece. This box is smaller than the overall outside dimensions by the thickness of the stock on each side.

In this case, then, the outside dimensions of the inner box are 15 inches wide by 19 inches long. In this design, the height of the inner box is 1½ inches less than the height of the finished drawer to allow room for a bottom support cleat.

Simple butt joints will be used, the front and back pieces lying between the sides.

Cut two side pieces 6½ × 19 inches. The front and back pieces must be narrower than the inner box width (15 inches) by double the thickness of the side-piece stock, so cut the front and back pieces to 6½ × 14 inches.

Set all four pieces on edge on a clean flat work surface and arrange them so that the front and back pieces lie between the sides with the corners flush and even. Apply glue to the butt joints and fasten them together, keeping the box in square. Corner or other clamps help that process. You can use nails and expect adequate results, but screws make for stronger construction; drill pilot holes and countersink.

Cut a rectangle of plywood 15 inches wide by 19 inches long for the drawer bottom. Set it in place on top of the box frame, check that all the edges are flush with the sides, and adjust or trim as necessary. There should be no overlapping, but slight undersizing will cause no problems. Apply glue to the frame edges, set the bottom piece in place, and secure it with fasteners (FIG. 9-16).

9-16 *Inner-box assembly, upside down.*

Now cut the pieces to make the outer box. The faces of the butt joints will remain in the same relative position, the front and back pieces between the sides. Cut two side pieces 20 inches long and a full width of 8 inches. Cut the front and back pieces 15 × 8 inches each.

Set the inner-box bottom on a smooth work surface. Stand the two outer-box sides against the inner-box sides and check to make sure they are flush at the ends and properly aligned. Apply glue along each end and draw a wavy line of glue on the meeting faces of the sides.

Clamp the outer sides to the inner sides, keeping the ends lined up and flush (they will want to slip apart). Fasten the outer sides along each end.

Follow the same procedure with the front and back pieces, completing the outer box. Drive fasteners into both end-grain sections, front and rear. The resulting joint arrangement is shown in FIG. 9-17.

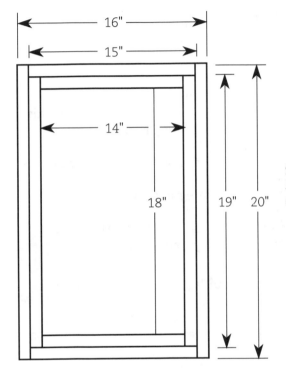

9-17
Box joint arrangement and dimensions.

Cut two strips of wood, either the same ½-inch plywood or solid wood, 1 inch wide and 15 inches long. Fit one on edge across the back bottom of the drawer and the other across the front. Cut two more 1 inch wide and 18 inches long, and fit them along the sides.

Apply glue and drive fasteners up into the drawer bottom and out into the drawer sides. These cleats, similar to the arrangement shown in FIG. 9-10, will give the drawer bottom plenty of support.

Step 6   Once the drawer assembly has been completed, you can install those parts of the guide system that mount on the drawer itself. Slide or guide hardware can be attached now, following the manufacturer's instructions. Note, however, that in a side-guide and runner system that employs dadoes cut into the drawer sides, those cuts would have been made before the drawer was assembled.

Install the pull or knob, set the drawer in place in the cabinet, and check for proper fit and operation. If anything is amiss, make whatever corrections are needed. Often a little beveling or easing along edges and corners makes for a better appearance or smoother operation.

Once the drawer is fitted, you can take care of any further embellishment your plans call for. As with cabinet doors, this may involve routing a design or applying decorative molding. Applying plastic laminate or wood veneer is typically done at earlier stages, but this varies depending upon the extent of the work and the overall design. Some may be done at this stage, provided clearance allowances were made early as required.

Now is the time to fit and install dividers, inset trays, sliding sections, covers, or other accessory items.

Step 7   The last step consists of final surface preparation followed by application of a finish. The exception is a drawer that has been entirely covered with a plastic laminate. Remove the drawer from the cabinet and mark it if necessary to show its location. Custom-fitted drawers, even though of the same nominal size, often do not interchange well. Remove all of the hardware and set it aside. Refer to chapter 12 on finishing for further information.

Drawer guides

You have a choice when it comes to guide systems. You can build your own as part of the drawer-cabinet assembly, or you can purchase various kinds of mechanical guides or slides. Many cabinetmakers frown upon using commercial guide hardware, perhaps feeling that it demeans both the maker and the cabinetry not to have it entirely fashioned of wood components in one of the traditional designs.

But manufactured systems are advantageous in a number of ways. Installation is faster and simpler, especially during the construction of built-in cabinetry, and labor saved is money saved. Other advantages include durability, long life, and continued and consistent smooth and effective operation of the drawer. Some varieties allow drawers to perform in ways that would not be possible with traditional built-in guide systems. Three examples are full-extension file-drawer slides, three-part constant-level full extensions that permit mounting of stereo turntables, and 100–150-pound-load slides.

This hardware also simplifies matters greatly for the home cabinet builder with only modest experience and skills. All you have to do is buy the right hardware for the purpose from a wide array of possibilities, follow the instructions, and install the parts. Note that there is also a wide variation in details and dimensions in these systems; you will need to have the hardware on hand before you start your project so you can plan and build to suit its requirements.

On the other hand, there are many other ways to accomplish the same purpose without spending money for slide hardware. And if you are building furniture-grade cabinetry, you may wish to follow the traditional methods.

Building *corner runners* is one of the simplest ways. Here the bottom edges of the drawer are guided along the corners formed by the sides and bottom of the cabinet. If there is a face frame that extends past the cabinet sides and leaves a gap between the cabinet sides and the drawer sides, install a filler strip to close the gap and guide the drawer accurately.

Where the drawer opening is bounded only by the cabinet stiles and rails, as in a stack of drawers, an extra part in the form of a deep L must be fitted front to back in the cabinet at each lower drawer corner (FIG. 9-18). This can be a single piece cut with a deep rabbet or two strips of wood glued and screwed together.

In all cases, a *kicker* should be installed front to back and centered over each drawer. The kicker allows the drawer to tip downward slightly as it slides out, so that it does not jam or drop out completely.

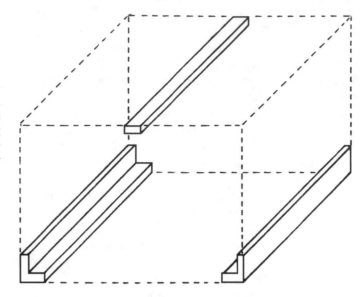

9-18
L-shaped cleats at drawer corners serve as runners, kicker centered above.

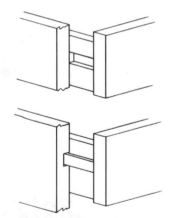

9-19 *Cleats mounted on sides to run in grooves in sides (above), or vice versa (below).*

Side guides and runners are commonly used in casework. This system consists of (1) grooves cut into the drawer sides that mate with rails mounted on the cabinet sides or (2) slots in the cabinet sides in which drawer rails run (FIG. 9-19).

In the first arrangement, a groove is cut lengthwise in each drawer side about halfway or a bit less down the side. The drawer sides must be at least ¾ inch thick, the groove depth about ⅜ inch. The width of the groove is not crucial. A cleat or rail, preferably of hardwood, is secured to each cabinet side, or front and back in rail or skeleton construction, properly positioned to accept the drawer. The width of the rails should be just a bit less than the groove width, the rail thickness just a little less than the groove depth. The object is to allow just enough clearance for smooth operation without binding or jamming, even in humid conditions, but not so much that the fit is sloppy.

In the second arrangement, the procedure is reversed, the grooves cut into the cabinet sides and the rails secured to the drawer sides. When the cabinet sides are not directly adjacent to the drawer sides (often the case), there are a couple of alternatives. One is to cut grooves in thick stock and mount them front to back, positioned to accept the drawer rails. Another is to mount two lengths of thinner stock one above the other on each side, leaving a slot between each pair that serves as the groove.

All of these rail-and-groove systems work well, and because of their design, they restrain the drawer from tipping, obviating the need for a kicker.

Another way to guide a drawer is with a *center guide* and runner. For this system, you need a certain space beneath each drawer and between stacked drawers. The bottom of the drawer must be set somewhat above the bottom edges of the drawer frame or opening.

In the simplest design, a strip of wood is fitted as a runner front to back in the cabinet, centered at the bottom of the drawer opening but protruding above the rail that forms the bottom of the drawer opening. Two more strips are attached from front to back on the drawer bottom, making a channel or slot just a bit wider than the runner (FIG. 9-20). These two strips comprise the center guide that aligns the drawer in the opening.

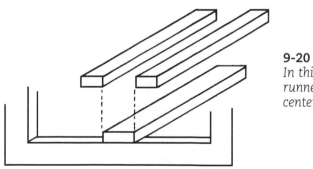

9-20
In this guide system, wood runners on bottom align with center guide in cabinet frame.

In a more complex construction, the center runner looks in cross section like a fat T and is shaped from a tough hardwood like maple. The two centering guides are mounted in the same way as in the method just discussed, and the back piece of the drawer extends below them. A T-guide notch that corresponds in shape to the cross section of the T-runner but a little larger for operating clearance, is cut in the skirt of the drawer back.

This aligns the drawer more closely and keeps it from tipping as it is opened.

Several variations on this scheme are popular. For example, the notched skirt in the drawer back is replaced with a molded plastic T-guide that attaches to the rear of the drawer. Some types do away with the runner guides and use only the T-guide. A T-guide can also be made from a thick block of hardwood, and the hardwood dovetail system (Fig. 5-16) works well.

Stop blocks, nylon bearing pads, or small rollers can be added to aid smooth operation. Two sets of guides and runners can be used, especially advantageous with very wide drawers. This minimizes the possibility that the drawer will go crooked and jam in opening.

Shelving

THE PRINCIPAL functions of a cabinet are to store articles or display them, often both, and the principal means of doing so is shelving. Although a shelf might seem a simple item, a knowledge of the design and construction of shelves is an important aspect of building home cabinetry.

Not all shelves are created equal, and in terms of square footage of storage space, shelving is certainly the most extensive element. Except for a few special-purpose storage units, like a gun cabinet, cabinets are not very useful without shelves. And while shelves are often made a part of many different kinds of cabinetry, they are also their own *raison d'être*. Whatever the function, to hold books or plants or china or fishing gear, shelving can stand alone as a complete piece of furniture existing for its own purposes and unassociated with other cabinetwork.

Shelves can take many forms, serve a multitude of purposes, and be constructed and installed in many ways. They range from unappealing but functional utility types through a great range of possibilities to ornate and highly imaginative furnishings. There is a lot of variation in detail, and as you might expect, there are right ways and wrong ways to build a shelf for a given purpose.

Shelf design

Several factors have to be taken into consideration when designing and building shelving. They have to be stiff and strong enough to carry their intended load. The arrangement should be flexible, for the greatest efficiency. The size must be sufficient for the intended purposes of the shelves, and that involves both length and width. Spacing has to be adequate for a variety of storage or display purposes. All of these considerations are interrelated.

Materials

Several materials work well for shelving. Solid wood is a reasonable choice, especially if the shelves are less than 5 or 6 inches wide. A soft wood like white pine is widely used for both

249

utility shelves and more decorative cabinet or furniture shelves. Hardwood such as oak is widely used, particularly where appearance is important and a natural or clear finish will be used.

The problem with solid wood, especially when used for adjustable shelves that are not securely fastened down, is its susceptibility to cupping, warping, and shrinkage. When the stock is wider than about 6 inches, these difficulties become more prevalent. The stock should be kiln-dried, of excellent quality, and acclimated to the microclimate of the jobsite before it is worked. Whenever possible, use vertical-grained softwood or quartersawn hardwood, to minimize these faults to some degree. Another possibility is to glue wide shelf stock from narrow strips of wood.

Particleboard makes good shelving provided it has ample support and is available in long lengths with one rounded edge for just this purpose. Because particleboard has no grain and its particles of wood are multidirectionally oriented, it does not have the lengthwise stiffness and rigidity of a wood plank. When pushed beyond its limits, it will simply break in half like a breadstick.

But the material is readily available, fairly easy to work, and relatively inexpensive. The high-density types have smooth surfaces, but cut edges require some edge treatment to fill or cover them. Particleboard is also dimensionally stable, and warping is not usually a problem. It is often used as a core to which a plastic laminate is applied. Carbide-tipped tools should be used for cutting and shaping.

Plywood is perhaps the most widely used shelving material in home cabinetmaking, and for good reason. It is stable, so problems with shrinkage, warping, and expansion-contraction are seldom encountered. Plywood has great strength and sufficient stiffness when used with the face grain oriented lengthwise to be used in fairly long lengths, depending upon its thickness. Cutting in this way allows maximum strength and rigidity for shelving purposes, makes the fabricating and finishing processes a lot easier, and looks better.

Softwood plywoods of cabinet grade are are most often used in enclosed cabinets, and either softwood or hardwood plywoods are used where appearance and decorative effect are part of the cabinetry design. Because of the way plywood is made, exposed edges must be further treated, usually by covering with an applied edge band. Plywood can also be used as a substrate for a plastic laminate covering, and it can be veneered with a variety of domestic or exotic woods.

Hardboard makes effective shelving if the grade and thickness of the material is properly related to the shelf length and width and the load that will be imposed. Tempered hardboard, which is quite stiff, can be used successfully as small compartment shelves, as in a multiple-shelf stationery cubby built into a writing-desk section of a storage wall.

This material is commonly available in ⅛- and ¼-inch thicknesses, and others are available. Thicker hardboard stock in Service grade can be used for increasingly longer and wider shelves for all sorts of purposes but is considerably less available. Hardboard is dimensionally stable and easy to work. It takes finishes well, can be used as a substrate for a covering, and need not be edge-treated. As with particleboard, using carbide tipped cutting and shaping tools is a good idea.

Glass, usually of the ¼-inch-thick plate or float variety, is often used for certain kinds of shelving. Typical applications are china cabinets, etageres, medicine cabinets, whatnots, and display cases. Glass shelves are much stronger than you might think. Properly arranged, they can be mounted with surprisingly little support to make attractive shelving sections. Glass has the advantage of allowing greater visibility than opaque shelves and can be artificially lighted to good effect.

Plastics see only limited use as shelving. Although sheet plastics of various sorts are fairly easy to work, they have several disadvantages, depending upon the intended application. The thicknesses commonly available for home consumption are too limber for most purposes, and most varieties have a great susceptibility to scratching. They also have a marked tendency to collect dust because of static-electricity buildup; this can be controlled to some extent by wiping with an antistatic solution. However, in certain kinds of display cabinetry the clear acrylics can be used successfully, especially where the displayed items are not moved about much, and the cabinet doors afford added protection. Also, translucent plastic shelves can double as light diffusers for indirect lighting hidden below.

Shelf depth

Proper shelf depth—the "width" of the shelf stock—is an important consideration if the shelving project is to fulfill its purpose. Shelves designed for particular purposes, such as storing single rows of canned foods or spice jars, holding a collection of figurines, or supporting an appliance or piece of equipment, should be sized according to the size and shape of those items. The usual practice is to allow about 1 inch of added shelf width and 2 inches or more of height for clearance, plus additional space for a back support cleat for a shelf above and doors or hardware that might interfere. Such shelves are often fixed in place but can be made adjustable for greater flexibility.

Shelves for miscellaneous storage and expected to hold practically anything must be as utilitarian as possible, or at least part of the value of the space they occupy will be lost. Those that are exceptionally narrow lack versatility. Those that are very wide may be awkward to use, although full frontal access along with racks, pullouts, and similar space-saver accessories help a great deal in that respect.

Shelves in kitchen wall cabinets are typically about 11 inches deep inside; those found in dining and living rooms (when found at all) may be as little as 6 inches or as much as 16 inches deep. Shelves in kitchen or equivalent base cabinets usually run from about 10 inches deep to a full 23 inches, depending upon cabinet construction and shelf placement.

Bookshelves should be at least 6 inches deep; note that nominal 1-x-6 boards will not work because they are actually only about 5½ inches wide. That width would be suitable only for small paperback books. An 8-inch depth is usually considered about right, and 9 inches is better. That depth will handle most books being marketed today with a little to spare.

The remainder—art books, "coffee table" books, ring binders, photo albums, horizontal format books, and similar specialty items—require shelves a full 12 inches deep and occasionally more.

As mentioned earlier, utility shelving is sometimes 16 to 18 inches deep, but anything deeper is likely to be more trouble to use than it is worth. There is an exception, however—a cabinet designed to hold linens, toweling, or blankets. Here, a depth of 24 to 30 inches is about right. Shelves in armoires and wardrobes are typically about 8 to 12 inches deep; 13 inches will also take care of audio records, including albums. Compact discs (audio or video) require 6 inches, boxed audio reel tapes 7½ inches. For audio- and videocassettes, the shelf depth depends upon the storing method.

Selecting the optimum length for your shelves is crucial to their well-being. In this context, "length" equals the distance between front-to-back supports. The actual length of a piece of stock that serves as a shelf can be whatever dimension you choose.

Shelf length

Unfortunately, you seldom know what loads will be imposed on a shelf. There are some exceptions, such as the small thin ones installed in a writing desk or the short narrow ones in a wall-hung whatnot; these will be loaded to a point far less than their capacity. But others, such as kitchen, utility, or especially workshop shelves or bookshelves, may become heavily burdened. This is particularly bothersome in bookshelves, where the load may be virtually constant for years.

Intermittent overloading will cause a shelf to bow, perhaps warp, and in extreme cases break or tear loose from its supports. Constant overload will creat a permanent sag that is most unattractive. Either condition is hard on the surrounding casework or frame.

Some generalities can be followed. First, except in circumstances where light loading is an obvious condition unlikely to alter with time, use shelf stock that is at least ¾ inch thick (1 inch nominal). If the loading is likely to be very heavy, such as storage of machinery or auto parts in a home shop, you could go to roughsawn stock that is an actual 1 inch thick or even construction-grade 2-inch planks.

When making general-purpose shelving, furniture-grade cabinet shelving, or kitchen shelves that are unlikely to hold heavy appliances, make sure that there is support at 3-foot intervals or less. This should also be a maximum for bookshelves 6 to 8 inches deep. Reduce this to 32 inches if the depth is over 8 inches.

Extrawide shelves, especially if they will hold heavy magazines, are best supported every 24 inches, or even less. In all cases, a support cleat running the full length of the back edge is of considerable help, especially in distributing the load. Stiffeners can also be applied to the front edges.

Shelf spacing
The spacing between shelves can also be crucial. If the shelves are stationary, care must be taken to make sure all are fully accessible. Where two or more shelves may be awkward to reach, as in the top of a tall armoire or in a kitchen base cabinet, the shelves can be of different widths for easier access.

For example, in a kitchen base cabinet, the floor serves as the first shelf and is full depth, usually about 23 inches. The next shelf might be only 15 inches or so deep, the upper one 10 to 12 inches deep, so that the contents are more visible and accessible. The vertical spacing between such shelves should be as great as can be managed.

Fixed bookshelves should be spaced at least 9½ inches apart, and the maximum you are likely to need is 14 inches. In large bookshelf sections, a mix of 10-, 12-, and 14-inch spacings is a good idea. In linear feet of shelf space, the wider spacings are generally less in demand than the narrower. The deep and wide-spaced shelves are best placed at the bottom of a shelving section, with the shallower shelves and smaller spacings above.

Spacing for fixed shelves in kitchen cabinets is difficult to determine because the requirements of different cooks and kitchen users are so variable. There must be headroom enough for tall glasses, pitchers, cereal packages, cooking oil bottles, and a host of other items of variable heights. One option is to provide a mix of spacings from about 8 inches to 14 or 15 inches and store whatever comes along in whatever way works best. Space-saving subshelves, racks, trays, and slideouts can be installed as the need arises.

The best way to minimize the problems of shelf spacing and take the most advantage of the total space available in a shelving section is to make all the shelves height-adjustable. There are a number of ways to accomplish this, discussed later. The advantage is obvious: The shelves can be placed at whatever height is best for the specific purpose and changed whenever necessary. Often more shelves can be installed in a cabinet or frame than would otherwise be practical.

There are some disadvantages to adjustable shelving, however. The shelves are loose and may be wobbly if warped or improperly made or installed. They have been known to come down abruptly when not properly anchored or overloaded or bumped. More labor is required if you make your own adjusting system, or more expense if you opt for adjustable-shelf hardware.

Another possible disadvantage is that open adjustable shelving, because of its appearance, may not fit a room decor or may not be in keeping with its surroundings. To many, this kind of shelving simply does not have the appearance of traditional fine furniture, a major detraction even though the installation may fulfill its intended functions in superior fashion. Both arrangements are found in many homes, each serving its own purpose.

Shelf installation

Shelving, no matter what its intended function, can be designed for installation in three ways. Built-in shelving essentially becomes a part of the house because it is attached permanently in place. The individual shelves may be either fixed or adjustable, but they remain as a part of a stationary installation.

On the other hand, shelving may be completely portable, as in ordinary small bookcases, the more complex sectional barrister style or something similar, or a part of other, perhaps multipurpose cabinetry, casework, or furniture that can be moved about at will. Here too, the shelves may be fixed or adjustable.

The middle ground is occupied by shelving sections that are multipurpose and considered semipermanent or semiportable. The shelves are often the adjustable type but may be nonadjustable and more or less readily removable. The shelving sides, dividers, supports or standards, and other components are held in place with locking hardware or other removable fasteners or tensioners. This is sometimes known as *knockdown* construction. The piece is neither permanent nor movable but is made to be taken apart easily to move it from one location to another.

Built-in shelving can be easily put together by any competent do-it-yourselfer, building partly in the shop and partly on the jobsite. The drawback, of course, is that when you leave, the shelving stays behind. Cabinetry shelving of all kinds can be made in the home shop, ranging from utility grades to fine furniture, for home use or for sale to help support the woodworking hobby. And while knockdown shelving and cabinetry used to be primarily the province of commercial manufacturers, the requisite hardware is now readily available to all through woodworking supply houses. The amateur cabinetmaker can now design and build custom shelving to suit any purpose.

Making shelves

The key to building good shelving is providing adequate support in the proper places. This depends upon four factors: shelf material, shelf depth (width of the stock), shelf width (length of the stock), and the maximum likely load. There is continual interaction among these four factors, and determining the details is not always easy. The best course is always to make shelving considerably sturdier than you think necessary. A substantial margin of safety does no harm.

As noted earlier, a ¾-inch thickness is the normal choice for shelf stock. Use thinner material only for short, shallow, light-duty shelves. The maximum length of shelves made of solid wood or plywood should be 42 inches between supporting points, provided there is also continuous support along the rear edge of the shelf.

If there is no rear support or the material is particleboard, reduce that length to a maximum of 36 inches, preferably 32 inches. For hardboard, oriented strand board, or similar products, use the manufacturer's recommendations.

If for some reason the shelf length must be longer or will take exceptionally heavy loads, build it from *four-quarter* (usually noted as 4/4; actually 1 inch thick) or heavier stock. The problem is usually not that the shelf is liable to break but that it will take on a noticeable sag over time. This is unsightly and difficult to correct.

The problem is common to bookshelves and can become a source of considerable difficulty in some constructions that include doors across the shelf openings or cupboard doors below. Unless the shelving remains flat, the doors may not operate at all.

There are numerous ways to support shelves, either in a cabinet or as part of a frame assembly. Where the shelves are fitted between solid side pieces of at least the same depth as the shelves, there are several options. The simplest method is to cut the shelf ends square and mount them with butt joints. Fasten each shelf with nails or screws driven through the side pieces after applying glue to the ends (FIG. 10-1). Screws will provide much more strength than nails, but this is still a weak arrangement that should be used only when the loading factors will be light.

10-1
Light-duty shelves made with simple butt joints and screws or nails.

One way to improve this arrangement is to install a *cleat* on the back wall of the cabinet, giving the shelf full support all along the back edge. Better still, secure cleats on the side pieces as well, to support the shelf ends (FIG. 10-2). This method is especially helpful when you can't drive fasteners through the side pieces from the outside and into the shelf ends (if you can, though, so much the better). And to provide even more support, you can nail or screw a face frame of sorts all around the perimeter of the shelf or add a "stiffener" to the leading edge (FIG. 10-3).

10-2
Shelf mounted on back and end cleats.

10-3
Stout hardwood stock applied to shelf outer edges.

You can make your own cleat material easily by ripping 1-inch-wide strips from a 1-inch (nominal) board, resulting in a strip measuring about 1 × ¾ inch. Position the narrow dimension beneath the shelf. An alternative, a bit more expensive, is to use a standard molding such as stop, screen, or quarter round.

Secure the cleats to the side pieces with nails or screws and glue and to the back wall in the same way if you can, depending upon the wall material. In a built-in arrangement, omit the glue and drive fasteners through the cleats and wall covering into the wall studs.

Another simple and commonly used method of supporting shelves is to cut dadoes in the side pieces and fit the shelf ends into them. An alternate is to use a stop or blind dado like the lower one shown in FIG. 10-4.

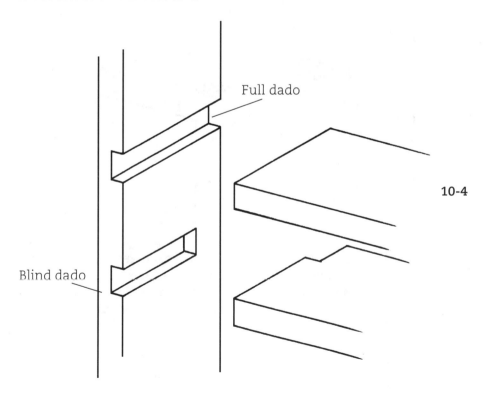

Full dado

10-4

Blind dado

If the shelving section depends upon the shelves themselves to provide part of the rigidity and solidity of the unit as a whole, the shelves must be firmly fastened with glue and screws. However, if the framework that holds the shelves is designed to be freestanding or will depend upon being attached to the structure for its principal support, the shelves can be left free in the dadoes.

If you need a rugged arrangement, mounting two or even three small steel *right-angle brackets* at each shelf end will provide it (FIG. 10-5). These brackets are easy to install, inexpensive, and unobtrusive, especially when they and the rest of the assembly are painted the same color.

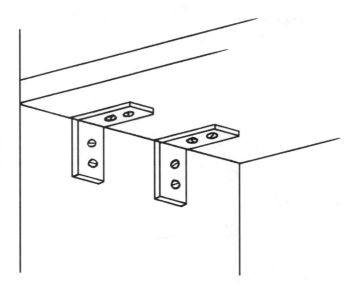

10-5
Steel angle brackets.

Small brackets with a pair of screws in each arm are more than adequate. Mount them to the side pieces first, then set the shelves in place and fasten them with screws. For a more finished appearance, you can mortise each bracket into both side pieces and shelf ends.

Often it is desirable to use long lengths of shelf stock and support them at intervals. There are several ways to provide that support. One method is to install a full-length back support cleat beneath the shelf, then tie each shelf to one or more stiles at the front. An alternative to the rear cleat if the cabinet back is accessible is to drive fasteners through the back and into each rear shelf edge.

In a shelving section with a full face frame, the stile is a part of that frame. The problem here is that the front-edge support is dependent upon a dab of glue and a couple of nails or screws. To add reinforcement, glue and nail additional support posts behind the stile and between each shelf (FIG. 10-6). The posts are not noticeable at a casual glance and do not interfere with items placed on the shelves.

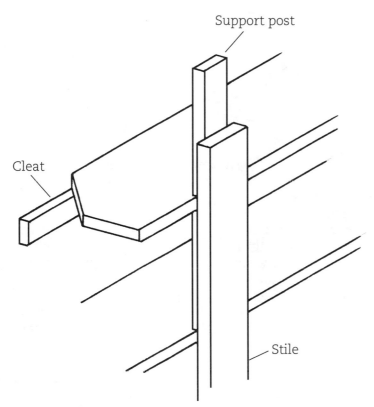

10-6
Built-in shelving system uses full-length rear cleat support and upright supports behind stiles.

Another way to provide support is to install full-depth *dividers* between shelves, spaced at appropriate intervals. To be fully effective in multishelf units, the dividers should be positioned directly above one another (FIG. 10-7). The dividers can be glued and nailed or screwed in place using simple butt joints. For a bit better appearance and to lock them in place, however, you

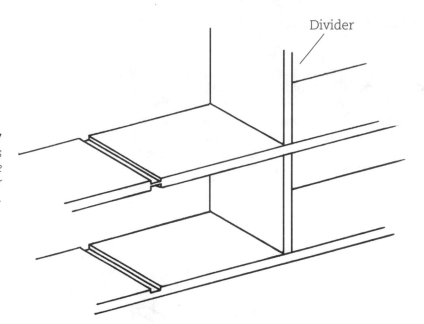

Divider

10-7
Dividers between continuous long shelves installed above one another with butt or dado joints.

can set them all in shallow dadoes; a depth of ⅛ inch is sufficient.

Another method that does away with cleats is *back standards*. At appropriate places along the shelves, mount vertical boards between them against the cabinet back, or in a built-in, against the wall. Solid wood pieces about 2 inches wide will work well. You can mount them as short lengths between shelves (FIG. 10-8), much like the dividers just discussed, and opposite front stiles like those discussed earlier. Or, you can make them full height and notch the shelves around them, then install small angle brackets or support posts.

Adjustable shelves are usually installed in one of three ways. They can be placed within cabinetry or casework that is self-supporting or in an open framework assembly that can be freestanding or more or less permanently attached to some part of the house. Or they can be set on brackets locked into *pilaster standards* or *track uprights* attached to the cabinet back or directly to the house wall (FIG. 10-9). In the simplest installation, the shelves are just laid across shelf brackets secured to the standards.

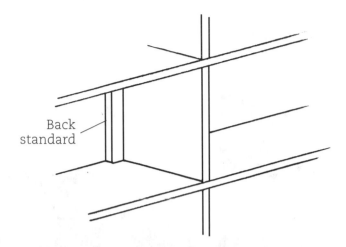

10-8
Standards installed at back of shelves, alone or with dividers.

Back standard

10-9
Typical standard arrangement.

You can make the shelves or the brackets or both, or you can buy them ready-made, no cabinetmaking required. And although standards or uprights can be surface-mounted, you can mortise them into wood strips that are in turn so mounted for a better appearance. Another type of standard can be mounted, either surface or flush, in pairs on the shelving side pieces to provide support at each end (FIG. 10-10)—a very popular arrangement.

10-10
Standards and clips supporting shelf ends in cabinet.

Another possibility is to cut dadoes in the side pieces in a continuous series about 2 to 3 inches apart on centers (FIG. 10-11). The dadoes must be cut to the full shelf depth and be unobstructed by face frame or trim molding. Then the shelves can be slid in and out of the slots at appropriate levels.

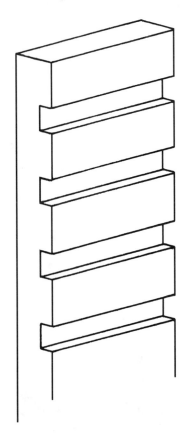

10-11
Side piece with ranks of dadoes.

One way to do this without making the dado cuts is to use a special form of plywood for the sides into which the grooves have already been cut. This material is usually termed *Texture 1-11* or T 1-11 ("tee one-eleven") and is chiefly used as exterior siding on buildings. It is available in several different groove spacings.

The back of this plywood does not have a good appearance, so it must be covered with another material for a finished look. In multisection units, make full height dividers of back-to-back lengths of Texture 1-11. Cover the cut edges with a molding strip or face frame (FIG. 10-12).

Shelf sections do not have to be mounted in a cabinet-style enclosure with solid end pieces. In many designs, a skeletal

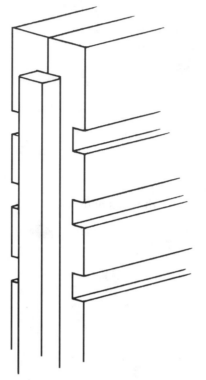

10-12
Adjustable shelving of back-to-back Texture 1-11 plywood, joint covered with trim molding.

structure that is primarily open serves to retain and support the shelves. Some types are freestanding, and others are meant to be attached to a wall. This style usually consists of a sturdy post or stile at each corner (FIG. 10-13).

Some of the same shelf attachment methods mentioned earlier can be used in skeletal construction. Angle brackets work nicely; so do cleats. The cleats may be short ones, extending only for the width of the individual corner supports, or they may run the full depth of the shelves, so that each end piece becomes a "ladder."

Metal shelf standards can be mounted flush or on the surface of the end supports. A good choice for fixed shelving is the corner dado joint shown in Fig. 7-19. This joint will also add to the overall strength of the shelf section.

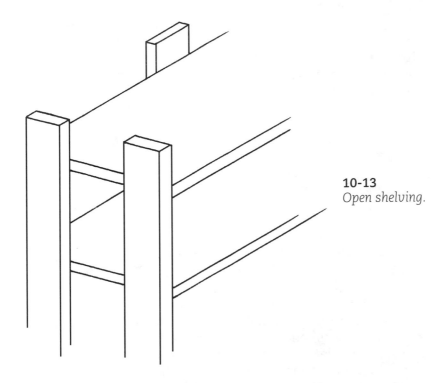

10-13
Open shelving.

Another way to support shelves, which works whether the shelf section is open- or closed-ended or completely enclosed in a cabinet, is to use either dowel pins or shelf pins made for the purpose.

For example, you can attach fixed shelves to the side pieces or corner supports by setting dowel pins blind in both members and fitting them together. This works especially well where both sides and shelves are made of *five-quarter* (⁵⁄₄ stock, 1¼ inches thick) or 1½-inch-thick stock. You can use ½-inch hardwood dowel stock for a solid and sturdy joint.

An alternative method is to drill through the side pieces and into the shelf ends, then drive hardwood pegs into the holes. Allow a bit of clearance at the hole bottom for glue. You can cut the pegs off flush or drive them deep and cap the holes with finish plugs or buttons. Another possibility is plated butt joints.

You can provide a much more flexible arrangement by drilling rows of close-spaced holes, either through or blind, in the side pieces. Insert short dowel pins, two or three for each shelf end, and rest the shelves on them at whatever level is desired. The same thing can be accomplished by using shelf pins (see FIG. 5-13), available in a variety of styles and finishes.

You can also purchase a special jig for drilling the pin holes with great accuracy, a difficult job otherwise. With either arrangement, you can make the shelves nonadjustable but removable by setting the pegs or pins in predetermined locations with no extra holes for adjustment.

There are so many ways to put shelving together and to install shelves in cabinets, built-ins, storage units, and furniture that it is impossible to describe them all. But by using some of the information and methods just covered and a little ingenuity and imagination, you can handle just about any shelving need. Chapter 12 will give you some further information and perhaps spark some ideas, since shelves are installed in both fixed and adjustable modes in multipurpose cabinets and in special-purpose cabinetry and casework where shelving is an integral part of the assembly.

Building cabinets

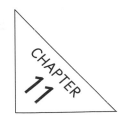

BUILDING CABINETS is really a relatively uncomplicated affair when you break the process down into its component steps. It does require care, patience, attention to detail, and accuracy—all the attributes that go into any woodworking project or any worthwhile endeavor.

Building a cabinet consists of constructing a framework of some sort, then fitting it out with doors, drawers, shelves, and tops as required, built as previously outlined. The specifics are infinitely variable, of course, but the basics of construction remain much the same.

You can make the construction details as plain and simple or ornate and complex as you wish, build your cabinetry rapidly for utilitarian purposes or lavish endless care and attention upon a piece of fine furniture, or strike any happy level in between. You can use a few simple techniques or a lot of complicated ones during the construction and expect excellent results either way.

You have already seen that there are numerous ways to build cabinet doors, drawers, shelves, and tops. The same is true of a cabinet framework, called a *carcass*. All you need do is select one that fits your circumstances. Outline your cabinet requirements, select the construction methods best suited thereto, design the cabinet with compatible components, and put it together step by step. No matter its size, kind, appearance, eventual purpose, or variable details, the fundamentals will remain the same.

There are several different ways to go about building cabinet carcasses. The end result is about the same in both appearance and function, and the method you select depends upon job circumstances, personal preferences, and the kind of cabinet involved.

Cabinet construction types

The two most basic construction methods are to build the cabinetry in place, a "built-in" arrangement, or to build it in the shop. With the first method, the entire cabinet assembly, except in most cases for the doors and drawers, is permanently constructed from scratch in its final location. Obviously this system is useful only where the cabinetry becomes a fixed, permanent part of the building. This method is often employed in building kitchen and pantry cabinets, dining-room servers, sideboards and china cabinets, and bathroom vanities and storage cabinets.

Freestanding and furniture types of cabinetry have to be built in the shop, then placed or installed wherever desired. But most cabinetry that lends itself well to jobsite construction can also be shop-built, and often is. Large assemblies are made in smaller units, then installed and joined as necessary. In theory, the assembly could perhaps be called removable, but the installation process usually custom-fits the pieces to their locations, and they are attached solidly to the structure, so they are considered permanent.

There are two principal methods of constructing shop-built cabinets. One is called the box-and-frame system, the other the casework system.

As the name implies, the *box-and-frame system* consists of a box constructed of thick sheet materials, usually plywood, with a built-up wood face frame attached to the front. The face frame is typically made as a complete subassembly, then attached to the front edges of the completed box. However, it can also be attached piece by piece to the box, a procedure that many beginners or even experienced woodworkers might find more agreeable.

In the *casework system*, a rectangular skeleton of wood strips is attached to a base of sheet material; then the sides and back are covered with thin plywood panels.

There are advantages and disadvantages to all of these methods. Building on-site obviously does not require a shop. Usually less material is needed because the walls, floor, or ceiling typically make up part of the cabinet. Beginners are apt to find this method easier and quicker than casework or box-and-frame methods. Pieces are individually fitted to the site, automatically compensating for misaligned parts of the building. You do not have the potential problem of fitting a completed cabinet into a given space or trying to mount a heavy, awkward assembly on a wall and getting it plumb and level.

But the installation is permanent—no chance to move it or remove it later. The quality level might be less than if the unit was shop-built under better conditions and with more sophisticated and accurate equipment. And you and the family might have to live with a scattering of tools, sawdust and shavings, materials, paint fumes, and occasional spates of racket as the job goes on.

As for the shop-built cabinets, quality level can be higher with a variety of power equipment available during construction. All the tools and supplies are handy in one spot that is designed, presumably, for just this kind of work. All the mess is confined to one area that can handle it well without bothering other parts of the house. A well-equipped shop operated even by an amateur is capable of producing fine furniture-type cabinetry.

Between the two shop-built methods, beginners will probably find the box-and-frame system (FIG. 11-1) easier to master. For a given article, this system typically takes a little less time and effort, requires somewhat less machining (much less sometimes), and does not require sophisticated equipment or techniques; the latter can be carried to whatever extent the cabinetmaker desires. About the only drawback of consequence is that the cost of materials tends to be a little higher for a given design because more or heavier stock is needed.

The casework system (FIG. 11-2) uses less material, so that cost is down a bit, and if screwed-together face frames are used, the amount of labor also goes down some. But overall, more labor is needed, the system is more complex and the techniques harder to master, and it is perhaps less adaptable to a full range of cabinet projects. Also, a lot of folks do not really care for the thin, lightweight paneling that this kind of construction features.

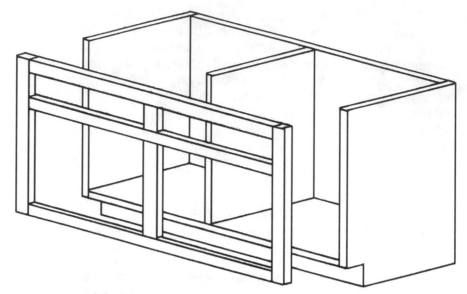

11-1 *Box-and-frame construction.*

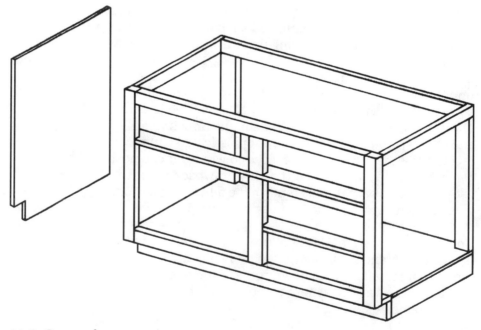

11-2 *Casework construction.*

A third construction method has recently been introduced in this country—the *European—Eurostyle*, or *32 mm* (millimeter) system (FIG. 11-3). Originally developed as a mass-production system, this kind of cabinetry has a distinctive appearance and requires a specialized type of imported hardware, mostly by Blum, that is available from mail-order woodworking supply houses. Some special equipment is also needed.

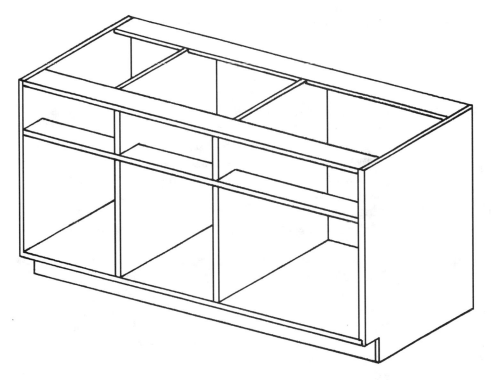

11-3 *Euro-style construction.*

Eurostyle cabinets do not have face frames and are very plain, smooth-faced, and rectilinear, reminiscent of the white steel cabinetry popular several decades ago. Their use appears to be almost entirely confined to kitchens and pantries, although adaptations could be made for other purposes. The same approximate appearance can be achieved by building with the box-and-frame method and installing overlay doors and drawers to conceal the entire frame.

Several cabinet projects are covered on the following pages, using both on-site and shop-built box-and-frame construction methods. These cabinets are designed for several purposes, but note that the construction details are similar. They can be modified and altered to suit a variety of other purposes, and using the same construction methods, you can design and build cabinets for whatever use you wish.

Built-in kitchen base cabinet

A kitchen-base cabinet assembly is likely to be the largest piece of cabinetry in most houses, although not necessarily the most complex. Because of its size and straightforward design, it makes a good beginning project.

Step 1
Start by making preliminary plans and working out the basic cabinetry design. Meaure the space where the cabinet will be built, decide how the cabinet will be used, then figure out what will be needed in the way of doors, drawers, and shelves. Try not to crowd the elements together—make them all roomy and workable. Include any special items in your plans, like a chopping block, pull-out pastry board or trash container, sink- or rangetop, or special racks.

Make a rough sketch of what the cabinet will look like as you face it head-on, as in FIG. 11-4. Jockey the cabinet elements around until you have an appearance that pleases you, then make another drawing, this time to scale. This will tell you if all the elements will fit in and give you a chance to balance out the drawer and door numbers, sizes, and arrangement accurately. You will quickly see if some of the elements are too large or small or if you need another arrangement. Give this stage plenty of thought and make any changes or adjustments now. Doing so later is difficult.

Step 2
With the plan established, it's decision time. Figure out what kinds of materials you will use, what decorative effects you want. Choose the hardware and countertop material and design, and select a finish. Then purchase all the ingredients. This is particularly important so that you can build to suit the materials according to your original plans and not get caught without some vital component.

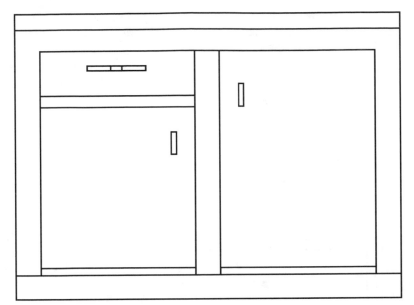

11-4
Example base cabinet when finished.

The first item is the *cabinet floor frame*. Start by checking the level of the floor at the cabinet site, from the wall outward for about 2 feet. You must first attach a cleat to the wall to support the rear edge of the cabinet bottom. The top edge of the cleat must be high enough to provide an adequate *kick space* or *toe space* at the front of the cabinet. Normal dimensions for this space are 3 to 5 inches high (measured from the surface of the finish floor) and 3 to 4 inches deep. If you select a height of 3½ inches, you can use a 1 × 4 as a toe board.

Make a mark on the wall to indicate the point where a level line extended outward 2 feet will meet the top edge of a toe board 3½ inches (or your chosen dimension) high. Run a level line along the wall for the entire length of the cabinet, outside to outside. If the cabinet butts against a wall at either or both ends, continue the line there.

If the cabinet does not butt against a wall, it will require an *end panel (outside bulkhead)* at each end, and the floor frame will need an end piece at each end. Subtract the thicknesses of both components from the overall length of the cabinet to get the length of the rear support cleat.

Step 3

If there is a wall at one end, subtract only one bulkhead and one floor-frame end thickness. If the cabinet is bounded by two walls, the support cleat will run the full length of the cabinet, wall to wall. Side support cleats will be used in this instance, so subtract the thickness of the toe board and the back cleat, plus the depth of the toe space, from the overall cabinet depth to get the length of the side support cleats.

Figure 11-5 shows you these arrangements. It all sounds confusing, but remember that you are working from the inside outward, so you have to make allowances for the thicknesses of the pieces that will be installed further along in the sequence.

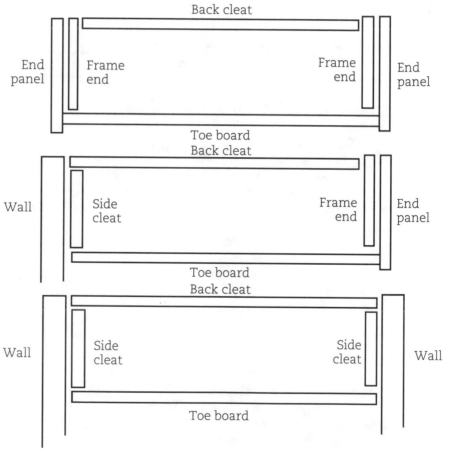

11-5 *Cabinet base-frame cleat arrangements.*

To arrive at the proper overall depth of the base frame from front to back, start with the overall depth of the cabinet. The industry standard is 24 inches. The countertop depth is greater by ¾ inch or more so that it will overhang the cabinet face.

These dimensions can be varied but seldom are in kitchen cabinets; special-purpose units can be whatever size you like. Subtract the depth of the toe space from the cabinet depth and you have the overall depth of the frame from the face of the toe board to the back wall. Figure 11-6 shows typical standard dimensions.

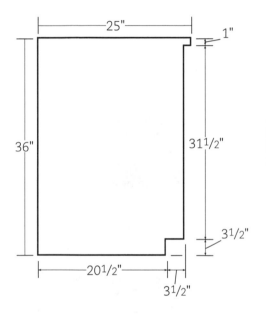

11-6
Standard kitchen base cabinet dimensions.

Once you have the dimensions and the pieces lined out and the level lines set, nail the back support cleat to the wall studs and sole plate, and nail up one or two side cleats as required.

Now you can go ahead with the base sides and the front or toe board. If side support cleats are used at both ends of the cabinet, there are no base sides; if one, there is a base side at the opposite end.

Nail one end of each base side to the ends of the back support cleat. Cut the toe board to length and nail it to the free ends of the base sides or to the cleats. Cleats will be level, but side pieces may not be because they follow the floor. Both side pieces and the toe board may have to be notched, shimmed, tapered, or otherwise adjusted so that the top edges of the whole base frame are level at all points and in all directions.

Once the proper position is established, secure the side supports and/or toe board to the floor by toenailing into the floor from the inside. An alternative, sometimes easier, is to nail wood blocks to the floor; then face-nail the frame into the blocks from the outside. When completed, the frame should be a solid, level part of the house.

Note that depending upon the arrangement of the parts, there may be exposed end grain at the toe-board–end-panel joint. If this is objectionable, fashion simple edge miter joints at those points.

If the cabinet is longer than 2 feet, nail additional floor supports in place, front to back within the floor frame (FIG. 11-7). Cut the pieces to fit closely, and nail them to the house floor or nailing blocks and to the toe board. Make sure that the frame remains level and square and the toe board does not bulge in or out because of improper cross-piece lengths.

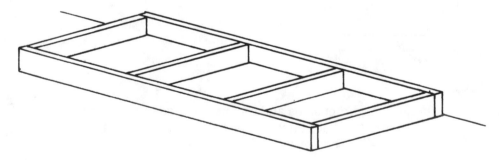

11-7 *Long base frames need additional cross members to support cabinet floor.*

Step 4   Cut and fit the cabinet floor. Each end should be flush with the side supports and fit snugly against the walls at the sides and rear. The front edge of the floor should overhang the toe board by an amount equal to the total depth of the toe space minus the thickness of the stock that will be used for the face frame (usually ¾ inch).

Mark the locations of all the front-to-back supports beneath the floor with accurate pencil or chalk lines. Take the floor up, apply glue to all the top edges of the frame, and replace the floor. The glue will make the floor panel slip around, so check the alignment carefully, then nail the panel down with 6d finish nails (FIG. 11-8).

11-8
Securing cabinet floor with glue and nails.

Now install the cleat that will support the rear edge of the countertop and side cleats if those are in order. Note that instead of side cleats, you can install full side panels. This will give you a flat, solid surface to which you can easily anchor shelves, accessories, the countertop ends, and the face frame. In some cases, this is a better solution than trying to attach parts to a hollow wall covered with plasterboard or lath and plaster.

Step 5

To find the cleat location, start with the overall height of the countertop from the finished floor surface. The normal height is 36 inches, but this can be varied for greater working comfort.

Do so carefully, though, because a change of only ½ inch can make a surprising difference.

Subtract the thickness of the countertop material from the height, and subtract the height of the base-frame and cabinet-floor material from that. Measure that distance up the wall from the cabinet floor and run a level line. Set the upper edge of the cleats to this line. Remember that the lengths of the cleats must be figured with allowances for the face frame and any back joints.

Step 6   If you are using end panels, they can be installed next (FIG. 11-9). Before trimming the panels to final size, check to see whether the cabinet floor is exactly at right angles to the back wall. If the wall is not plumb, trim the back edges of the panels to match so that their forward edges are plumb and square with the cabinet floor and the top edges are level. Set the panels in place and glue and nail them to the base-frame side supports at the bottom and to the ends of the counter-back support cleat. If the cabinet butts against a wall, nail the panels to the wall studs.

Step 7   If you are using side support cleats instead of side panels, secure a vertical face-frame support between the bottom edge of each side cleat and the cabinet floor. This will give you a solid nailer to which the end stile of the face frame can be attached later.

If there are divider panels (called *interior bulkheads*) that separate the cabinet into sections, they can be installed now (FIG. 11-10). Cut and fit the panels so that the front edges are flush with the cabinet-floor front edge and are plumb, with the back edges fitting snugly against the wall and notched around the countertop support cleat. Secure them with glue and toenails.

Step 8   If shelving will be installed, establish shelf heights now and draw in appropriate level lines to mark their locations. Cut cleats to support the back edges of the shelves and nail them to the wall studs. If you can, stagger the shelf heights slightly in

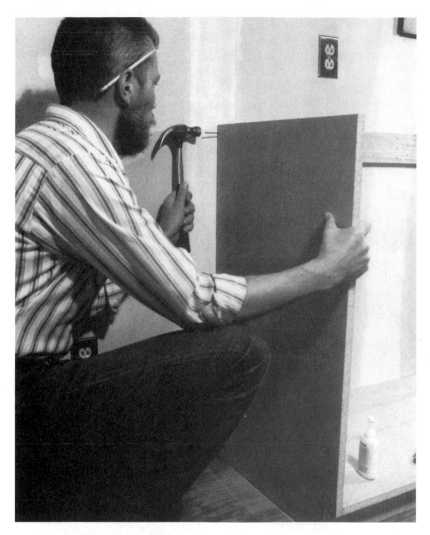

adjacent sections, then nail the side pieces or divider panels to the ends of the shelf cleats.

You may also wish to put cleats in place on the divider panels to support the shelf ends. Or you can nail through the side or divider panels directly into the shelf ends. This works well as long as the loads are not too great.

11-10
Divider panel, notched around the upper back cleat, being checked for proper fit.

Cut and fit the shelving and glue and nail everything in place (FIG. 11-11). Make sure the shelves are level front to back as well as side to side.

Step 9 The face frame comes next. This can be built on the workbench and attached as a unit, but in this example is put together piecemeal. Solid-wood stock ¾ inch thick works well and obviates the need for any added edge treatment. The material here is standard 1 × 4 (3½ inches actual width). Well-dried relatively stable lauan was used in this cabinet so that shrinkage would not be a problem.

Install the top rail first (FIG. 11-12), full length across the cabinet face. Set the top edge of the rail flush with the top edges of the side and divider panels (or ends of the side cleats and upright nailers). The ends of the rail should be flush with the outside surfaces of the side panels or butted snugly against the walls. Secure the ends first with glue and nails. Check that any divider panels are plumb and properly aligned, and nail the rail to them.

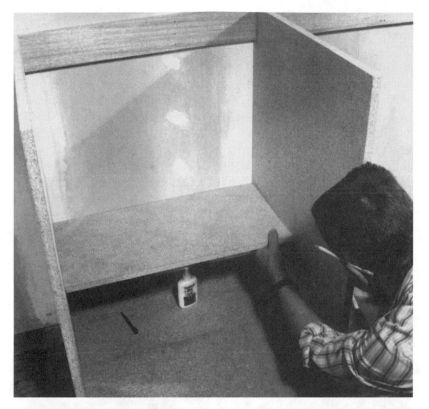

11-11
Shelf is installed using simple butt joints glued and nailed.

11-12
Top face-frame rail being nailed in place.

The stiles at the cabinet sides are next. Lauan of exactly matching thickness and ripped to 1½ inches wide was used in this example. Fit the stiles into place butted tight against the bottom edge of the top rail and with their bottom ends flush with the bottom of the cabinet floor. The outer edges of the stiles should be flush with the outer surfaces of the side panels or set tight against the walls. Fit them carefully and glue and nail them in place with 4d nails. Toenail at the inside angle of each upper flat butt joint with 3d finish nails where the stile joins the upper rail (FIG. 11-13). Follow the same procedures for installing stiles over the edges of the divider panels. Additional stiles may be needed to separate door or drawer openings.

11-13
Toenailing stile and rail corners.

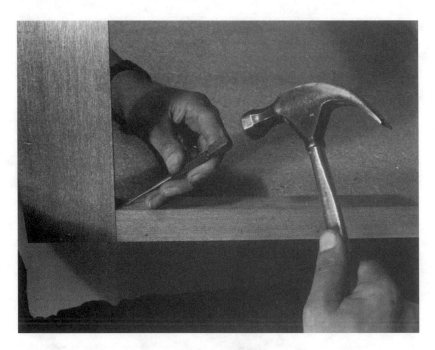

Install any secondary rails next. In some cases, the rail may actually be a shelf edging. Just cut the rail to length and glue and nail it in place across the shelf edge, and toenail the flat-butt-joint angles as usual.

If the rail is a divider between drawers, for example, back support should be added (FIG. 11-14). Cut and fit the rail first, tightly. Then cut a longer, narrower piece that will fit crosswise

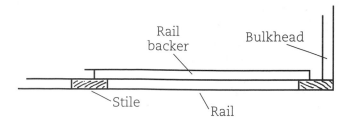

inside the cabinet, behind the rail to be secured to the back of the rail and the stiles. Glue and nail the backer to the rail, then glue the two pieces in place. Clamp the assembly into the cabinet (FIG. 11-15), nail the backer at each end to the back of each stile, then toenail each end of the rail to the stiles at each flat-butt-joint angle.

11-15
Drawer-divider rail backer clamped in place before fastening.

Finally, install the bottom rail. In this example, the rail is no more than an edging. Attach a piece of ¾-inch stock across the cabinet bottom with glue and nails to cover the raw edge.

If any exposed raw edges remain on shelving or other parts, apply an edge molding to them. You can use wood strips or molding attached with glue and nails or veneer tape secured with glue.

Step 10

Step 11   This step is optional but worthwhile. Adding gussets to each corner (FIG. 11-16) formed by the side panels, divider panels, back support cleat, and front top rail will strengthen the assembly considerably and afford some additional anchoring points for the countertop should they be needed. Cut some triangles of solid wood or plywood; fit them to each corner flush with the top edge of the cabinet, and secure them with glue and screws.

11-16
Upper corners of cabinet strengthened by gussets.

Step 12   Slip the cabinet drawers into place and check for fit and alignment. This may involve mounting a slide or guide system or installing runners and kickers. Whatever the case, doing this work now is usually easier than doing it after the countertop has been installed. Refer to chapter 9 for information on drawers and guide systems.

Step 13   Fit the cabinet doors, making any necessary adjustments, then hang the doors. Install any special hardware, accessories, or specialty items. Refer to chapter 8 for door details. Check the entire assembly to make sure that it is complete and according to plan.

Step 14   Remove the doors, drawers, and hardware preparatory to putting on the countertop and applying the final finish. There are several possibilties for countertops, as noted in chapter 4.

To prepare for a plastic laminate or a ceramic-tile top, fit a sheet of ¾-inch-thick plywood to the cabinet top and secure it to the top rails and the top edges of the side and divider panels, flush against the wall at the rear, flush at the sides, and overhanging the cabinet front by 1 inch (this dimension can be varied).

Note that for ceramic tile, some cabinetmakers and tilesetters prefer to use a double thickness of plywood or plywood topped with cement backer board. This results in a solider tiling job with less chance for grout lines to crack.

For a self-edged countertop, you can apply the edging directly to the plywood if a narrow edge is desired. For a wider edge, attach a strip of ¾-inch stock to the underside of the countertop edge with glue and screws to fill it out to 1½ inches wide (more can be added if you wish).

Apply the plastic laminate band to the edge first, flush with the bottom surface and extending upward about ¹⁄₁₆ inch above the surface of the plywood top. Do the same at the sides if applicable. Then trim the protruding edge exactly flush and square to the plywood surface with a laminate trimmer. Trim the edge corners.

Fit the laminate to the plywood top, allowing about ¹⁄₁₆ inch to overhang the edge band at front, sides also if applicable, otherwise flush at sides and rear. Apply the contact cement, allow curing time; set the laminate on dowels or waxed paper strips; position it exactly; and remove the dowels or paper bit by bit, pressing the laminate into place.

Apply pressure over the entire surface with a roller or beating block and hammer to ensure full contact and adherance. Then trim the laminate edge either at a bevel or square and flush with the edge band (the bevel is preferred, since there is less chance of chipping).

Alternatives are to lay the countertop laminate and apply metal moldings around the edges, fit a metal molding at the rear, install backsplash sections at the rear, or trim the lead edges with wood molding instead of metal or laminate. In the latter case, a hardwood molding is typically attached to the lead edge of the plywood with its top flush with the laminate surface.

A tile countertop may be edged with matching tile, either a special narrow bullnose or sink-cap tile or a full-width band cemented to a wide wood backing. Metal edging can also be used, as can plain wood molding attached to the plywood edge with the top flush with the tile surface. The finish might be natural, stain, or paint; tung-oil varnish works very well.

Laying the tile is a matter of laying out the pattern, making whatever tile cuts are required, spreading the adhesive or mortar, and setting the tiles. After a curing period, the joints are grouted, preferably with an epoxy grout. Vinyl countertop cover is applied by fitting the sheet carefully, then gluing it down with a water-resistant adhesive. Trim the edges with metal moldings.

Solid wood is sometimes used as a finish countertop. Make the top as a single piece or in appropriate sections, gluing strips together with waterproof glue. A hard, close-grained wood like maple is preferred; a porous wood is not recommended. Attach the top solidly from underneath through corner gussets and brackets; brass or stainless-steel screws are a good idea here. Apply a special nontoxic clear finish that is made for the purpose (sometimes called *salad-bowl finish*).

Yet another possibility is to install a plywood substrate top as for a laminate and glue ⅜-inch-thick (or thereabouts) solid tongue-and-groove hardwood strip or parquet-tile flooring to the plywood. Use a flooring design that does not have grooves as part of the pattern or beveled edges that leave grooved joints between the pieces. Lay the material with a water-resistant parquet floor-tile adhesive. Apply a matching wood edge band. You can also run the same material up the wall at the rear to form a backsplash.

If you have selected artificial or real stone for your countertop material, have the material professionally installed. Confer with the supplier before building the cabinets to make sure of all the dimensions and anchoring points and that there is ample support in the cabinet structure for the considerable weight involved.

There are more similarities than differences between the built-in and the box-and-frame base cabinet. The biggest difference is that you do not have anything solid to build to or against. This makes nailing a bit harder, so you might want to opt for screws instead. This makes a ruggeder assembly that is easier to put together, although more labor is involved. There are several ways a box-and-frame unit can be constructed. This set of procedures is only one.

Step 1

Make the decisions and lay out the plans, just as for a built-in unit. Decide upon all the dimensions, select the materials and hardware, and draw up plans.

Step 2

Build the cabinet base. This consists of a toe board for the front, a back strip, and two side pieces; nominal 1-x-4 solid-wood stock is suitable for this, or you can rip solid wood or ¾-inch-thick plywood to other widths. For units longer than a couple of feet, include cross pieces. Assemble the base ladder-fashion (see FIG. 11-7).

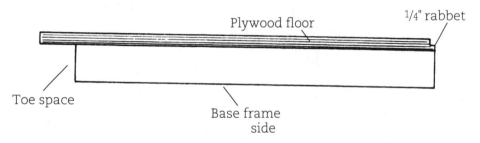

Plywood floor

¼" rabbet

Toe space

Base frame side

11-17 *Cabinet floor with rabbeted rear edge for back panel, set on frame with toe-space overhang.*

In this design the base assembly is shorter than the overall width of the cabinet by the thickness of both side panels, and the toe board extends beyond each base side piece by the thickness of one side panel. The ends of the toe board can be cut square, leaving the end grain exposed, or you can miter them to fit later against a mating miter on the side panel.

Step 3 Check that the base frame is square by measuring the diagonals. When they are equal, the frame is in square. Cut a piece of sheet stock for the cabinet bottom. It should fit flush at the back of the base frame, flush at each side, and overhang the toe board by the depth of the toe space minus the thickness of the stock that will be used for the face frame, typically ¾ inch.

The bottom can be either particleboard or plywood, and a ½-inch thickness is commonly used; ⅝-inch or ¾- inch is also suitable. Along the back edge, cut a rabbet ¼ inch wide to a depth of half the thickness of the stock (FIG. 11-17).

Step 4 Cut the side panels out and miter the vertical toe-space edge to 45 degrees (FIG. 11-18) if necessary. The material used here is ¾-inch-thick plywood, although particleboard can be used.

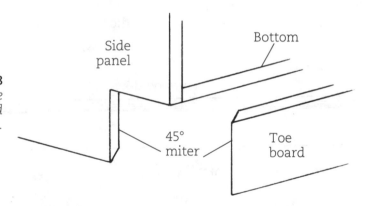

11-18
Mitering toe board to side panels conceals end grain and makes a neat joint.

Cut a rabbet in the rear inner edge of each side panel ¼ inch wide and to a depth of half the thickness of the panel stock. Set the panels in place against the base-frame sides, true them up, and fasten them securely.

Step 5 Cut a back brace from nominal 1-inch stock. Its length is the same as the interior width of the cabinet. Fasten the brace in place across the cabinet back flush with the upper edges of the side panels and inset ¼ inch from the rear edges (FIG. 11-19).

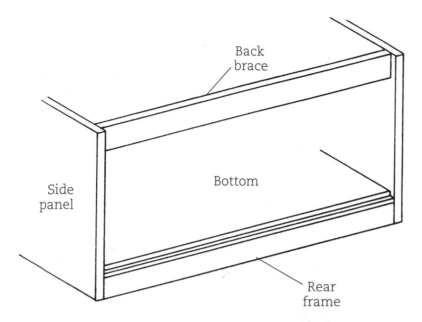

Back
brace

Side
panel

Bottom

Rear
frame

11-19
View from rear—back brace in place, set back to allow for back panel.

Tip the cabinet on its face and align the side panels square with the bottom. Cut a back piece; ¼-inch plywood is a common choice; hardboard can also be used. Fit the back so that it lies in the rabbets cut in the bottom and the side panels with the top edge flush with the top edge of the back brace. Glue and nail carefully with 3d finish nails or brads canted slightly into the rabbets.

Stand the cabinet up on its base. Cut and fit divider panels; plywood and particleboard ½ inch thick are common choices here. Notch the upper rear corners to fit snugly against the back brace (FIG. 11-20). Secure the dividers with nails or screws through the back brace and the back panel.

Step 6

Then tip the cabinet on its back, check the alignment of the dividers, and drive fasteners up through the cabinet bottom. This must be done with precision so that the divider material does not split or the fasteners break through into the open.

If shelves are in order, this is a good time to install them. Cut them to fit and install them carefully so that the divider panels do not become misaligned. Butt joints or support cleats can be

Step 7

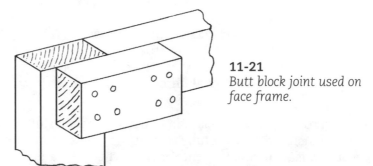

11-20
Divider panel notched around back brace and flush against the back panel.

used here; dadoes must be cut before the side and divider panels are installed.

Step 8   Double-check the face dimension of the cabinet. Decide on the joinery method you will use in assembling the face frame. Mortise-and-tenon joints are traditional, doweling is an option, and plate joining is probably the best bet.

Using one of the new pocket-hole drilling guides, you can also construct even an intricate face frame with glue, pocket holes, and cabinet screws. The butt block system is an acceptable alternative too (FIG. 11-21). If you have not used any of these procedures before, practice with a few pieces of scrap before tackling the cabinet itself.

11-21
Butt block joint used on face frame.

292   Custom Cabinets

Lay out and cut all the pieces for the face frame. Nominal 1-inch stock is the common choice, but veneered pieces are sometimes used, especially if the cabinet is of the furniture type rather than a kitchen or utility unit. Arrange the pieces in order on a flat clean work surface.

Fashion the joints and assemble them dry to check for fit and assembly sequence. Working with the parts facedown is often a good idea, and necessary if you use pocketed screws or butt blocks. Assembling the most complex section first and working from there is normal practice. When all the fits are satisfactory, assemble the pieces permanently with glue and fasteners as required. Clamp as necessary and allow the assembly plenty of time to cure.

Step 9

Tip the cabinet over on its back and set the completed face frame in place. Check for fit. The ends should be flush with the side-panel faces, the top edges flush, and the upper edge of the face-frame bottom rail should be flush with both top and bottom surfaces of the cabinet floor.

Make adjustments. Run a bead of glue along all the cabinet-front edges and set the face frame in place (FIG. 11-22). Nail the frame to the cabinet with 4d finish nails, making sure that no part of it slips out of place. Drill pilot holes for the nails or use a nail spinner at points close to the ends of rails or stiles to avoid splitting. Apply edging to any visible raw edges.

Step 10

Complete the cabinet by installing doors and drawers as well as accessories and specialty items, and put on the countertop. Prepare the surfaces and apply a finish.

Built-in wall cabinet

A built-in kitchen wall cabinet is constructed in much the same way as the base cabinet discussed earlier. A brief set of procedures follows; refer to the base cabinet discussion for more details.

This unit is made of ¾-inch particleboard and solid wood stock and has a standard overall depth of 12 inches. It is located a

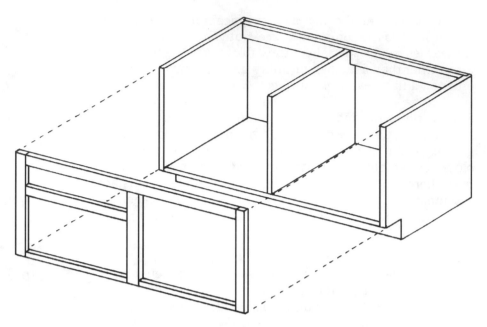

11-22 *Face frame made separately, then attached to forward edges of side and divider panels and floor.*

standard 18 inches above a base cabinet, in this case a built-in dining-room sideboard or server.

The purpose is storage of china and glassware on one side, audio equipment on the other. An identical unit could be built in a living room, kitchen, or elsewhere for other purposes. The cabinet height can be whatever is needed; in this case, the top was set well below ceiling level for convenient access.

Step 1 After establishing dimensions, drawing up the plans, and gathering the necessary materials, lay out the cabinet pattern on the wall with a pencil, rule, square, and straightedge. Show all the parts outlined in full size, making sure all are level and plumb.

Step 2 Cut the cabinet top to length and to a width equal to the overall outside depth of the cabinet minus the thickness of the face frame; here, 11¼ inches. Nail or screw the piece to the ceiling joists or support cleats (FIG. 11-23).

294   Custom Cabinets

11-23
Securing top piece on support cleats.

Cut and fit the back and side cleats that will support the full-width cabinet bottom. Align them with the level guidelines and nail them to the wall studs. If the studs are not in the right places for proper attachment, put in hollow-wall fasteners. Then cut the cabinet bottom and check it for proper fit.

Step 3

Run a bead of glue along the top edges of the support cleats and set the bottom piece in place. Nail it down close to the points where the cleats are fastened to the wall structure, through drilled pilot holes (FIG. 11-24).

Step 4

11-24
Nailing bottom shelf on support cleat.

Step 5   Cut the two cabinet side pieces to proper width and height. Fasten them in place between the top and bottom pieces by nailing to the wall studs, shimming and trimming as necessary to keep them plumb and squared. Apply glue to the top and bottom edges of each, and toenail to the top and bottom pieces.

Step 6   Cut the support cleats for the shelves in the left side of the cabinet. For each cleat, apply glue to one end, butt it tight against the left side piece, and nail it to the wall studs or install hollow-wall fasteners (FIG. 11-25). Set each cleat exactly to the level guideline.

11-25
Putting shelf back-support cleats in left-hand section.

Step 7   Cut and fit the left-hand divider panel; its length and width is the same as for the side pieces. Mark transverse lines on the top and bottom pieces, square to the leading edges to indicate the divider-panel position. Check the panel for fit; it must be plumb, with the front edge vertical.

Apply glue to the top and bottom edges and ends of the shelf cleats. Set the panel in place and drill a pair of pilot holes through the divider at each cleat end, but do not drill into the cleats.

Keep the panel snug against the wall. Nail the divider to the cleat ends (FIG. 11-26), nail up through the bottom piece into its bottom edge, and toenail the top corner to the top piece. If there is room to work, nail down through the top piece into the upper edge of the divider.

11-26
Installing left-hand divider panel before nailing to shelf-cleat ends; note nails in pilot holes, ready for driving.

Cut and fit the shelf support cleats for the center section of the cabinet. Apply glue to the ends and fasten the cleats in place, set to the level guidelines. These shelves are placed at different heights than the left-hand ones, so nails can be driven through pilot holes in the divider panel into the center cleat ends. Then

Step 8

cut and fit the right-hand divider panel and install it in the same manner as the left-hand one.

Step 9   Mark level lines on the divider panels extending from the top edge of each cleat end to the outer edge of the panels. These will be the guidelines to follow when you position the shelves. Cut the shelves to fit snugly between the panels. For each shelf, apply glue along the top of the support cleat and to the shelf ends.

Slip the shelf into place (FIG. 11-27) and nail the back to the cleat after drilling pilot holes. Align the shelf with the guidelines on the panels and nail through the panels into the shelf ends. Use three or four 6d finish nails per end, driven straight in. To secure the left ends of the left-hand shelves, toenail through pilot holes at the corners into the left side panel.

11-27
Installing shelf in center section.

Step 10   Cut and fit the top rail, which in this case is also a fascia closing the gap between the cabinet and the ceiling. Fit the ends snugly to the walls. The rail extends down over the edge of the top piece. Apply a bead of glue across this edge and down the side and divider panels by the extent of the overlap. Nail the rail in place, making sure that it remains level.

Step 11

Cut the face-frame stiles, one for each side of the cabinet and two more to cover the divider-panel edges (these stiles are sometimes termed *mullions*). In this design, the stiles extend below the cabinet bottom to cover the ends of the side cleats that support the bottom piece. Measure and cut each to fit its own spot to cover any dimensional irregularities.

Check the fit, apply glue, and nail each one to the panel edges (FIG. 11-28). Drill pilot holes and toenail into each shelf corner. The divider-panel stiles are centered on the panel edges.

11-28
Installing face-frame stiles on center section.

Step 12   Cut the short sections of bottom rail to fit snugly between the stiles. The top edge should be flush with the upper surface of the cabinet bottom and the lower edge flush with the ends of the stiles. Apply glue and face-nail the rails to the cabinet bottom, then toenail with 3d nails at each bottom corner to the adjacent stile.

Step 13   Cover the exposed raw edges of the shelves (FIG. 11-29). Here, solid wood strips ¾ inch wide and ⅜ inch thick were used, snugly fitted and glued and nailed in place.

11-29
Applying matching wood-strip edging to raw shelf edges.

That completes the cabinet construction. In this case, the right-hand compartment was left unfinished to be filled later with a stack of audio equipment and fitted face panels. The plan calls for three matching doors, however. Note too that adjustable shelving could have been installed instead of fixed shelves, a situation that is true of most cabinetry having side and divider panels at least ¾ inch thick.

Box wall cabinet

A box wall cabinet (FIG. 11-30) is perhaps the simplest cabinet to build. Any practical dimensions can be used, and depending upon the materials used, decorative features, construction quality, and finish, such a cabinet can be put to a variety of uses. There are only a few simple steps involved, and these can be altered as necessary to suit conditions.

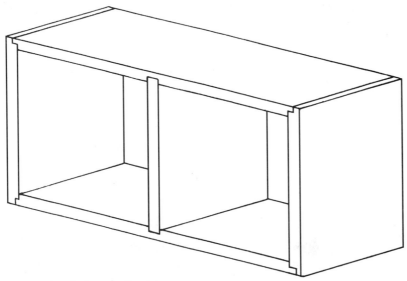

11-30 *Simple box wall cabinet.*

Cut two matching side panels. Rabbet the top and bottom inner edges to half the thickness of the stock; with ¾-inch stock, a ⅜-x-⅜-inch rabbet is usual. Rabbet the back inner edge ¼-x-¼ inch.

Cut two matching pieces for the top and bottom. Rabbet each inner end to mate with the side panels, and rabbet ¼ -x-¼ inch along the back upper edges. Cut a dado across the center of the inner face of each piece wide enough to receive the divider panel (½ inch, for example) and to a depth of half the thickness of the stock (typically ⅜ inch).

Assemble the five pieces in whatever way is most convenient, depending upon the size and shape of the unit. Try a dry run first, then apply glue and nail the parts together. Make sure that the resulting box is perfectly square.

Cut and fit a back panel of ¼-inch plywood or hardboard. Apply glue to the rabbet and secure the panel in it with brads or 3d finish nails. If you use hardboard, drill pilot holes. Note: If the cabinet is fairly large and will be hung on a wall, make the back of ½- or ¾-inch plywood and change the depth of the rabbet to suit.

Cover the exposed raw plywood edges with veneer tape or solid-wood strips. If the cabinet will be painted, you may wish simply to fill and sand the edges.

Install standards or tracks for adjustable shelves and add doors if you wish.

Box-and-frame kitchen wall cabinet

Building a box-and-frame kitchen wall cabinet (FIG. 11-31) is done in much the same way as those discussed earlier. A variety of construction details might be employed, the end result being about the same. The following arrangement uses rabbet and dado joints.

Cut two matching side panels from ¾-inch sheet stock (typically a hardwood plywood). For kitchen-cabinet purposes, the standard depth is 12 inches. Subtract the face-frame thickness (usually ¾ inch); the height can be whatever is required for the specific cabinet location. Cut a ¾-inch-wide, ⅜-inch-deep dado across the inner face of each side panel ½ inch up from the bottom edge and another ½ inch down from the top edge. Cut a ¼-x-⅜ rabbet along the back inner edge of each.

Cut two matching pieces from ¾-inch plywood for the top and bottom. They should be ¾ inch shorter than the outside width of the cabinet and ¼ inch narrower than the depth of the side pieces (11 inches here). If there is a divider panel, cut a dado ¾ inch wide and ⅜ inch deep at each appropriate location across the inner face of the top and bottom pieces.

Cut a back panel from ¼-inch plywood. The width should be the outside width of the cabinet minus ¾ inch, and the height should equal the overall cabinet height minus 1 inch.

Assemble the basic box facedown. Set the back in place and check for fit. The back should overlap the top and bottom edges with its edges flush with the top and bottom surfaces and fit snugly into the side rabbets. Trim as necessary with a block plane. Remove the panel.

Cut a rigid-back or hanging strip from nominal 1-x-2 or 1-x-3 stock (hardwood is best) to fit snugly between the side panels

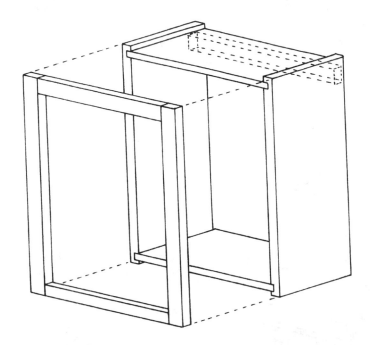

and tight against the top at the rear of the cabinet. Note: In a large, heavy cabinet of this sort, another rigid-back is often positioned similarly at the bottom, above or below the bottom piece.

With a correct fit of all the pieces ensured, glue and fasten all the parts together. Use 4d finish nails at the dado joints and 3d finish nails for the back.

If there is no divider, the face frame consists of only four parts. Cut two matching stiles to the the full cabinet height. The width is typically 1½ inches, but you can use any appropriate dimension.

Cut a top rail; this is usually the same width as the stile, but you can vary it. Cut a bottom rail, here really an edging strip for the bottom shelf. Both rails must fit tightly between the stiles. Assemble the pieces with whatever joinery system you have selected, then fasten the face frame to the cabinet with glue and nails.

Finally, install shelves and doors and proceed with the finishing.

Simple bookcase

Few pieces of cabinetry are simpler than a plain utility bookcase or shelf set (FIG. 11-32). All you need is a couple of nominal 1-inch 2-grade pine planks (2-inch construction grade for heavy-duty use) and some ¼-inch plywood.

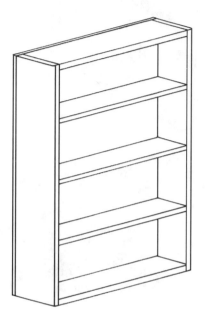

11-32
Plain utility shelves with butt joints and nailed-on back.

Cut the two side pieces to the height of the bookcase. Cut a top and a bottom piece, plus the number of shelves, to the inside width of the case. Set the pieces on edge and nail them together ladder-fashion.

Square the box by checking the diagonals (equal means square). Cut a piece of plywood to match the height and width of the case and nail it to the back. Done.

Quality bookcase

Making a quality bookcase is not much more difficult than a simple one. Select some decent material with a pleasing appearance, say ¾-inch hardwood plywood or some prime dry knotty pine. Determine the overall dimensions and calculate the piece dimensions from them. For this sort of case, a height of 4 to 5 feet and a shelf width of 28 to 32 inches is about right; a shelf depth of 8 to 9 inches will handle most books.

Cut two matching side pieces. Rabbet the top inner edges ¾ inch wide and ⅜ inch deep. Cut ¾-inch dadoes ⅜ inch deep at all the intermediate shelf locations, plus one for the bottom piece located about 5 inches up from the bottom ends. Rabbet the inner rear edges 14 × ¼ inch.

Cut a bottom piece ¼ inch narrower than the depth of the sides and ¾ inch longer than the inside width of the case. Cut a top piece and all the intermediate shelves to the same dimensions.

Assemble the case to check for proper fit. Cut and fit a back piece of ¼-inch plywood. It should drop into the side rabbets and cover the back edges of the top and bottom pieces, flush with the upper and lower surfaces.

Disassemble the case, apply glue, and reassemble in whatever sequence you find most comfortable. Use 6d finish nails at the joints and brads or wire nails to secure the back. At this point the assembly should appear as shown in FIG. 11-33.

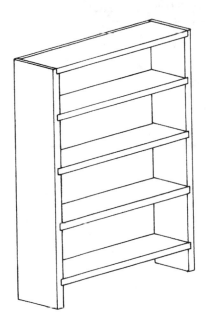

11-33
Basic bookcase, dado and rabbet joints.

Cut a second top piece that will extend outward ¾ inch at each side and forward about ¾ to 1 inch at the front. Fasten it centered on the case top with the back edge flush with the case back surface. You can nail it in place from the top down, but a better way is to drive screws up through countersunk pilot holes in the subtop.

Apply ¾-inch-wide half-round or similar molding of matching wood to the raw side and front edges of the finish top. Miter the corners to 45 degrees, and cut the ends of the side pieces off square and flush with the back surface. (An alternative is to shape the edges of the finish top with a router.) In the same way, apply a ¾-inch cove or similar molding to the underside of the lip of the finish top at front and sides (FIG. 11-34).

Cut and fit a front and two side base pieces. The width of these pieces (height when installed) should be such that the top edge of the front piece meets and aligns with the bottom edge of the bottom shelf. Make 45-degree miter joints at the front corners. Glue and fasten the base pieces. You can face-nail or drive screws or nails from inside the case. Apply a ¾-inch cove, shoe, or similar molding to the top of the base pieces, mitered at the corners (FIG. 11-35). An alternative to this construction is to make the base pieces about ¾ inch wider and mold the top edges to a suitable shape with a router.

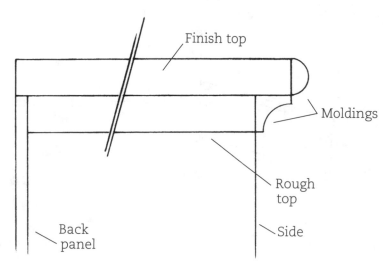

11-34
Finish top and trim moldings on basic bookcase.

Finally, cover all the raw shelf and side edges with veneer edging. Solid-wood strip edging can also be used, in which case

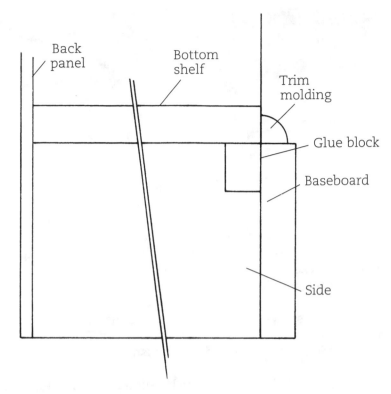

Back
panel

Bottom
shelf

Trim
molding

Glue block

Baseboard

Side

11-35
*Baseboard and trim molding
on basic bookcase.*

allowances for its thickness must be worked into the set of
piece dimensions.

Bookcase wall

Building a large bookshelf unit to cover a whole wall, or a large
part of one, is not difficult, just repetitive and time-consuming.
But it is the only practical way to store a large number of
volumes.

The unit shown in FIG. 11-36 extends from floor to ceiling and is
about 15 feet wide, is made of ¾-inch particleboard faced with
lauan, and has a paint finish. The shelves are 9 inches deep and
32 inches wide, fixed in a staggered pattern of different heights.
The plasterboard wall was taped and primed beforehand.

The first step is to build a solid base. The easiest method is to
form a ladder of nominal 1-x-4 or 1-x-6 solid-wood stock,
depending upon the desired height of the base. An alternative
is strips ripped from ¾-inch plywood.

Building cabinets   307

11-36
Typical full-wall bookshelf arrangement.

A "rung" of the ladder should lie directly under each divider panel. The face board should extend ¾ inch beyond each end of the base. Anchor the base solidly to the floor by fastening nailing blocks to the floor inside the base frame and nailing the cross pieces and the face to them.

Figure 11-37 shows the arrangement and installation sequence of the main components of the booksehelves. It runs left to right, which can be reversed if you wish.

With a plumb bob, ascertain the location of the first top piece and fasten it to the ceiling, preferably to joists but otherwise with anchors.

Ceiling line

2	6	9
3	5	8	11
4	7	10

Base 1

Floor line

11-37 *Assembly sequence, full-wall bookshelves.*

Cut the first side piece, which covers the end of the base and extends up to the ceiling. Fasten it to the base and to the end of the top piece.

Cut the first bottom piece and install it butted against the side piece, tight to the wall, with the front edge flush with the outer surface of the base face.

Cut the first divider panel and stand it in place plumb and square. Fasten it to the ends of the top and bottom pieces. Then fasten the next top piece to the ceiling, and so on until you install the second end piece.

Mark the shelf locations on the side and divider pieces with level lines front to back and across the back wall. Cut a series of back and end support cleats from nominal 1-x-1 stock or a small molding. Fasten the cleats solidly with nails, screws, or anchors.

Cut a series of shelves and secure them in place on the cleats with glue and 3d nails driven through pilot holes. They should fit snugly but not so tight that they drive the dividers out of line.

Cut and fit the top face-frame rail, which extends up to the ceiling or ceiling-joist level and down over the top piece by about 1½ inches in this design. Apply glue and nail the rail to the top piece edges and to the sides and dividers at the overlap. Drill pilot holes to avoid damaging the particleboard.

Cut and fit the side stiles; the bottom ends should be flush with the underside of the bottom piece. Cut and fit the divider stiles the same way. A width of 1½ inches is typical. Apply glue and nail them to the side- and divider-panel edges. Also toenail into the shelf corners through pilot holes.

Apply edging to all the shelf raw edges. Here, ½-x-¾ base shoe molding was used, but other molding shapes or flat wood strips could also be used. Cover the rough edge of the bottom piece with a ¾-inch molding as well.

Finally, fill and sand, and apply a finish.

Shadow boxes and wall display cabinets

A *shadow box* is really nothing more than a covered shallow tray that can be hung or mounted on a wall, usually fairly small. Wall display cabinets are usually larger and deeper, but they serve the same purpose—to display just about anything.

The small generic shadow box shown in FIG. 11-38 is made of four strips of mahogany ripped 2 inches wide and rabbeted ⅛ inch deep and ⅜ inch wide on the rear edges. The corners are fitted together with edge miter joints and the frame assembled with glue and finish nails, aided with a set of corner clamps. The back is ⅛-inch hardboard, smooth side in, attached with glue and small wire nails.

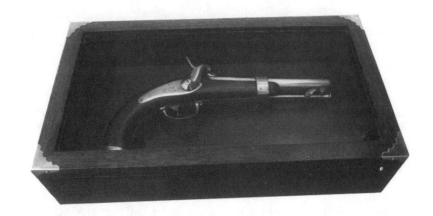

11-38
Typical small shadow-box display cabinet.

The cover is made of 1-x-1-inch mahogany strips fitted with miter joints. A ⅛-inch groove ¼ inch deep was cut along the inner centerline of each piece. The four pieces were presanded and given a coat of clear sealer; then three legs were assembled with glue and nails, clamped in corner clamps. A sheet of ⅛-inch glazing-grade acrylic plastic was slipped into the grooves, and the last frame piece was fastened in place.

The box was finished with polyurethane, the interior of the tray covered with black velveteen, and brass corners and hinges were attached.

Construction of the large wall-hung display-storage case shown in FIG. 11-39 was considerably different. It has the specific purpose of housing a collection of N-scale model railroad cars

and engines, and was sized to accomodate them and the
standard lengths of flexible track on which they stand.

To begin, the cabinet sides, top, and bottom were ripped to
width from clear pine S4S flat molding stock. At full width, this
material would also work for an HO-scale cabinet. The back
edges were rabbeted ¼ inch deep and ⅜ inch wide. A groove was
cut across the bottom and top pieces ⅛ inch in from the front
edge and ⅛ inch wide. This groove is ¹⁄₁₆ inch deep in the bottom
piece, ⅛ inch deep in the top. A ¼-x-¼ rabbet was cut in the front
edges of the side pieces.

The frame was put together with the sides between the top and
bottom, and overlap butt joints were hand-cut to conceal the
side rabbets (FIG. 11-40). Glue and ring-shank panel nails were
used in pilot holes.

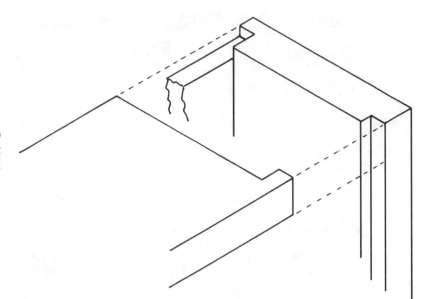

11-40
Detail of coped corner butt jiont and rabbeted back panel in large shadow box..

The back was cut from ¼-inch tempered hardboard with the smooth face spray-painted with several coats of gloss white enamel. It was set in place without glue and secured with a number of 4-¾ Phillips pan-head sheet-metal screws set in clear holes drilled only through the hardboard.

The shelves were then cut to length from stock clear pine doorstop molding with a rounded edge at the front and squared back edge (several standard widths are available). The shelves were prefinished with clear polyurethane and the lengths of track secured with dabs of clear silicone adhesive.

They were installed by drilling through pilot holes in the sides at predetermined points, setting the shelves, and fastening them with ring-shanked panel nails. Clear holes were then drilled through the hardboard back panel, and two intermediate rows of 4-¾ Phillips pan-head sheet-metal screws were driven into the back edges of the shelves for further support and rigidity.

A pane of ⅛-inch glazing-grade acrylic pane was cut and the raw edges (very sharp) filed and smoothed. A small knob was attached at the midpoint close to each side. Closing the case is a matter of slipping the upper corners of the pane against the side rabbets all the way up into the top groove, then swinging the bottom edge in so that the whole pane rests against the bottom of the side rabbets and lowering it into the bottom groove.

The procedure is just like installing a sliding door in its tracks, except that this panel does not slide, just rests there (FIG. 11-41). The fit is surprisingly tight and uniform, and the pane keeps the cabinet interior fully visible but entirely dust-free. As a bonus, this kind of plastic does not accumulate dust particles.

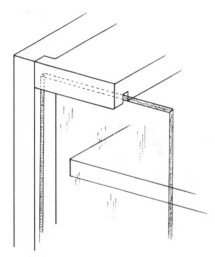

11-41
Clear acrylic front panel of large shadow box slips into top and bottom grooves and rests against side rabbet faces.

Furniture-grade cabinet

The difference between an ordinary kitchen base cabinet and a furniture-grade cabinet lies mostly in matters of degree. Change the dimensions a bit, use high-quality cabinet-grade materials and hardware, make a few alterations in design and construction details, and you have, for example, a fine credenza.

To construct this cabinet, select a quality material such as ¾-inch birch, walnut, or mahogany hardwood plywood and matching solid-wood stock. Lay out the dimensions carefully; an overall size of about 2 feet high, 4 feet wide, and 18 inches deep is typical for such a piece. The basic assembly is shown in FIG. 11-42.

11-42
Basic assembly of credenza.

Cut dadoes in the sides and divider panel to receive the bottom panels, and rabbet the inner back edges of the side panels ¼ inch deep and ⅜ inch wide to receive the back panel. The back panel will lie against and cover the back edge of the divider and bottom panels and the back top support rail.

Cut a notch in the divider panel to pass that rail, and mortise the upper back corners of the side panels to accept the rail ends (see detail in FIG. 11-43). Do the same at the upper front corners to accept the front top support rail. Drill a series of holes in the inside faces of the side panels and corresponding holes in both faces of the divider panel to hold the pin-style supports for the adjustable shelves.

Attach the side and divider panels and the bottom panels with glue and screws. Align and square the parts and install the front and back top support rails with glue and screws. Install the two-piece front bottom support rail in the same way. Set the back, cut from ¼-inch plywood, into the back rabbets and secure it with glue and wire nails or brads.

Cut and fit the baseboards with miter joints at the front corners (FIG. 11-44). These pieces can be S4S stock boards with a stock molding applied after they are installed or wider stock that has been shaped with a suitable top profile before installation. Attach the baseboards with glue and an ample number of screws driven from inside through the sides and bottom support rail; drill clear holes for the shanks.

314   Custom Cabinets

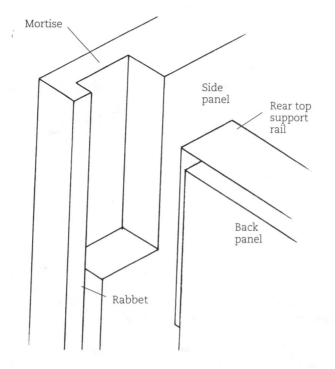

Mortise

Side panel

Rear top support rail

Back panel

Rabbet

11-43
Detail of support rail.

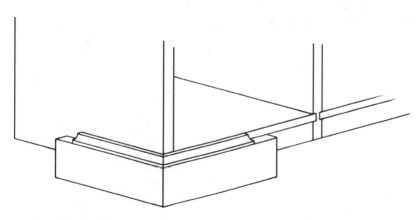

11-44
Detail of baseboard and trim.

Finally, install battens of ¾-inch-square stock along the top inner edges of the side panels and the upper edge of the divider panel on both sides. Apply glue and screw them to the panels.

The details of the top panel depend upon the materials. If hardwood plywood is used, the edges must be covered. Squared edges can be covered with veneer edging, but molded edges cannot.

If a shaped edge is desired, as is usually the case, apply a wide (2 to 3 inches or more) edge band of preshaped matching hardwood around the front and sides and a squared length across the back edge. Use miter joints at the front corners and butt at the rear, with the rear length between the side pieces.

Make the edge joints with plates, tongue-and-groove, or a similar reinforcing system. Alternatively, leave the back edge of the plywood square and apply veneer edging. Then apply a relatively narrow hardwood molding of suitable profile to the other three edges.

If the top is made of a glued-up series of hardwood pieces, neither edging nor matching is a problem. After the panel has cured and been surfaced, square the back edge and shape the sides and front edge with a router to some agreeable pattern.

Install the top with glue applied to the battens and top support rails (carefully at the front to avoid squeeze-out). Drive screws up through clear holes drilled in the battens and at a few points in the top support rails to fasten it (FIG. 11-45).

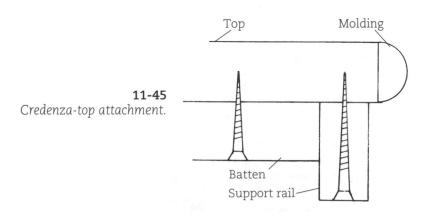

11-45
Credenza-top attachment.

Make a set of shelves and two or four doors, fit them, and proceed with the finishing. The completed project might look something like the cabinet shown in FIG. 11-46.

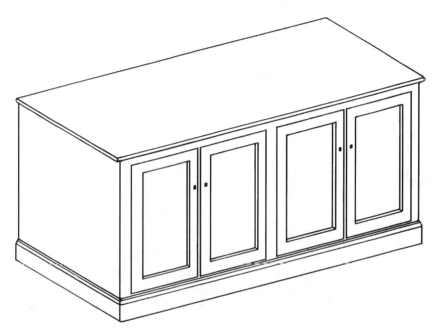

11-46 *Approximation of final appearance of credenza.*

CHAPTER 12

Finishes & finishing

THE LAST STEP in each cabinetmaking project (with the possible exception of some rough-and-ready utility types) is to prepare the surfaces and apply a finish. This is the frosting on the cake, the final bit of work that can either make or break the completed piece.

A poor finishing job can ruin the appearance of an otherwise excellent cabinet. Conversely, no amount of expert finishing can salvage a poorly made piece. So once you have labored mightily to produce a well-crafted cabinet, fouling up the finishing makes no sense.

It behooves you, then, to take care in selecting compatible combinations of materials and procedures to produce the best results. Knowing just what that combination will be before you even start a project is not only a good idea but often essential. And the decisions will often affect the interior of a cabinet as well as the exterior.

A huge amount of information is available from numerous sources regarding specific finishes and finishing procedures, and the field is an extensive and involved one. There are books on this subject alone, and you can tap such sources as dealers, distributors, and manufacturers of products; government agencies; and timely magazine articles. Many craftspersons spend years and a great effort perfecting their finishing techniques to a high degree of excellence and learning just what materials and techniques produce the best results under many circumstances and on a wide range of different surfaces.

Because of the size and complexity of this subject, skimming the surface is all that is possible here. The following guidelines are general but should see you through most average finishing jobs or at least point you in the right direction to find further information. For special or unusual circumstances or some of the more exotic treatments such as pickling, distressing, or antiquing, or difficult techniques like simulated wood graining, additional research will be necessary.

Note too that the field of applied finishes is in a state of great flux nowadays. Most of the familiar finish formulations that we know and have grown up with will soon be unavailable to us. By the time you read this, such old favorites as oil-based stains, spar varnishes, lacquers, and other finishes may be gone. They will be supplanted by synthetics of low or zero toxicity using water or other benign agents as vehicles and for thinning and cleanup. A few such products are available now, but there is not much of a track record to judge them, and application methods and procedures will undergo constant changes for the near future.

No matter how carefully you select your materials or work, there are usually some imperfections on the cabinet surfaces that have to be taken care of before a finish can be applied. Avoiding an occasional dent, crack, torn grain, fissure, pinhole, or other defect is difficult.

Repair work

Patching up these blemishes is often taken care of before the first sanding operations begin, but in some cases it is easiest to do the job between the rough sanding and the preparatory sanding stages. Minor imperfections are usually best taken care of between prep and finish sanding operations. But often as not there is no "best" time or practice, and just what to do depends upon the job circumstances and your preferences.

You can sometimes remove small dents in wood or plywood by *steaming*. This expands and reshapes the fibers, and is usually successful only if the dent is shallow and the wood is not torn or abraded. Place a damp cloth folded into several thicknesses over the dent and bring a hot iron in contact with it for a second or two. Repeat until the dent disappears. If the wood does not come level, you will have to resort to a filler.

Nail or worm holes, cracks, rough spots, and similar defects can be covered with a *filler*. The material you use may depend upon the type of finish that will be applied later. If the surface will be covered with an opaque coating, almost any kind of filler will do the job.

A ready-mixed *plastic wood, wood dough* or *putty,* or a *wood-filler powder* mixed with water all work fine. *Glazing putty* can be used in some circumstances but is apt to remain soft and may be attacked and degraded by the solvents in some kinds of finishes. *Spackle* works particularly well and comes ready-mixed in cans or tubes as well as powder form to be mixed with water. *Vinyl-paste spackle,* ready to use from the can, is excellent.

Follow the directions that come with whatever product you select, filling all the imperfections with a small *putty knife* or artist's *palette knife.* Overfilling to compensate for shrinkage usually just results in extra work in sanding. You you will probably have to make a couple of applications of filler unless the defect is very small.

If the finish is to be natural, transparent, or semitransparent, the filling situation becomes much more problematic. Some fillers will not take a stain, for example, and others will absorb more than the wood. Most fillers will be quite obvious beneath the finish unless they are carefully matched, and that's not easy.

If the finish will be natural, the filler must exactly match the color of the workpiece at the application point, and this typically means a variety of shadings in different locations on a piece of any wood species; perfectly uniform coloration is not a common characteristic of most woods. With semitransparent finishes, the filler must match the combined coloration of the workpiece and the finish so that the patches are invisible.

Then there is the problem of the wood changing color, usually darkening, over time while the color of the patches remains constant. A certain amount of experimenting on scrap pieces is necessary to achieve satisfactory results.

Wood dough is often a good choice in this situation. It will take stain, though not necessarily to the same extent that the workpiece does; it may be more or less. But it can sometimes be prestained to match the workpiece before finishing so that afterward (one hopes) it will absorb the finish to the same degree as the workpiece.

Another method is to apply a prestained matching wood dough after staining the workpiece but before applying a clear topcoat. This has to be done with care so that virtually no sanding of the filler is needed—tricky, but possible. There are wood-dough fillers that come in various colors to match different species of woods. These can be used as is or sometimes combined to form custom colors that will work satisfactorily.

Shellac sticks are widely used and are available in many colors to match most woods. The solid shellac is buttered into the defect and smoothed off with a special blade called a *burn-in knife,* electric or heated over an alcohol burner . The shellac can be applied to the wood after it has been sealed, when the finish will be clear or natural, or after staining; it will not absorb stain. It can also be applied after the final finish coat and is often used for finish repair work on cabinetry and furniture.

Wax or *putty sticks* are available in a wide variety of colors and are very popular for covering defects, especially filling nail holes. They are easy to use, and two or more sticks can be combined to make custom colors. You can apply this filler by rubbing the head of the stick over the defect until it is filled, then wiping away the excess.

However, better results can be obtained by shaving a bit of wax off the stick with the tip of a small penknife blade, adding another bit from another stick for a color mix if necessary, then pressing the wax into the defect and packing and smoothing it with the side of the blade. With a little practice you can make unnoticeable patches.

The filling is almost always done after the last finish coating has thoroughly cured, but there may be occasions when it can be done prior to final topcoating. The topcoat material must be compatible with the wax.

Another widely used filler consists of *fine sawdust* saved from cutting and sanding. Mix the sawdust with white glue to form a thick paste and press it into place. If the dust and the mixing tools are clean, the mix will exactly match the workpiece color, and it is suitable beneath clear finishes. It is always good under opaque finishes.

However, it may not work well with stain unless you stain the sawdust itself, making a mix of stain and varnish or some other clear medium that is compatible with the stain but will dry hard. Otherwise the wood particles, being coated with glue, will not absorb the stain in the same way as the workpiece surface and will probably be obvious. On the other hand, it might not; much depends upon the specific finishes and wood species, and you will have to experiment.

Filling holes and imperfections in resawn or rough-cut wood, which is sometimes used to build rustic cabinetry, can be done with any suitable putty or dough. Use a small knife with a flexible blade to apply the filler. Before it dries, brush it lightly with a fairly coarse-bristled brush; an old toothbrush works well. With a bit of practice, you can create an almost identical texture, and the patch will be hardly noticeable.

Knots often require some special treatment, especially in resinous softwoods. If there are cracks, they can be filled as usual. Often they are slightly raised above the surrounding surface, so they must be taken down flush. This is apt to be easier said than done because they are often very hard. Hand sanding may work, but a power disk sander or even a rotary file may be needed. In any case, work with care so as not to mark up the surrounding surface. And if you sand a bit too deep, you can always fill.

After the surface has been finish-sanded, the knot should be sealed off with a coat of shellac or a special sealer. When this is dry, lightly sand again, feathering the sealed area out into the surrounding surface, but do not cut through the sealer over the knot. Apply a second coat and repeat the sanding. This process will keep resin and discoloration from bleeding into the finish coatings.

Covering screw holes can be done with fillers. But in most cases a better option is to glue *flush* or *button plugs* into the screw holes, which should have been counterbored previously for just that purpose. For clear or semitransparent finishes, the plugs should sharply contrast with the workpiece (as with walnut and maple) or be exactly the same so that they are practically invisible.

Although you can purchase plugs made from several popular species of wood that will match like species reasonably well, the best approach to near invisibility is to cut your own with a *plug cutter*. Select the plug stock carefully, preferably using scraps left over from making the cabinet itself. Often you can even match up the grain pattern and shadings of coloration, then set the plugs in a matching grain orientation. With opaque finishes, all this fuss is immaterial.

The hardest part of finishing a cabinet is preparing the surfaces, and this is also the most crucial part of the job. The quality of the bare surface is the quality and appearance of the finished article. More often than not, the applied finish not only does not hide defects but magnifies them. You can see problem areas that you never even noticed before. This means that the utmost care has to be exercised throughout the process.

Surface preparation

Surface preparation for an applied finish almost always consists of sanding. "Almost," because a few experienced cabinetmakers prefer to smooth by scraping rather than sanding, using *steel cabinet scrapers*. This is a process you might like to try as you gain woodworking experience; more about that later.

The sanding is done after all forming and shaping has been done but not necessarily after assembly has been completed. Sometimes it is easier to do at least some of the sanding on individual pieces beforehand. There are three stages of sanding; rough, preparatory, and finish. In some finishing processes light sanding is needed between coatings too, but that comes later.

Sandpaper comes in several grades, weights, and types. The backing may be paper, cloth, or a synthetic. Paper is the most commonly available and least expensive, and is the usual choice for hand and electric pad-sander use. Paper backings are designated by weight, or thickness, from A through E. The A weight is too flimsy for woodworking purposes, and E is like cardboard, too heavy. The C grade, sometimes called *cabinet paper,* is just right. Cloth backing comes in J and X weights, J being the lighter and more common.

There are several abrasives. Flint, found on cheap papers, does not hold up especially well. It is recognizable by its pale yellowish vanilla color. Garnet is the usual choice, reddish-brown to orangy in color and ideal for hand sanding.

For power sanding, the tan to dark brown or black aluminum oxide is the better choice because it will withstand the heat generated by the machine and the friction of the process. Silicon carbide, a deep charcoal color, is used primarily on sandpapers that can be used either wet or dry, and is widely used in the auto-body industry. However, it is also valuable in cabinetry because the very fine grits are readily available. The paper is also tough and long-lasting.

Sand papers are also classed as *open-coat* or *closed-coat.* The difference is that the particles of grit are spaced considerably farther apart on open-coat paper. Choose open-coat paper when sanding softwood or any surface that might tend to clog and fill between the particles as it is abraded away. For hardwoods, use a closed-coat paper. A new kind of paper just becoming available is coated with a stearate to prevent clogging and loading; greatly increasing useful life.

All papers are designated by the size of the grit, and using the correct size is crucial to good finish work. There are two systems: *grit number* and "aught" (0) or "oh" size. The smaller the number, the larger the grit particle. Sizes start at 12 (4½) and run up to 600 (12/0), but not all kinds of papers are available in all sizes. Table 12-1 shows the sizes most commonly available. For surface preparation, 60 (½) would be about the coarsest you might need, 220 (6/0) about the finest.

The key to sanding wood surfaces is to start with the finest grade that will start the job and work your way to the finest to achieve a perfectly smooth surface, without skipping any grit

Table 12-1 Available abrasive grits.

Garnet	Aluminum oxide	Silicon carbide
- - -	1200	- - -
- - -	600-12/0	600
- - -	500-11/0	500
- - -	400-10/0	400
- - -	- - -	360
- - -	320-9/0	320
280-8/0	280-8/0	280
240-7/0	240-7/0	240
220-6/0	220-6/0	220
180-5/0	180-5/0	180
150-4/0	150-4/0	150
120-3/0	120-3/0	120
100-2/0	100-2/0	100
80-1/0	80-1/0	80
60-½	60-½	60
50-1	50-1	50
40 1½	40 1½	40
36-2	36-2	36
30-2½	30-2½	30
24-3	24-3	24
20-3½	20-3½	20
- - -	16-4	16
- - -	12-4½	12

numbers along the way. This will take you through the three sanding stages; rough, preparatory, and finish.

The purpose of *rough sanding* is to remove a relatively largeamount of unwanted material, getting rid of high or rough spots, ripples, ridges. Sometimes this step is not really necessary, especially with well-constructed cabinets or casework made with top-grade materials that are relatively smooth and defect-free to begin with. The rough sanding may consist of smoothing off a few patches or moderately rough spots.

The papers most often used for this are 60 once in a while, 80 more commonly, and 100 if it will do the job satisfactorily. These are classed as medium grits, but they cut quickly and leave deep scratches, so proceed with care.

Always sand with the grain of the wood, never across it. The the fiber-tearing scars left by cross sanding are most difficult to remove. Check the surface often as you work to note the result and more important, to brush away the dust and loose grit particles. Those particles pop off the paper and can leave deep scratches.

Clean the paper by slapping it against the back of your hand. The tendency is to oversand, and that can cause more work later, so back off a little earlier than you think necessary, at least until you get a good feel for the process.

Tackle *preparatory sanding* with fine-grit paper. Start with 120, go to 150, then 180. This will leave a much smoother surface than the coarser grits and eliminate most of the scratches but not all of them. Depending upon the nature of the surface, the 180-grit paper will leave scratches, albeit fine ones. This phase is also meant to slightly round or "ease" sharp edges and corners slightly and produce a uniformly flat, relatively smooth surface.

Again, keep the surface free of sanding dust and stray grit particles, and always sand with the grain of the wood. If you have compressed air in your shop, use a blowgun and low pressure—20 or 30 pounds or so—to force dust out of corners and crevices. If you don't have a compressor, consider using a portable air tank. You can charge the tank at your local service station, and one load will last a good while. A good alternative is to vacuum with a shop vacuum and brush or a small hand vacuum (not the cordless type, which do not have sufficient power).

Sanding with the 180-grit paper may produce a satisfactorily smooth surface, depending upon the nature of the material. If an opaque finish preceded by a sander-surfacer coat will be applied, further and finer sanding of that coating may be needed.

Finish sanding, the last phase, is done with 220-grit paper, perhaps followed by 240. Going as high as 280 would be unusual on a raw surface (common enough between finish coatings in some finishes). The purpose at this stage is to render the surface satin-smooth.

You can quickly determine the relative smoothness of a surface by a combination of two methods once you gain a little experience. By running your fingertips lightly over the surface in various directions, you will be able to tell whether your sanding job is done and if not, where a bit of touchup is needed. The other method, easier for some, is to shine a strong light across the workpiece almost at surface level and sight across it. Even tiny imperfections will show up as either highlights or shadows.

This stage of surface preparation is crucial. Unless you have a completely smooth and satiny surface, the applied finishes may turn out to be something less than the high quality you had anticipated. That in turn may spell a need for further work between finish coats or even stripping and starting over. The final steps in sanding do seem endless sometimes and are always tedious, but stick with the job if you want a flawless finish.

All three stages can be, and frequently are, done entirely by hand with a sanding block or a sanding plane. If you need to remove lots of material during the rough-sanding phase, a *belt sander* will get the job done quickly. But because of the rapid cutting action, a lot of care must be taken; be sure to practice on some scrapwood before tackling your new cabinet. Some pros who have developed a touch for using this machine will even use it during the second and early-third stages of sanding.

An *orbital sander* will work fairly well in the rough sanding stage and better in the preparatory stage. It is generally not recommended for fine finish sanding, especially on a soft surface. The machine may leave hundreds of little whirligig scratches that are hard to erase.

The machine of choice in the past has been a *pad* or *finish sander* operating with a straight in-line motion; it should be oriented lengthwise to the grain. This machine, while still useful, has been superseded by another called a *random orbital sander*. It operates smoothly and at high speed, and can be employed for preparatory and even early finish sanding.

The last few licks are almost always done by hand, since this seems to produce the best finish. Some woodworkers experienced at this process will sometimes sand without a block, using only fingers on the paper. This is not a recommended procedure because when done by an inexperienced worker or anyone who does not have a well-developed sense of touch, the usual result is a series of shallow but visible ripples caused by uneven or excessive finger pressure. On the other hand, this is a good way to ease sharp edges and corners, with a couple of fingers curled gently over the paper. By all means, try this method, but proceed with caution until you develop a feel for it.

Machines, blocks, and sanding files are the best for open flat surfaces, but there are plenty of situations where they will not work, such as tight corners or the surfaces of routed grooves or patterns. There are several aids that can be of help in unusual circumstances. Ordinary *emery boards,* normally used for smoothing fingernails, work well for some touch-up jobs. You can use specially shaped concave or convex *sanding grips* to work those kinds of surfaces, and the new *triangular high-speed pad sanders* allow you to poke into the tightest of corners.

For sanding round elements, try *cloth-backed sanding strip,* typically 1½ inches wide and sold by the roll. Round or flat *sanding cord,* available in a number of widths or diameters and grit sizes and sold by the 50-foot spool, is perfect for getting into little grooves and slots.

Prefinishing

Several other processes may be considered either part of surface preparation or an early phase of final finishing. Although most cabinet finishing involves only the straightforward application of a familiar liquid coating, there are occasions when one of these special prefinishing techniques is part of the design.

The purpose of *bleaching,* as you might expect, is to render a dark wood lighter or a light wood almost white. It is used where a very light-colored finish is desired or as a base for honey-colored finishes. Bleaching can also be used to lighten darker parts of a workpiece so they will blend in better with the overall surface.

A bit of *lemon juice* or household *laundry bleach* can be used for very mild spot bleaching. This sometimes works satisfactorily and sometimes does not. But working with commercial bleaches can be tricky and dangerous. A great deal of caution, full safety equipment, and strict safety rules are mandatory.

There are three principal chemicals that can be used for bleaching wood. The weakest and simplest to apply is a solution of *oxalic acid* crystals in hot water. Another consists of a solution of *hydrogen peroxide,* which is applied in concert with a liquid *caustic soda,* each applied immediately after the other or both used at once. The strength of the bleach can be varied by varying the proportions of the two, dilution of one or the other, or both.

These bleaches can be injurious immediately upon contact. No matter how small the job, outfit yourself with rubber gloves, full face shield, full-length rubber apron, and sleeve protectors. Make sure of plenty of ventilation and work completely away from any flames (including pilot lights) or spark-producing equipment. Mixing and application must be done in strict accordance with the manufacturer's instructions.

The surfaces to be bleached should be properly dried and cured before the process starts. After applying the bleach, wash off the residue and allow the workpiece to dry thoroughly at a minimum temperature of 70 degrees F for at least 24 hours. Then do a final sanding with fine-grit paper before applying a finish.

Take great care when bleaching glued surfaces that the glue does not begin to dissolve and the joints weaken. If you know that the surface will be bleached, use a waterproof or water-resistant glue.

Bleaching

Another potential problem is that excessive moisture may lift the grain badly or even cause the workpiece to warp. Keep the process as short as you can; two or three separate sessions might be preferable to one long one if you have trouble reaching the right color. Never let moisture stand on the surface, and when you wash off the bleached surface, wash the opposite side as well to equalize the moisture content on both surfaces. This will help to minimize warping.

Sizing

Sizing is sometimes recommended when a particularly smooth surface and smooth finish coating is desired. The traditional sizing solution is made by mixing animal glue and warm water in a ratio of ¼ pound to 1 gallon. Commercial sizings are also available.

Apply the solution in a thin coat over the entire surface with a brush and allow it to dry for at least a full day. Then do a final sanding. This takes some judgment; only a tiny amount of the sizing should be taken off and it is not at all tough. If you sand it all away, its value is lost. If you leave too much on, it may interfere with the finish coatings.

The idea is to bond all the tiny wood fibers tight to the body of the workpiece to allow a smoother finish. The process works best with fibrous woods that tend to develop feathery surfaces when sanded.

Washing

Washing has nothing to do with cleaning the surfaces of the workpiece. Rather, it is the application of a prefinish, called a *washcoat,* consisting mostly of a thinner to which has been added a small amount of an ordinary finish.

Any finishing material can be used, but it should be compatible with topcoat materials to follow. Shellac, oil-based stain, and varnish are commonly used for washcoats, typically in a ratio of about 20 percent finish and 80 percent thinner normally associated with the particular finish.

Washcoats are used for a variety of purposes. The coating only partially seals the wood, so it is effective in evening out stain coatings between porous, absorbent areas. It is applied to the raw wood before staining.

Washcoating also can be done after a stain has been applied, which prevents the topcoat from picking up stain color and streaking or muddying. A washcoat is also sometimes used after a surface has been treated with a glaze or a paste wood filler to prevent color mixing or material pickup.

The washcoat seals the surface just enough without interfering with previous or future coatings. A washcoat also allows you to add color to pores in the wood, add or change colors in the edges of carvings and moldings, or do color patternings without changing the wood color and without one element of the decorative process interfering with another.

Sealing

Sealing is similar to washcoating, but the coating is typically not as thin as a washcoat and is meant to seal the surface entirely rather than just partially. The sealer penetrates the wood to a certain degree and leaves a hard surface that can be touch-sanded prior to application of the following coats. This allows the first coat after sealing to flow on evenly and take a uniform gloss or sheen because the wood surface now has little or no absorbent qualities. The sealer also prevents bleed-through of stains and colors on the wood surface, as from knots.

There are numerous commercial sealers available, most of them thin and clear—thinned with water, mineral spirits or turpentine, or lacquer thinner. You can mix your own sealer. One of the most popular formulations over the years has been one part of 4-pound-cut shellac to seven parts of denatured alcohol. Another common solution is 50 percent varnish and 50 percent mineral spirits or turpentine.

You can use a *lacquer sealer* under any topcoat. However, if the topcoats are to be lacquer-based, use only lacquer sealer beneath them.

Surfacing

Surfacing is a process of applying one or more relatively heavy coatings to a raw wood surface that has some imperfections that cannot readily be sanded out, such as wavy grain, pocks, ripples, or ridges of hard latewood between valleys of soft earlywood that refuse to come smooth. The surfacer builds up in a layer and is then sanded off the high spots, evening out the surface.

The process is especially useful when an opaque, fairly thick finish is to be applied. If the surface unevenness is slight, you can mix one part of orange shellac to one part denatured alcohol and brush on two or three coats a couple of hours apart. Then sand to level the surface. Recoat if necessary. This surfacer can be used under clear or opaque topcoats.

If substantial filling is required, you can use a coating called a *sander-surfacer,* which is available more readily from auto-body supply houses than hardware or paint stores. This is a thick, opaque, primerlike liquid that can be sprayed or brushed on, formulated especially to be easy to sand off.

Properly applied and sanded, a sander-surfacer can make a fine, smooth surface from a ragged one. Be aware, though, that it raises an unholy amount of dust. Wear a mask.

Note that surfacing cannot be used successfully where staining is involved.

Pickling

Pickling is a simple prefinish that goes in and out of fashion but has been moderately popular for decades. The process consists of wiping or brushing on a paint or a special pickling stain. If you use an oil-based paint, which works the easiest, thin it with about ½ pint of mineral spirits or turpentine per quart. The most common color is white or off-white, but no law says you can't use a color.

After the finish sanding is done, coat the surface with a thin layer of the pickling solution. Wipe the surface immediately, moving with the grain; good-quality absorbent paper towels will do. When the appearance suits you, stop. There is no great hurry; if the surface starts to get tacky, you can just moisten it with a small amount of thinner.

You can also use a latex paint thinned in the same ratio. However, the surface will tack up faster, and moistening with a bit of water does not always help much. Also, the moisture is likely to raise the grain of the wood. This means that you will have to sand again before topcoating, which is not necessary with oil-based pickling.

There are two kinds of *glazing*. One is a finish coating that uses an almost full-strength semitransparent glaze paint manipulated with brushes, sponges, or rags to create various patterns and is applied over a primer and a solid-color base coat. Prefinish glazing, on the other hand, is a process that uses thinned paint, somewhat in the manner of a washcoat. However, it is thinned considerably less than a washcoat or a stain. As with pickling, it is topcoated with a clear finish for protection.

Glazing

Glaze can be used directly on raw wood but is usually applied over a washcoated or sealed surface. Its purpose, again like a washcoat, is to darken wood color or change its tone. The coating can be feathered out into patterns or applied only to corners and crevices or molding sides for a light-dark contrast or an aging effect.

Special tools allow you to marbleize the surface or create graining patterns. The typical procedure is to brush the glaze onto the surface in a uniform layer and wait for the sheen to disappear, indicating that the thinner has almost evaporated. Then wipe with the grain (or manipulate the patterning tools) until you are satisfied with the appearance.

Many woods are open-grained, having visible open pores and grain lines. Often it is desirable to disguise this open grain so that the surface of the final finish will be perfectly smooth. This is done with a special material called a *wood filler*.

Filling

Many woods, like white pine or cherry, do not need this treatment because the finish coatings will come out glass-smooth when properly applied and sanded. Other species are only moderately porous, like the birches and some of the maples, and they can be filled with a relatively thin liquid wood filler. Very porous woods like mahogany or lauan, walnut, or the oaks require a liberal application of thick paste wood filler to create a smooth surface.

Commercial wood fillers can be obtained for different filling processes, and they may be lightly colored to match the color of the wood. White zinc pastes can be used too. These fillers can be tinted with colors to suit the application, and they are also available in natural tones. If the finish will be opaque, a vinyl paste spackling compound can be effectively used, especially on a rough and pocked surface like some kinds of particleboard.

Once cured, fillers will not take stains, so coloring has to be part of the initial application. Colored fillers should always be tried on a piece of sizable and representative scrapwood to make sure that the effect is the desired one. You can make your own colored filler by adding just a bit of mineral spirits or turpentine to the filler base, then mixing in very small amounts of color until you get the right tone or shade.

Depending upon the viscosity of the wood filler, you can brush, spray, rub, or roll it onto the surface. A good method with thick paste wood fillers is to put the stuff on with a stiff-bristled brush in a circular motion, then rub with a pad or the heel of your hand to drive the paste well into the pores and force air out.

After the sheen has disappeared, meaning that the thinner has evaporated, immediately rub off the excess filler. You must rub across the grain so as not to pull the now-tacky filler out of the pores; do not scrub the surface or rub too hard. If insufficient filler remains in the pores and the surface is still dimply, you can make another application later.

You can apply wood filler to a raw sanded surface or a sealed one. In the former case, the surface should be completely clean and dry, all sawdust cleared away. Vacuuming is the best method because this will suck small dust particles out of the pores. Use a tack rag to pick up any leavings, then apply the filler.

If the filler is a neutral or natural color, it should match the wood. If the wood is to be stained, that will be done with the filler itself, and the filler will be a different color than the natural wood surface.

Applying the wood filler to a sealed surface can produce different results. You can match the filler color to the wood, and it will go unnoticed. Or you can color the filler differently—the contrast should be fairly strong to be effective—and this will highlight the pores and grain lines. In either case, allow plenty of time for the filler to cure before applying a topcoat.

Once the cabinet surfaces have been sanded smooth, last-minute details or adjustments taken care of, and prefinishing steps completed, the time has come to get on with the final finish. There are numerous materials.

Choices in applied finishes

Probably the most familiar finish is paint. There are many brands, kinds, names, and formulations of paints and enamels for a variety of purposes, and they can be confusing. And not only are different paints intended for different purposes; there can be a certain amount of incompatibility among some of them.

Paints

When selecting a paint, settle upon one or two name brands that are readily available in your area and have a good reputation, and stick with them. Within the line of products offered, choose those that are most appropriate for your intended use. Most paints require a primer undercoat; use primer and topcoat combinations that are either made or recommended by the same manufacturer.

You can buy paints off the shelf in a wide array of colors, and you can have an infinite number of shades and tones custom-mixed. You can opt for *high-gloss, semigloss, satin,* and *flat-finishes*—all may be called something slightly different (*matte* instead of flat, for instance). The higher the gloss, the harder and slicker the coating. The glossier the coating, the more it will reflect light and consequently reveal even minor defects; matte coatings hide defects.

Paints are mostly available in either oil-base alkyd or water-base latex and acrylic formulations. You can apply water-base over oil-base paints. A favorite combination is an oil-base primer with an acrylic topcoat. You can apply an oil-base topcoat over a water-base primer for indoor use.

Paints are opaque and hide the surface completely. A quality paint sprays or brushes on, levels well, fills well, adheres well. Durability is a function of quality (but not necessarily cost), and a top-grade paint will hold up well. For cabinetwork, a semigloss latex enamel is often a good choice.

Consult your favorite paint supplier and get his or her recommendations for the paint to match your requirements. Use the product according to the manufacturer's instructions. For best results, make the application in as dust-free an environment as you can manage, calm air, and in a temperature range of 60–80 degrees and a humidity of 40 to 60 percent.

Stains

Stains are widely used to provide color and a rich undertone unavailable with other finishes and to bring out the grain and figure of wood. No other finish will do as much to enhance the natural characteristics of any wood. Not only the color but the general appearance can be changed remarkably when a stain is applied. And because different stains react to different woods in various ways, some experimenting should always be done before you use a stain on a completed cabinet. That's not a good time for surprises.

Most stains consists of three parts; a *coloring agent,* a *binder* that sticks that agent to the surface, and a *solvent* or *thinner* that serves as the vehicle to carry the color and binder (and eventually evaporates to leave them as the finish). A few types, however, do not use a binder. The coloring agent is either a pigment or a dye; occasionally both are used.

The stain is referred to by the kind of vehicle used. A *water stain* is made with a dye, while oil stains might use a pigment. A *pigment-oil stain* is composed of pigment, linseed oil, and turpentine. A *penetrating-oil* stain is made of soluble dyes and special oils. The oil stains are most commonly used in cabinet finishing.

Water-base stains have their adherents, but the problem with them is that they raise the grain of the wood and are tricky to use. *Spirit stain* is made by dissolving dye in alcohol, and a non-grain-raising stain is composed of glycol, alcohol, and soluble dyes. Excellent results can be obtained with these stains, especially color fastness, intensity, and clarity, but they are not easy to use and require some practice.

Other possibilities are *varnish* or *polyurethane stains* with a vehicle of brushing varnish or a polyurethane and *lacquer stains* with a lacquer base, usually intended for spraying. The advantage of these two types is that the stain and topcoat are combined, saving a step. A couple of specialty items are *wiping stains*, designed especially to be wiped onto a surface with a cloth pad, and *gel stains*, which are paste-like and can be applied very evenly. Both types are worthwhile and advantageous in certain circumstances.

You will see some additional terms with regard to stains. *Transparent stains* add a bit of color to the wood and bring out the grain pattern; they are so thin that they hide no details. *Semitransparent stains* contain a greater proportion of pigment, so they add a lot of color and also obscure some of the fine details in the grain or figure. *Opaque stains*, also called *solid-body stains*, are like paint, hiding everything.

Water stains are inexpensive and easy to mix and apply. Just mix the powder thoroughly with water and apply the solution with a brush or a small roller, with the grain. You can mix colors and tones, but be sure to try them on scrapwood before applying them to a cabinet. The stain will appear darker when wet but lighter as it dries, so wait for the final effect.

Water stains are relatively quick-drying and fairly fade-resistant, and color effects can be deepened by adding coats or varied by playing around with the application pattern. The disadvantages are that the coloration can be streaky or more variable than desired, and the solution can raise the grain of the wood/or cause problems with glue joints.

Pigment-oil stains, widely available in a good range of colors, are probably the most commonly used stain finish in home cabinetmaking. There is a decent range of colors, they are ready to use from the can and easy to apply. If you follow the instructions on the label and work in midrange temperature and humidity conditions, you should have no difficulty in achieving even, streak-free coatings.

Color penetration is not very deep, especially in close-grained woods, but scratches, dents, and other blemishes become pronounced. Grain raising or fiber swelling is not a problem, and you can mix this type of stain with a filler for a one-shot application of both. Oil stains do fade somewhat, sometimes becoming muddy or dusty-looking.

Penetrating-oil stains, which sink more deeply into the wood, are also readily available at most paint stores in several tones. You can mix custom colors by adding pigments, and application is the same as for ordinary oil stains. They do tend to fade more, however, and are not used under a lacquer topcoat because they may eventually bleed through.

Other types of stains are less readily available in local paint stores but can be purchased at woodworking stores and mail-order houses.

Shellac

Shellac was once a favored finish but is not much used today because it lacks the toughness and durability of other finishes. Nonetheless, it remains a good choice in some instances as a final finish, perhaps with a wax coat, and makes a fine sealer.

Although shellac will bring out figure and grain, it is colorless when cured and will add no tone to the wood. This means that it is especially effective as a natural finish on light or white woods like birch, some maples, and white pine. It is easy to apply, fast-drying, and has a short recoat time.

The disadvantages are a comparative lack of surface toughness, a strong susceptibility to water spotting, and no resistance to alcohol (its own solvent) and numerous other liquids. The usual formulation is one part 4-pound-cut shellac to one part alcohol. Apply several coats for a good finish.

Oil has long been a popular cabinet and furniture finish, and with good reason. It is inexpensive, simple to apply, can be readily recoated to freshen the appearance, and does not have a dust-collecting problem as it cures. Oils work especially well on certain hardwoods like walnut, rosewood, and teak, and on some softwoods like redwood. They can be used on any species of wood. This finish is not done with any of the assorted furniture oils and polishes on your grocery store shelves, though, and there is some confusion about what a finishing oil is. Some are not even oils.

Oil finishes

Strictly speaking, there are only three *true oils* that you can use for finishing. With one exception, to be useful as a finish, the oil must be a curing type, one that hardens within a short time to form a coating. Most oils, such as motor oil or vegetable oil, do not cure at all. Two oils do—*tung oil* and *linseed* oil. Tung oil is sold pure and processed. Linseed is available raw, with a long curing time, and boiled, curing under good conditions in a couple of days or less. These oils can be used for any finishing purposes.

True oil

The exception is pure mineral oil, the type you buy in a drugstore. This will not cure but can be effectively used for one chore—oiling wood butcher-block cutting boards set into kitchen countertops. The oil will protect the wood without hardening, will not go rancid, and is easy to reapply when the previous treatment is wiped or washed away.

These oils are simply wiped on and allowed to set for a few hours. Then the excess is wiped away and the surface allowed to cure for a while before handling or use. A full finish takes many coats and results in a soft, low-sheen appearance with little depth but fine patina.

Periodic reapplication over the years adds to the patina, but care must be taken to avoid a sticky buildup by carefully wiping away any excess. You can make a slightly modified oil finish that works very well by mixing one part turpentine with two parts boiled linseed oil.

Polymerized oil   A form of tung or linseed oil that has undergone a special heat treatment, called *polymerized*, has a different chemical makeup because of the treatment. Multiple coatings result in a hard, glossy finish. Polymerized linseed is sometimes used for gunstock finish, but neither kind is readily available and seldom appears in quantity; it is also expensive.

Oil-varnish   *Oil varnishes* have been very popular over the past two decades or so. Usually known as *Danish oil, antique oil,* or *teak oil*, the commercial products like Watco Danish Oil are a blend of true oil and varnish, sometimes with an additive or two in some sort of proprietary mix.

You can easily make your own by mixing 50 percent boiled linseed oil or tung oil with 50 percent good varnish, then thinning a bit with mineral spirits if the mix is too thick and sticky. The degree of sheen in the resulting finish can be varied somewhat by the sheen of the varnish used.

Oil varnishes are applied in the same way as true oils. Wipe the mix on with a cloth pad and allow it to set up briefly. Because of the varnish the surface will become tacky, so don't dawdle. Wipe off all the excess before the tacky stage. If you are caught short, dampen your cloth with a bit of mineral spirits. Be sure to wipe away all the excess, because the oil will leave the surface gummy. After several coats you will have a reasonably hard, fairly tough, satin-sheen surface, made so by the hard synthetic resins such as polyurethane or phenolic contained in the varnish.

Wiping varnishes   Although often advertised as oil or tung oil finishes, *wiping varnishes* contain far more varnish than oil. Familiar products like Formby's Tung Oil Finish may contain any kind of varnish cut two or three times with thinner, along with some oil and perhaps other additives.

You can make your own plain wiping varnish by mixing one part varnish (any type, any gloss) with two parts mineral spirits. For thinner coatings and faster drying with virtually no dust pickup, use three parts thinner. You can add oil or not, about one-half to one part of either tung or linseed oil adds to the "wipability" and is interesting to experiment with.

These finishes, whether commercial or home-brewed, work extremely well and are ideal for home applications. Just wipe the finish on liberally with a small cloth pad and leave it wet; do not wipe off the excess. Allow it to cure overnight and touch-sand dry with fine paper of 320-grit or smaller, just to scuff the surface a tiny bit and pop off whatever few dust nibs might have settled in. Then recoat, and repeat the process at least six or seven times.

The result will be an amazingly hard, tough, glossy surface with very little effort, no mess, not much odor, and no cleanup. An added advantage is that you can recoat this finish any time to restore its original character, using the same approximate solution of the same or other products. And if you don't care for the glossy finish, go over it with extrafine steel or brass wool, pumice, or some other dulling agent, then apply some wax.

There are many *paste waxes* available for wood finishing, such as Trewax or Johnson's Paste Wax. Those suitable for protective coatings on woodwork are typically blended from paraffin, carnauba, beeswax, and a solvent such as turpentine. Some varieties, however, are a straight wax of one kind. (Note that most liquid polishes contain little or no wax, a small percentage of mineral or silicone oil, and solvent.)

Waxes

You can apply wax directly to raw wood; it will act to some degree as a filler and afford a small protection. Waxes can also be applied over some fillers, some sealers, and most topcoat finishes.

Waxes will impart a satin sheen and make a low-friction surface that resists scratching and is modestly liquid-resistant. Under most conditions, the wax film will last for several months and can be reapplied at any time. So-called wax buildup is a myth. It simply does not occur when a paste wax containing a solvent is applied; the remains of the old coating blends with the new. Waxes will often darken the wood a little, and they emphasize grain and figure when applied over raw wood or a dulled clear finish.

Stain waxes can be used in the same way as clear waxes but will result in a slightly colored finish. Stain waxes have a small amount of pigment added to them, and several natural tones are available. The color and tone that results after the wax is applied depends upon the wax color and the wood color.

Experiment on scrapwood before applying stain wax to a completed project; the same wax applied to white pine and red oak will look different. Remember also that wood surfaces will darken to a variable degree with age, which will add to the effect. You can apply multiple coats to raw wood to gain the desired effect, then maintain the finish with a clear wax.

Sealers

Several brands of special *sealer* finishes are available. These penetrate the surface of the wood to a small degree and act as a clear protectant with a reasonably tough and durable surface. They also seal out stains, so are sometimes used as a sort of primer or first coat, then topcoated with another finish such as polyurethane.

Sealers are intended for application to raw wood. The first coat generally exhibits a dull or flat finish because most of it sinks into the wood. Two or three coatings will result in a satin or glossy finish (depending upon the product). Sealers can also be tinted to provide either natural tones or lively tonal effects of bright colors.

Finishing procedures

There are dozens of finishing procedures and practices, and no one method or finish is necessarily "best" for a given cabinetmaking project. Even the experts argue about the best way to achieve the best finishing results, and many have pet theories, methods and even "secret formulas." Probably the best teacher is practical experience. Given time, experimentation, and practice, most woodworkers will eventually settle upon a set of procedures and materials that afford them the most satisfactory results.

There is no way to discuss all the ramifications of wood finishing here. Volumes have been devoted to the subject, and you can probably find more information at your library. The following information is basic and will at least give you some starting points from which you can evolve your own processes through experience, experimentation, and research. The methods and materials used here have served well in the past and make useful and interesting finishes. But because of the way the whole area of applied finishes is evolving and changing, methods and procedures will continue to evolve.

Shellacking

Although shellac can be applied to any wood, it is at its best on close-grained woods where a smooth and natural effect is desired. Sand the surfaces until they feel silky to the touch, as smooth as possible. Dissolve one part of 4-pound-cut orange shellac with one part of denatured alcohol.

Allow plenty of area ventilation and wear a mask; shellac fumes are strong. Apply with a top quality full-bristled brush in a smooth, even coat. Avoid back-brushing, go with the grain of the wood, and do not return to dress up any spots that have already been covered.

Allow the first coat to dry for about 4 hours. Smooth the surface with fine steel wool or an equivalent abrasive pad, clean the surface with a tack rag, and recoat. Again allow 4 hours or so for drying. Repeat the procedure.

Three coats should be considered a minimum, but you can apply as many as you wish. Rub the last coat very lightly with 4/0 steel wool or an equivalent pad, going with the grain, and complete the job with a coat of high-quality paste wax, well buffed.

French polish

The traditional treatment known as *French polish* has many variations and can produce a natural finish, clear or tinted, of great depth and very high gloss when properly applied. It comes up best when applied to a workpiece slowly revolving in a lathe, but with a polishing pad and elbow grease, the results are also good on flatwork, even a fairly large expanse. The success of the finish depends in part upon the pressure with which the finish is applied and the consequent heat from friction.

Mix a solution of about 1 cup of shellac to 1 tablespoon of linseed oil. Dampen a small pad of cheesecloth with a bit of the polish and rub the surface of the workpiece with the grain in long, hard, even strokes. (On a turning workpiece, hold the pad against the rotating surface, the tool rest moved away; application will be across the grain and will fill it.)

Keep the pressure as even as you can and try to avoid streaking. Replenish the solution on the pad frequently as it begins to run dryish and sticky. Allow some curing time, and start again. Usually at least four or five applications, maybe more, are needed to bring up a good finish.

You can vary the proportions of the polish until you find a combination you like or works well on a particular wood. You can also tint the mix with japan colors or aniline dyes.

Oil finish

Oiling is an effective way to provide a natural finish on hardwoods and works better with close-grained than open-grained woods. It is one of the better ways to emphasize grain and figure and at the same time affords some protection. The following recipe is a good one if you enjoy finishing in the traditional way.

Mix one part turpentine and two parts boiled linseed oil. Place a pan about one-third full of water on the stove and bring it to a steady rolling boil. Place the container of turp and linseed into the water and leave it there for about 15 minutes. Keep a sharp eye on it; don't allow the mixture to boil. You want it just thoroughly thinned and quite warm.

Saturate a rag with the mix. If it is too hot to handle, use tongs and a neoprene glove. Wipe the whole surface of the workpiece until you have a uniform, consistent coloration.

Next, fold a cheesecloth pad into a comfortable size and rub a small section of the surface as hard as you can for several minutes. Then move to the next small section and repeat. Continue this process, always in small areas, until you have rubbed out the whole surface. If there is any oil left standing on the surface, wipe it away.

Allow the piece to cure (and your arms to revive) for at least 24 hours and repeat the process. Two applications are a minimum, and typically four or more will give better results. The coatings following the first one will go faster and easier and require less oil. If you don't favor the armstrong method, you can substitute a buffing machine fitted with a felt buffing pad, but take care not to damage or mark the surface.

After a couple of months have passed, repeat the application. This will fill whatever areas had a greater absorption capacity than others and help to even out any dulling or streaks that might have developed. Thereafter, a light application every year will keep the finish looking presentable.

Wax finish

A wax finish is the easiest and least messy of all the finishes to apply, requiring no equipment except a few clean rags. Rather than hand buffing, you might use a power buffer; a low-speed one with a lamb's-wool pad of the same sort used to buff automobile finishes works well.

A good wax finish depends upon a smooth, clean surface, all imperfections filled with burnt-in shellac or a similar filler. If you select a stain wax, be sure to try some on a scrap first. Apply a liberal first coat with firm, even strokes both with and across the grain; a circular motion is often easiest. Allow the wax to set up until a haze is visible, then buff. If there is any unevenness of sheen, apply a second coat. A third is seldom necessary.

Note that once a wax finish has been applied, you cannot successfully apply other finishes.

Stain finish

Staining is a popular method of finishing cabinetry because of its ease of application and the wide range of colors and effects. As well as the familiar wood tones like walnut and red oak, you can select colors like chrome green, bright red, Prussian blue, and lemon yellow. Different stains, including dyes and japan colors, are mixed and applied somewhat differently. Follow the manufacturer's instructions, but don't hesitate to experiment.

In general, you apply oil stains by brushing the mix on with even strokes or applying it with a pad or roller. Wet the surface thoroughly, allow it to set up for a few moments, then wipe the stain with the grain to blend the coloration and take up the excess. Depending upon the pigmentation and the amount of solvent in the mix, you may be able to wipe out any unevenness or darken the tone (lightening is not possible). Allowing the stain to cure for several days before applying a topcoat is a good idea.

Apply penetrating oil stains in the same way. They go on easily and evenly, and after they have set for a while, just mop up the excess. Allow a several-day curing period if you can, then apply any kind of topcoat but lacquer.

Apply alcohol stains with a pad, smoothly and quickly. They dry and take a set rapidly, and a blotchy or streaky appearance is all too easy to get. However, these stains can be worked to achieve a clean, uniform appearance, and you can also create some rather startling effects. Some practice on scrapwood is recommended. Experience in handling the stuff is the best teacher.

Water stains are also tricky and have the added disadvantage of raising the grain of the wood. Test the stain on a piece of scrap to make sure you have the desired tone. Dampen the whole surface with a slightly moistened sponge immediately prior to application. Moisten end grain more than the face so that it will not absorb a markedly greater amount of stain than the surface and appear too dark.

Put the stain on with a soft, fine-bristled brush or a new fine sponge. Allow about 24 hours for drying, then touch-sand lightly with very fine paper. Allow the stain to cure for another day or so, clean with a tack rag, and apply a topcoat.

Varnish finish

Varnish has long been a popular finishing medium that can be applied over raw wood, sealers, fillers, stains, paint or even a prevoius coat of varnish. A polyurethane varnish does not do well covering itself. Various formulation of varnishes are used for different purposes, so be sure to select one that suits your project.

On raw wood, first apply a cut coat of varnish as a sealer. A common solution is 1 pint of thinner to 1 gallon of varnish, but some workers prefer to cut even more, sometimes as much as 50–50. Stir the mix thoroughly but smoothly. Never shake varnish, cut or otherwise; it will fill with bubbles.

Apply a cut first coat with a good brush, stroking with the grain. After allowing plenty of drying time, scuff-sand the surface to remove any nibs and cut whatever gloss may appear. Apply subsequent coats with a quality varnish brush.

Work on small sections, and stroke first across the grain, then immediately brush the fresh varnish out with the grain. Always work from dry to wet and let the varnish flow of its own accord; scrubbing it around will not work. Avoid backbrushing and touch-up, and let lap marks settle of their own accord.

Lacquer finishes, the hallmark of museum-quality furniture and show cars, are seldom suited for ordinary home application. Most are applied by spraying, which requires expertise and special equipment and involves numerous hazards.

Lacquer finish

There are a couple of exceptions. You can successfully spray relatively small items with lacquer from aerosol spray cans if you set up properly for the job. The other possibility is a brushing lacquer finish.

Start by applying a special sanding sealer intended for use with lacquers, or as a second choice, a coat of shellac. Touch-sand the surface to remove nibs, then apply the brushing lacquer with a top-grade, long-bristled, ox-hair varnish brush.

Load the brush to about the halfway mark but do not scrape or slap any off on the side of the can; just let any overload drip off. Then flow the liquid onto the surface with long, even strokes with the grain and in only one direction, working from the wet area out to the dry. Move quickly but smoothly and avoid overlaps or brush-outs. Lacquer cures rapidly, so you don't have time to fiddle.

Recoating is done in the same way. Subsequent coats will bond with the earlier ones. You can apply as many coats as seems desirable, each one adding to the depth of the finish. You can also apply colored or tinted coatings first, then topcoat with clear lacquer. With a little practice, you can achieve some fine-looking finishes.

Paint finish

Paint, long used on all sorts of home cabinetry, provides a durable, attractive finish when properly done. It is one of the easiest and least expensive finishes and has the greatest number of available color variations (hundreds, in fact) and decorative possibilities.

A perfectly smooth, defect- and blemish-free surface is crucial. Paint will not hide defects. The glossier the finish, the more the paint will highlight them. Light colors will show imperfections more than dark ones, and bright light makes matters worse.

A paint finish starts with a sealer, primer, undercoat, or sander-surfacer. Terminology varies, and so do manufacturers' recommendations. On porous, open-grained wood, apply a filler as well unless you especially want the pores to show. When the first coat has cured, make a thorough inspection for imperfections. Take care of repair work, then sand the surface thoroughly with a fine-grit paper. Occasionally spot-priming or even a second coat is needed.

When this surface is as near perfect as you can get it, apply the first coat of the finish paint. Follow the manufacturer's application instructions, using a clean quality brush. You will obtain best results by using a professional grade of brush with bristles of the right kind for the type of paint you are applying.

Brush with the grain, and keep all backbrushing and touch-up to a minimum. Flow the paint on smoothly from dry to wet areas. You have to let plenty of liquid move off the brush; a common problem with water-base paints is brushing the coating out too thin.

After allowing plenty of curing time, check the surface once again for defects and make necessary repairs. Vinyl-paste spackle works well for this, but you may have to coat the repairs with a thin layer of sealer. (Note: Do not use shellac for a sealer under water-base paints.) Go over the surface with a very fine paper or abrasive finishing pad to cut the gloss, knock off any dust nibs, and provide a little "tooth" for the next coat.

Then apply another coat of finish paint. In most instances, two coats plus a primer will do the job nicely, but occasionally a third is needed for optimum appearance.

Topcoat finishes are applied to achieve a "traditional" furniture finish. In cabinetwork, the topcoat material is either a varnish or a lacquer, clear or semitransparent, with the grain and figure visible beneath.

There are three goals in developing such a finish: to provide surface protection, achieve a satin-smooth surface, and (a subjective one) to achieve certain visual effects that enhance the natural beauty of the wood when seen under varying light conditions.

There are several such finishes, but among the most popular are the *deep luster,* the *high-sheen satin,* and the *dull satin.* All three are started by applying two or more topcoats, sanding between coats to ensure as smooth a surface as possible. The total thickness of these coatings should be relatively great because the finishing process involves quite a bit of sanding. A thin layer would be in danger of being cut through.

The deep-luster finish is achieved by first sanding the last topcoat with successively finer grades of wet-or-dry (silicon carbide) sandpaper, using small amounts of water as a lubricant. Start at 280, go to 320, then 360, and 400, cleaning the surface thoroughly as you work.

Do the last sanding with 500-grit paper, clean again a couple of times to get rid of the last few minute particles, dry the surface with a soft cloth, and allow plenty of time for complete drying. Then use a deep-pile lambs'-wool buffing pad on a low-speed rotary polisher to remove the last vestiges of tiny scratches and bring the surface to a polish. Finish by polishing the whole surface with a high-grade furniture cleaner-polish, and maintain the appearance over time with the same.

You can accomplish the high-sheen satin finish by taking almost the same steps. The last two, though, are different. After the final sanding with 500-grit paper, apply a mixture of rubbing oil and FFF pumice to the surface. Hand-rub the whole surface with a block of wood wrapped in felt, always moving with the grain.

Continue the process, replenishing the pumice and oil as necessary, until you have the surface as smooth as you think you can make it. Clean the surface, change felt pads, and apply a mixture of rubbing oil and *rottenstone.* Check the surface often by cleaning a small patch and polishing it with a dry cloth. When you reach a smoothness and sheen that you like, quit.

The dull satin finish is easy. Stop sanding when you have completed the 400-grit session. Clean the surface thoroughly with a high grade furniture cleaner-polish. Then apply a liberal coat of paste wax, allow it to cure for a half hour or so, and buff thoroughly. Maintain the appearance with paste wax.

A fourth type of topcoat finish that has always been in favor is the *generic rubbed finish,* which has lots of variations. You can achieve this finish on either varnish or lacquer topcoats without much trouble or effort. The result, not a high gloss, will be satin smooth, and you can select whatever degree of sheen appeals to you.

There are four basic steps to a rubbed finish; rubbing out, cleaning, polishing, and protecting. Rub out with fine-grit wet-or-dry papers and either water or rubbing-oil lubricant. Start at 280 and work up without skipping any sizes; you can go to 600, even 1200 if you can find it.

This phase does not have to be long and drawn-out. Just remove any traces of nibs, bumps, or other surface irregularities and get a nice smooth surface.

Polishing comes next, using oil and either (or both) pumice and rottenstone, as outlined earlier. You can do this by hand with a felt-covered wood block or a felt pad attached to an inline-motion pad sander.

Clean up with a soft cloth, warm water, and an ordinary detergent soap. Dry with a soft clean cloth, cleaning out all cracks and crannies, nooks and corners. The last step is to treat the surface with a paste wax or a liquid furniture polish, wiped on well and buffed.

Maintain the finish with whatever you used at the outset. Silicone polishes work well because they are relatively hard and water-resistant.